WORLD XIs

Published by Melbourne Books
Level 9, 100 Collins Street,
Melbourne, VIC 3000
Australia
www.melbournebooks.com.au
info@melbournebooks.com.au

Copyright © Richard Smith 2024

Title: WORLD XIs: Best Cricket Teams of all Eras
(1870s – 2020s)
Author: Richard Smith
ISBN: 9781922779274

All rights reserved. No part of this publication may be reproduced, stored in a retrieval system, or transmitted in any form or any means electronic, mechanical, photocopying, recording or otherwise without the prior permission of the publisher.

 A catalogue record for this book is available from the National Library of Australia

WORLD XIs
Best Cricket Teams of all Eras
1870s – 2020s

Richard Smith

M
MELBOURNE BOOKS

CONTENTS

INTRODUCTION	7
1800s	9
1900–WORLD WAR ONE	38
1920s	66
1930s	94
1940s AND 1950s	123
1960s	151
1970s	179
1980s	208
1990s	236
2000s	264
2010s AND 2020s	294
SUNDRY LISTS	324
THE AUTHOR	328

INTRODUCTION

I have been a cricket tragic for as long as I can remember. My earliest cricket memory is the 1977 Centenary Test and David Hookes hitting Tony Greig for five boundaries in succession. I would spend hours poring over books on the history of cricket and the associated statistics as well as choosing 'best of' teams with my cricket-mad grandmother. The idea for World XIs evolved from this obsession with the game, the deep history and statistics.

The idea of the ultimate World XIs is to choose a 'best of' team from the various eras of world cricket. While many of these eras align with their respective decades, there are some that are combined due to the relatively small amount of cricket played in a decade. For example, the 1910s saw Test cricket cease from 1914, and matches didn't recommence until 1920 due to the Great War. Accordingly, these few years (1910–14) have been combined with the 1900s decade.

Qualification for a player's selection is determined according to the following rules based on Test matches:

1. A player can only be selected in one era.
2. The era in which a player can be selected is the one they played the most Test matches in.

3. Where a player played matches equally between two eras, then it is the era the player made the most runs or took the most wickets, depending on whether they are considered more a batter or bowler. For example, as Dennis Lillee played 35 Tests in the 1970s and 35 Tests in the 1980s, the determining factor will be the number of wickets he took in each era, as he was primarily a bowler. As he took 184 wickets in the 1970s and 171 in the 1980s, he qualifies for the 1970s team.
4. In the unlikely event the qualification is still not resolved, the era will be determined by the year they made their Test debut.

For each decade, the ultimate players will be listed in batting order.

It has been a very enjoyable task for me to research the great players from the distant past up to the present and make the selection calls for each era as well as learn more about each player. In fact, now that World XIs is done I am feeling a little bit lost without the daily companionship of the world's greatest cricketers.

1800s

March 15, 1877 at the Melbourne Cricket Ground is when and where it all began, when Test cricket started its long and proud tradition. Australia defeated England by 45 runs with Charles Bannerman retiring hurt on 165 in Australia's first innings.

Cricket tours were more of a business venture in the 1800s, with players promoting the tours and keeping the profits. The 1877–78 tour of England by Australia is an example of the arduous and business-like nature of some of the tours undertaken. No Tests were played but the team was together for over a year, beginning November 2, 1877. They assembled in Melbourne and toured Australia to raise funds for their England leg, visiting Brisbane, Toowoomba, Sydney, Newcastle, Maitland, South Australia and Victoria; all in the days before airline travel, or planes at all for that matter. In January they visited New Zealand, returned to Victoria, then went on to San Francisco for a train journey across to New York.

The Australians arrived in England in May of 1878 and played 39 matches. Back in the USA and Canada, another six matches were played as they made their way across the continent again. Finally, on arriving home, the team was met by a flotilla in Sydney Harbour on November 30, 1878 and they were paraded through the streets to the Town Hall. And modern-day players reckon they have a packed schedule! Each player earned £750 for their efforts, definitely a financial success for the times.

England dominated Test cricket in the 1800s and won 53.1% of the Tests they played, while Australia won 35.7% of the time and South Africa lost all eight Tests they were accredited with.

The player who bestrode cricket in the 1800s was England's good doctor, WG Grace, who was paid £1500 plus expenses to him and his new wife for one Australian tour in 1873–74 before the advent of Test matches. His Test statistics do not amount to much by today's standards as we shall see, but his First Class record was monumental. He was a natural choice as captain of the 1800s XI.

In fact, all the Test batting averages of the time reflect the standard of pitches encountered by batters. Pitches were never covered, and if it rained that was just bad luck for the batting side. Being caught on a 'sticky' changed the course of many a Test. On the other hand, the bowling averages and strike rates of the 1800s bowlers benefited from uncovered pitches.

The 1800s XI is well balanced, with two all-rounders batting in the top-six in WG Grace and Australia's George Giffen, and the great English batter Ranjitsinhji (the only batter in the XI to average in the 40s) anchoring the middle order. Anecdotal evidence points to Australian Jack Blackham being the standout keeper of the day.

Australia provides the pace attack with Fred Spofforth and Charles Turner, and England the spinner with Johnny Briggs. England also brings the medium pace of George Lohmann, who has one of the best statistical records of all time (over 100 Test wickets at a bowling average of 10.75 and strike rate of 34.1). It was hard to leave out Australia's off-spinner Hugh Trumble, but Briggs has the better overall record.

It was also a difficult choice to leave out Test cricket's first century-maker in Charles Bannerman, but he really only played one innings of significance in three Tests. Australia's Joe Darling, who took his place, had a longer Test career.

Most Test Runs in Period

Player	Mat	Inn	NO	Runs	HS	Avg	100	50
A Shrewsbury (E)	23	40	4	1277	164	35.47	3	4
G Giffen (A)	31	53	0	1238	161	23.35	1	6
J Darling (A)	18	33	1	1139	178	35.59	3	4
AC Bannerman (A)	28	50	2	1108	94	23.08	0	8
WG Grace (E)	22	36	2	1098	170	32.29	2	5
SE Gregory* (A)	24	42	3	1096	201	28.10	3	4
AE Stoddart (E)	16	30	2	996	173	35.57	2	3
TW Hayward* (E)	15	24	2	976	137	44.36	3	3
KS Ranjitsinhji (E)	12	22	4	970	175	53.88	2	6
PS McDonnell (A)	19	34	1	955	147	28.93	3	2

*played more Tests after 1899

Most Test Wickets in Period

Player	Mat	Wkts	Avg	BBI	BBM	5 i	10 m
J Briggs (E)	33	118	17.75	8/11	15/28	9	4
GA Lohmann (E)	18	112	10.75	9/28	15/45	9	5
G Giffen (A)	31	103	27.09	7/117	10/160	7	1
R Peel (E)	20	101	16.98	7/31	11/68	5	1
CTB Turner (A)	17	101	16.53	7/43	12/87	11	2
FR Spofforth (A)	18	94	18.41	7/44	14/90	7	4
T Richardson (E)	14	88	25.22	8/94	13/244	11	4
GE Palmer (A)	17	78	21.51	7/65	11/165	6	2
H Trumble (A)	19	63	25.63	6/30	12/89	3	1
JJ Ferris (A)	9	61	12.70	7/37	13/91	6	1

Results

Team	Mat	Won	Lost	Tied	Draw	Win %
England	64	34	20	0	10	53.1
Australia	56	20	26	0	10	35.7
South Africa	8	0	8	0	0	0.0

1877 – 1899 XI

1. Joe Darling (AUS) vc
2. WG Grace (ENG) c
3. Andrew Stoddart (ENG)
4. KS Ranjitsinhji (ENG)
5. Arthur Shrewsbury (ENG)
6. George Giffen (AUS)
7. Jack Blackham (AUS) wk
8. Johnny Briggs (ENG)
9. Charles Turner (AUS)
10. Fred Spofforth (AUS)
11. George Lohmann (ENG)

1. Joe Darling (AUS) vc

Test Record

Bat	M	Inn	NO	Runs	HS	Avg	100	50	Ct
	34	60	2	1657	178	28.56	3	8	27

Darling's career is nearly evenly split either side of 1900, but as he played 18 of his 34 Tests pre-1900, he narrowly qualifies for selection in this era. As it turns out, his performances were better in this era too, averaging 35.59 against 19.92 post-1899.

In fact, when I sat down to choose the 1877–99 team, I assumed Darling would be a walk-up starter. He is, after all, spoken of as a 'great' from the turn of last century. However, on closer inspection it turns out his most productive series was when England toured Australia in 1897-98. Australia crushed England 4–1 in the Test series and Darling topped the averages with 67.13 (and a total of 537 runs for the series). He also scored all of his three centuries in this series, making him the first ever to do so in a single series. The balance of his career produced 1120 runs at the much more modest average of 22.40.

Nonetheless, Darling's overall record puts him at or near the top of the pile of his contemporaries with the added bonus of his leadership, ensuring him a place in the 1877–99 XI. He was a schoolboy prodigy at Prince Alfred College, where he once scored 252 just before his fifteenth birthday, surpassing George Giffen's schoolboy record. Farming on his family's properties then took much of Darling's time, and it was not until the 1893–94 season that he turned out for his state.

In the 1894–95 summer, Darling was chosen to make his debut for Australia against the touring English. He played all five Tests and performed solidly, averaging 28.67 with a top score of 74. The series was drawn 2–all.

Darling was elected as captain by his teammates for the 1899 tour of England in a clear recognition of his leadership abilities. In the five Test series, four matches were drawn, and Australia retained the Ashes by winning the Lord's Test. This was the first of three tours that Darling would lead to England. His final tour in 1905 was notable for the fact he lost all five tosses and eventually resorted to challenging the English captain, Stanley Jackson, to a wrestling match (which was, of course, declined).

Darling is remembered as one of Australia's great captains, known for his integrity and fair play as well as being a strong disciplinarian who did not have a fondness for drinking. Despite his legendary status, he led Australia 21 times, winning only seven and losing four.

After the 1905 English tour, Darling retired to his Adelaide sports store. He sold the shop in 1908 and moved to Tasmania where he resumed farming, becoming actively involved in community affairs. He held a seat in the Tasmanian Parliament from 1921 until his death in 1946. He and his wife also had 15 children, which must have been interesting for her when Joe was away on those long tours of England.

2. WG Grace (ENG) c

Test Record

Bat	M	Inn	NO	Runs	HS	Avg	100	50	Ct
	22	36	2	1098	170	32.29	2	5	39
Bowl	M	Inn	Wkts	Avg	BBI	BBM	5i	10m	SR
	22	13	9	26.22	2/12	3/68	0	0	74.0

Grace played before and around the time Test cricket was kicking off and thus did not play a lot of Test matches. Perhaps his First Class record gives a better indication of his quality. Across 870 First Class matches, he scored a massive 54,211 runs at 39.45 with 124 centuries and a high score of 344. Grace also collected 2809 wickets at just 18.14 and a best bowling in an innings – the perfect ten, 10/49. (There is some speculation about his record, but these numbers give a fair indication.)

Grace dominated cricket in the second half of the nineteenth century – both on and off the field. He was, and is, a household name, known even by those who are not cricket lovers, and is largely the reason that cricket took off in popularity when it did.

He was 32 when he made his Test debut, scoring 152 in his first innings. Grace regularly skipped tours of Australia and next made his mark in the 1886 Ashes series in England when he made 200 runs in the three Tests at an even 50 average, with his highest Test score reaching 170.

Grace captained England in 13 of his 22 Tests with eight wins and three losses. His final Test as player and captain was in 1899 when he was just short of his 51st birthday – making him the oldest to captain a Test team.

Some say Grace cut a few corners when it came to the niceties of cricket; some say he cheated. There was one occasion in an exhibition match when Grace was bowled early in his innings. He calmly replaced the bail and informed the bowler the crowd had come to watch him bat, not the bowler bowl, and he continued his innings.

Grace was also fond of extracting every last cent out of the game that he could. When still a medical student, Grace was paid £1500 to tour Australia in 1873–74 (when the average annual salary in England was around £1000 for a well-off middle-class person). He also attracted regular testimonial matches, including one that raised £1458 so Grace could buy a medical practice. In 1891–92, one-fifth of the cost of transporting the English side across Australia was spent on Grace alone. One estimate puts the value extracted from the game by Grace at £1 million in today's terms. Whatever the amount, it could be argued it was money well spent for the profile Grace gave the game of cricket.

Naturally, Grace is an inductee in the ICC Hall of Fame.

3. Andrew Stoddart (ENG)

Test Record

Bat	M	Inn	NO	Runs	HS	Avg	100	50	Ct
	16	30	2	996	173	35.57	2	3	6

Bowl	M	Inn	Wkts	Avg	BBI	BBM	5i	10m	SR
	16	6	2	47.00	1/10	1/10	0	0	81.0

In Stoddart's obituary, *Wisden* described him as, 'A splendid batsman to watch. Mr Stoddart had all strokes at his command, but was especially strong in driving and hitting on the leg side. Again and again he proved his greatness by his ability to make runs under conditions which found other batsmen at fault, his play, both on fiery and on soft wickets, being quite exceptional.'

Stoddart came to notice in 1886 when he scored a world record 485 in 370 minutes for Hampstead against Stoics, all after spending the entire night before the game playing poker. He then made his Test debut in the only Test of England's 1888 tour of Australia, where he contributed just 16 and 17, being dismissed by Charles Turner on both occasions.

His next opportunity came on England's Australian tour in 1891–92 when he led the English run scoring with 265 runs in three Tests at 53, including his maiden century of 134 in the third Test at Adelaide.

In the 1893 Ashes series in England, Stoddart managed 162 runs at a respectable average of 32.40. Here, he also achieved a high score of 83 in England's innings win in the second Test at The Oval.

Stoddart was captain when England came Down Under in the summer of 1894–95, and he led his side to a 3–2 victory. He added 352 runs personally at an average of 39.11, which included his highest Test score of 173 in England's 94-run win in the second Test at the MCG.

WG Grace was back at the helm when Australia toured England in 1896, and Stoddart played in two of the Tests. He knocked up 103 runs at 34.33, but failed to pass 50. England were thrashed 1–4 in Australia in 1897–98, and Stoddart played just two Tests for 81 runs at 20.25. Here ended his Test career.

Stoddart also played 10 rugby union Internationals as a centre for England – twice against Scotland, three versus Ireland, four against Wales and one against the New Zealand All Blacks.

Sadly Stoddart, burdened by financial worries, took his own life at the age of 52.

4. K.S Ranjistinhji (ENG)

Test Record

Bat	M	Inn	NO	Runs	HS	Avg	100	50	Ct
	15	26	4	989	175	44.95	2	6	13
Bowl	M	Inn	Wkts	Avg	BBI	BBM	5i	10m	SR
	15	4	1	39.00	1/23	1/24	0	0	97.0

Kumar Shri Ranjistinhji, or just Ranji for short, was an Indian prince who played the game as if he were also cricketing royalty. A magician with the bat, Ranji was both orthodox and unorthodox and was responsible for popularising play on the leg side, particularly the leg glance.

Ranji was born in a western Indian state in 1872 into a family with a distant familial connection to the ruler of the state of Nawanagar. The ruler chose Ranji to be his successor and supported him financially in his early life despite the fact that Ranji often lived beyond his means.

In 1888, Ranji moved to Cambridge where he was exposed to a higher level of cricket and began to play the game more seriously. He worked hard at his batting and eventually found his way into the Cambridge XI and earned his blue. No doubt his race may have been counted against him at the selection table from time to time.

After some success, Ranji was selected for Sussex and drew large crowds to watch him bat. He was soon in contention for the English side but some opposed his selection on the grounds of race. Eventually he was selected (some argue it was a financial decision, as he would draw bigger crowds) in 1896 and began cautiously with 62 in the first innings; but with England following on, he scored 154 not out including a century in a session. England's next best was 19. *Wisden* named him one of the cricketers of the year for 1896.

Despite being distracted by the possible succession in Nawanagar and suffering from asthma, Ranji continued to score heavily and was selected to tour Australia in 1897–98. In the first Test he amassed 175, England's then-highest Test score, and he ended the series with 457 runs at an average of 50.77.

Taking some time out in India to pursue his claim to the throne of Nawanagar, Ranji did not return to cricket until 1899. He had lost none of his touch, becoming the first batter to score over 3000 First Class runs in a season at an average of 63.18. He was not as successful against the touring Australians, however, and his best was 93 not out in the first Test. He still averaged 46.33 in the Ashes series.

By this stage, Ranji was learning to adapt his game to counter the leg side fields' opposing captains, who were now setting to him. He continued to evolve, becoming a more than competent driver of the bowling.

In the early 1900s, Ranji spent more time away from cricket pursuing his claim, and when he did play he was distracted and his form fell away. However, in 1904 he was back in form and led the First Class averages with 74.17.

Ranji was accepted as the ruler of Nawanagar in 1907 and became Colonel His Highness Shri Sir Ranjitsinhji Vibhaji II, Jam Sahib of Nawanagar, GCSI, GBE. He did return to England from time to time to play cricket sporadically for Sussex but, despite some success, never played for England again.

5. Arthur Shrewsbury (ENG)

Test Record

Bat	M	Inn	NO	Runs	HS	Avg	100	50	Ct
	23	40	4	1277	164	35.47	3	4	29
Bowl	M	Inn	Wkts	Avg	BBI	BBM	5i	10m	SR
	23	1	0	-	0/2	0/2	0	0	-

Arguably the greatest batter of his generation, Shrewsbury topped the county averages playing for Nottinghamshire on seven occasions, including his final season in 1902 when he turned 47. The great WG Grace was once asked who he would most want in his side and he responded simply, 'Give me Arthur.'

Shrewsbury was born in 1856 in Nottinghamshire and trained as a draughtsman following school. His early county career was delayed by ill health and he debuted in 1875, finishing fourth on the county's averages in a wet summer.

In 1881–82, together with Alfred Shaw and James Lillywhite, he organised a tour of the USA, Australia and New Zealand. As an organiser, he was presumably a walk-up start for the first Test against Australia where he made just 11 and 16. His best performance was in the third Test where he made 82 and 47, with the next best English score being only 23. Each of the promoters profited to the tune of £700 from the tour.

Australia toured England in 1884 and Shrewsbury top scored in the first Test for England with 43 but did not exceed this score in the next two Tests. Organising another Ashes tour in 1884–85, Shrewsbury was second on the English averages at 50.17 and managed a profit of just £150. He was also captain and led his country to a 3–2 Ashes, claiming victory.

Shrewsbury's batting was built around an impregnable defence and, as a result, he was effective on the rain-affected 'sticky' pitches of the day when pitch coverings were not used. The best-known of these knocks came against Australia at Lord's in 1886, when he scored a masterly 164 against the might of Fred Spofforth on a pitch deemed 'impossible' by his peers. He averaged over 60 in the three Test series.

The Australian summer of 1887–88 saw Shrewsbury organising another tour Down Under. The tour, however, was a financial disaster as the Melbourne Club organised a competing tour. The two touring parties did combine for a single Test where Shrewsbury top scored for the visitors with 44. The tour allegedly lost over £2000.

In 1893, he repeated the feat of top scoring on a sticky wicket, this time against Charles 'The Terror' Turner with a well-made 106 – once again at Lord's against Australia. Shrewsbury's final Test was the third of the same series where he made 12 and 19 not out.

Sadly, though, he shot himself in 1903 (the second of this XI to do so) after a bout of depression associated with his thinking he had an incurable disease. Shrewsbury was known as a quiet, humble man and his passing was mourned all over the cricket-playing world – but especially in Nottinghamshire, the county which he served for nearly three decades.

6. George Giffen (AUS)

Test Record

Bat	M	Inn	NO	Runs	HS	Avg	100	50	Ct
	31	53	0	1238	161	23.35	1	6	24
Bowl	M	Inn	Wkts	Avg	BBI	BBM	5i	10m	SR
	31	43	103	27.09	7/117	10/160	7	1	62.0

George Giffen's presence looms large over the latter part of nineteenth-century Australian cricket. His longevity is shown by the fact he was still figuring highly in First Class batting and bowling figures when he was aged in his forties. Just shy of his 44th birthday, he could still manage match figures of 81 and 97 not out and 15/185 against Victoria. Giffen is still the only Australian to have done the double of 10,000 runs (11,757) and 1000 wickets (1022) in First Class cricket. He is thus considered one of Australia's all-time great all-rounders (he is admitted to the Australian Cricket Hall of Fame) and was one of the first picked for this XI.

Giffen's *Wisden* obituary describes him as possessing a wonderfully fine defence with a great variety of strokes and being exceptionally strong at driving. His right-hand bowling was rather below medium pace, but delivered with considerable spin and a well-concealed change of flight and pace. He was also a noted fielder in any position, his large hands helping both his catching and spin bowling.

Aged 22, he debuted at Melbourne in the 1881–82 English series. It was not a particularly notable debut with 2 wickets and just 14 in his only turn at bat. However, the selectors saw enough in him to choose him for the 1882 tour to England and he played in the only Test, making two and a duck, and was not required to bowl.

Giffen's fortunes improved from his slow start to the point where he was a key member of the Australian side, although his job as a postal worker occasionally meant he had to miss some matches. He also declined to play at other times because his brother Walter was not chosen. It is apparent Giffen had a higher opinion of his brother's ability than many others did.

After missing a couple of Tests, Giffen opened the bowling for Australia in the 1884–85 series and dismantled the English batters, taking 7/117 from a massive 52 overs. He was not shy of long spells; in the fifth Test he bowled 74 overs in England's only innings.

On the 1886 tour of England, Giffen topped both the overall (all tour matches) batting and bowling averages. He did not return again until the 1893 and 1896 tours, choosing to sit out the intervening series.

Back on Australian soil, Giffen dominated the 1894–95 series against England, scoring the most runs (475 at 52.78) and taking the most wickets (34) of either team. He also racked up his highest Test score of 161 in the first Test in Sydney, which proved in vain as England won by ten runs. He also took eight dismissals in the match. Giffen was given the honour of captaining his country in the last four Tests of the series with the series drawn 2–all.

Giffen was treated as a hero by the Australian public, particularly in his home state of South Australia where he received a watch and chain valued at a hundred guineas on his return from the 1882 Ashes victory. As many others were, he was treated to a testimonial match which raised £2020 for his benefit.

7. Jack Blackham (AUS) wk

Test Record

Bat	Mat	Inn	NO	Runs	HS	Avg	100	50	Ct	St
	35	62	11	800	74	15.68	0	4	37	24

John 'Jack' Blackham, known as the 'Prince of Wicketkeepers', won the race for selection against Billy Murdoch for the keeping spot in the first-ever Test in 1877. So began a long and distinguished career behind the stumps for Australia. This choice of Blackham over Murdoch was somewhat controversial with the Victoria–New South Wales rivalry rearing its head. In fact, the great New South Wales fast bowler Fred Spofforth refused to play in the first Test as he preferred his mate Murdoch as keeper. However, once Spofforth had bowled in the second Test with Blackham keeping, he had no qualms about him remaining there for the rest of his career.

Blackham was the wicketkeeper who made it fashionable to do away with a long-stop and to stand up to the stumps even to quick bowlers such as Spofforth. This is reflected by the high proportion of stumpings in his tally of dismissals (37 of his dismissals were catches and 24 were stumpings).

He was described by an English magazine just before the 1890 tour as the 'greatest wicketkeeper the world has seen'. *Cricket*, a weekly magazine, wrote that, 'He stands up without the slightest fear, no matter how fast the bowling. There is no pretence or show about his keeping but he takes every kind of ball with the greatest of ease.'

Confirmation of Blackham's greatness is provided by the man himself, WG Grace, who, when asked who the best wicketkeeper he had ever seen was, replied, 'Don't be silly, there has only been one – Jack Blackham.'

Including the 1878 tour, when no Test was played, Blackham made all of the first eight tours of England at a time when others would occasionally skip a tour due to employment pressures or other reasons. His role as a bank clerk must have allowed him great flexibility to pursue his love of cricket, especially when playing for Australia.

Blackham captained Australia on the 1893 tour of England and several times in Australia. Across six matches he had the balanced record of two wins, two losses and two draws. However, he was not as well-regarded for his captaincy as his wicketkeeping. It is said he was often filled with gloom in the dressing room and dragged others' moods down with him. He also struggled to manage the colonial factions and a train trip to Sussex ended in blood being shed in fisticuffs as rivalries boiled over.

Blackham's last Test was the first of the 1894–95 Ashes series where he split his thumb, and while he tried a comeback for Victoria he was forced out of First Class cricket. It was in this Test match he made his highest Test score of 74 and shared a ninth wicket partnership of 154 with Syd Gregory. This remains a record all-time ninth wicket partnership for Australia.

In 1996 Blackham was one of the ten inaugural inductees into the Australian Cricket Hall of Fame.

8. Johnny Briggs (ENG)

Test Record

Bat	M	Inn	NO	Runs	HS	Avg	100	50	Ct
	33	50	5	815	121	18.11	1	2	12

Bowl	M	Inn	Wkts	Avg	BBI	BBM	5i	10m	SR
	33	49	118	17.75	8/11	15/28	9	4	45.1

Johnny Briggs was a left-arm spin bowler who played his county cricket for Lancashire where he is still the second leading wicket-taker for the county. He was also the first player to reach 100 Test wickets.

Selected in early teams for his fielding as much for his batting or bowling, Briggs first played for Lancashire in 1879. By 1884, his batting was such that he was selected for the 1884–85 touring party to Australia. He played in all five Tests, averaging 25.29 with the bat including his one Test century, taking just three wickets. This was the first of six trips he would make to Australia.

From there, his bowling improved markedly and he became known for his flight, control and prodigious spin on the uncovered wickets of the day.

In the 1886 Ashes, Briggs led the wicket tally for the series with 17 wickets at just 7.76 in the three Tests despite not bowling in the first Test. He collected 11/74 in the second Test to bowl England to victory by an innings.

Briggs played in what are now recognised as the first Test matches against South Africa in 1888–89, and took 15/28 in the second Test – of which 14 were bowled. He was named one of *Wisden's* Cricketers of the Year in 1889.

Back in Australia in 1891–92, Briggs led the wicket tally for either side with 17 wickets in three Tests, and performed the third ever hat-trick in Test cricket at Sydney when he cleaned up the tail.

He again led the wickets taken when Australia was back in England in 1893, as he took 16 playing in two of the three Tests.

Perhaps his most famous performance was against Australia in 1894 when England were the first Test team to win after following on. Set 177 to win, Australia were 2–113 at the close of play but rain overnight turned the wicket into a sticky. Together with Bobby Peel, he bowled England to a victory of 10 runs.

Briggs remained a useful batter down the order and C.B Fry described his trademark shot as a 'whizzing uppercut that travels over third man's head', not out of place in a modern T20.

As one of the professionals (or 'players') for Lancashire and England, Briggs was required to bowl long spells, often unchanged for most of the day. No play meant no pay, so Briggs often tried to play through illness or minor injuries.

His bowling and health gradually declined (he suffered a seizure in a Test in 1899), although he did take all 10 wickets in an innings against Worcestershire in 1900.

Briggs suffered from a form of epilepsy for which there was no cure and he died aged 39 in early 1902.

9. Charles Turner (AUS)

Test Record

Bat	M	Inn	NO	Runs	HS	Avg	100	50	Ct
	17	32	4	323	29	11.53	0	0	8
Bowl	M	Inn	Wkts	Avg	BBI	BBM	5i	10m	SR
	17	30	101	16.53	7/43	12/87	11	2	51.2

Charles 'The Terror' Turner was born in Bathurst in 1862 to Charles Biass Turner, an innkeeper, and his wife Mary Ann. He was schooled at Bathurst Grammar and Commercial School where he was not chosen for the School XI. Undeterred, Turner worked hard at his bowling while he found employment with Cobb & Co.

By 1882–83 he had made his debut for New South Wales and moved to Sydney to advance his cricket prospects. The 1886–87 Australian series proved a watershed for Turner. He made his Test debut, taking 6/15 in 18 overs in his first bowling innings. Across the two Tests he took 17 wickets and began his lethal bowling partnership with J.J Ferris who took 18.

In his 12 First Class games in the 1887–88 summer, Turner nabbed 106 wickets at 13.59, including 5/44 and 7/43 in the only Test against the English. This remains an Australian record in a season; no other bowler has ever exceeded 100 wickets in an Australian First Class season.

Turner continued his supreme form on the 1888 tour of England where he took 314 wickets at 11 across all tour matches. In the three Tests he played, Turner bowled in four English innings and took at least five wickets in each.

When next facing the old enemy on the 1890 English tour, Turner resumed his partnership with Ferris and they both took 215 wickets across the whole tour. Turner's return in the two Test matches didn't live up to his high standards, with just six wickets.

England were back in Australia in 1891–92 after a five-year absence and Turner again topped the Australian wicket tally in the three Tests with 16, Australia winning the series 2–1. This was enough to see Turner again chosen for what turned out to be his final tour to England in 1893, collecting 11 wickets in three Tests. He played the first four Tests of the 1894–95 series but was dropped from the side for the final Test despite taking 3/18 and 4/33 in the fourth Test. Turner declined to tour England in 1896 despite being selected, thus ending his Test career.

Turner was more medium to medium-fast than outright fast (he was measured at 55 miles or 88 kilometres per hour on the 1888 tour, a modern-day Nathan Lyon) so the moniker 'Terror' probably relates more to the difficulty batters had dealing with his bowling than the terror of being injured by a fast ball.

In talking about his own bowling, Turner commented, 'I go more for the wickets than for catches. In bowling I have always made it a point to commence to a new man with a view of finding his weak points, and then go for him with a "break" … It is a nonsense to suppose you can get a man out by straight or fast bowling. If you send them dead for the wicket you are knocked about all over the place.'

The Terror was inducted into the Australian Cricket Hall of Fame in 2013 alongside Glenn McGrath.

10. Fred Spofforth (AUS)

Test Record

Bat	M	Inn	NO	Runs	HS	Avg	100	50	Ct
	18	29	6	217	50	9.43	0	1	11

Bowl	M	Inn	Wkts	Avg	BBI	BBM	5i	10m	SR
	18	30	94	18.41	7/44	14/90	7	4	44.5

Such is the regard that Fred 'The Demon' Spofforth is held in Australian and world cricket, that he was an inaugural inductee into the Australian Cricket Hall of Fame and a member of the ICC Hall of Fame.

George Giffen described him thus: 'What a sight it was to see Spofforth bowling when a game had to be pulled from the fire like a brand from the burning! He looked the Demon, every inch of him, and I verily believe he has frightened more batsmen out than many bowlers have fairly and squarely beaten. When the Demon meant business, the batsmen had to look out for squalls.'

Born in 1853 at Balmain, Spofforth spent part of his childhood in New Zealand before returning to Sydney just in time to watch the 1864 English touring team. Spofforth later noted he was inspired by George Tarrant to bowl fast as he 'always sent the stumps flying when he bowled a batsman out'.

Spofforth played for a couple of clubs before making his New South Wales debut in 1874, taking 3/56 and 3/67. Only two First Class matches were played in the 1875–76 season, but the *Sydney Mail* wrote that his '… pace was something not likely to be forgotten by those who had to stand up against it.' He was also athletic, able to run 100 yards in under 11 seconds.

Boycotting the first-ever Test match over his mate Billy Murdoch being overlooked as wicketkeeper for Jack Blackham, Spofforth made his debut in the second Test taking four wickets in total. He then toured with the 1878 Australian side (a tour with no Tests) and he took 6/4 and 4/16 against the MCC.

England toured again in 1878–79 and Spofforth bowled Australia to victory in the only Test with figures of 6/48 and 7/62, including the first-ever hat-trick in Test cricket.

An injured finger meant he missed the only Test of the 1880 tour, but he returned for the 1882 tour to again bowl Australia to victory in the only Test. This was the famous Test that gave rise to the Ashes, and Spofforth took 7/46 and 7/44, pushing Australia to the win. England collapsed from 2/51 to all out for 77, chasing 85 to win. It was Spofforth who had declared 'this thing can be done', then went and did it.

Spofforth continued to take wickets against the English with 18 wickets in 1882–83 (four Tests), ten wickets in 1884 in England (three Tests), 19 in 1884–85 (three Tests) and 14 (three Tests) in 1886. In the latter two series, he was comfortably the leading wicket-taker for Australia. His last Test was in the 1886–87 series and he declined selection to the 1888 tour of England.

In 1885, Spofforth moved to Victoria to take up a job with the National Bank of Australasia. There he married the daughter of a wealthy tea merchant and they moved to England in 1888, where he played on occasion for Derbyshire and Hampshire.

Initially employed as the Midlands representative of the Star Tea Co, he rose through the ranks to become managing director and he died in 1926 a wealthy man in Surrey.

11. George Lohmann (ENG)

Test Record

Bat	M	Inn	NO	Runs	HS	Avg	100	50	Ct
	18	26	2	213	62*	8.87	0	1	28
Bowl	**M**	**Inn**	**Wkts**	**Avg**	**BBI**	**BBM**	**5i**	**10m**	**SR**
	18	36	112	10.75	9/28	15/45	9	5	34.1

*not out

Although he played relatively few Tests, Lohmann is statistically one of the greatest bowlers to have played Test cricket. Over 100 wickets in just 18 Tests at an average of 10.75 and a strike rate of a wicket every 34.1 balls (the best ever for bowlers with over 20 wickets) are pretty impressive numbers. His peak rating under the ICC player rankings system is the second highest of all time. With stats like these it is little wonder Lohmann is an inductee into the ICC Hall of Fame.

Lohmann bowled at a little above medium pace but had deadly accuracy and could swing or cut the ball both ways. This, combined with his ability to vary both the angle and pace of the ball, meant he was rated the most difficult of bowlers by his contemporaries.

Debuting in the first Test of the 1886 Ashes series in England, Lohmann took a solitary wicket and went wicketless in the second Test. However, he decimated Australia in the third Test with 7/36 and 5/68 as England won by an innings. Lohmann's career was up and running.

A further 16 wickets came his way in two Tests in Australia in 1886–87 and then nine in the only Test of the 1887–88 Australian tour. By his tenth Test he had 50 wickets and it took only six more to bring up his hundred.

In 1892 at an age of 27, Lohmann contracted tuberculosis and thereafter had to spend English winters in South Africa. This also meant his Test appearances became more sporadic, although he tore

South Africa apart in 1896 taking 35 wickets in three Tests at an average of just 5.80. This included 15/45 in the first Test (including a hat-trick) and career-best figures of 9/28 in South Africa's first innings of the second Test. The South African matting wickets were obviously to his liking, but there is no doubt the illness curtailed his career.

Lohmann's final Test was against Australia in 1896 when he took three wickets. A pay dispute where Lohmann demanded double the standard pay of £10 per Test saw him withdraw from the second Test. As his health declined, he moved to South Africa full time and played for Western Province for a couple of seasons.

Lohmann's health never really improved, and he died aged 36 in 1901.

1800s Second XI

1. Charles Bannerman (AUS)
2. George Ulyett (ENG)
3. Percy McDonnell (AUS)
4. Billy Murdoch (AUS) c
5. A.G. Steele (ENG) vc
6. Alick Bannerman (AUS)
7. Gregor Macgregor (ENG) wk
8. Bobby Peel (ENG)
9. Hugh Trumble (AUS)
10. Tom Richardson (ENG)
11. J.J. Ferris (AUS)

1900

World War One

Part of the Golden Age of world cricket (generally considered to be 1890–1914) where we gaze back at the era with misty-eyed nostalgia as some of the great names of cricket loom – Fry, Barnes, Noble, Hill, Armstrong and of course the immortal Trumper. Perhaps history does rewrite the complete truth, but we look back on this period as one of competitiveness and also of fair play, with the 'spirit of the game' being first and foremost. An era when cricket was played by exquisitely flowing batters and creative bowlers, magicians with the ball.

Australia had the best win rate during this period, winning 47% of the Tests they played. England were next best with a 42% strike rate, while South Africa finally got on the board with a Test win but won just 25% of the matches they played.

The Ashes between England and Australia again dominated the decade, with England winning the bragging rights after claiming the Ashes 4–1 in Australia in 1911–12 as Australia suffered from internal fighting between the Board of Control and the players over matters such as team management.

The era was also highlighted by a three-way Test series between England, Australia and South Africa; played in England. England dominated, beating Australia 1–0 and then thumping South Africa 3–0. Australia also edged South Africa 2–0.

Run scoring for the era was led Australia's Victor Thumper. A young Jack Hobbs also burst onto the scene during this time, but he was not eligible for selection in the 1900s XI.

On the bowling side, Englishman Sydney Barnes was the overwhelming leader of the Test wickets tally with 189 in just 27 Tests – a strike rate of seven a match.

The most difficult selection decision was to leave out Australia's Charlie MacCartney, whose career blossomed after the war. In the end, there were just not enough spots available to select him in the middle order – Wilf Rhodes's bowling gave him the nod at the top of the order. This XI is also top-heavy with spinners, with all-rounders Rhodes and Warwick Armstrong included and Colin Blythe's numbers for the era too good to ignore, so he grabbed one of the specialist bowling spots. The third all-rounder in the side, Monty Noble, would be called on to provide some medium-pace bowling to complement pacemen Barnes and Tibby Cotter.

Of course many a career was cut short, interrupted or delayed by World War One. Two of the XIs paid the ultimate sacrifice – Tibby Cotter and Colin Blythe.

Most Test Runs in Period

Player	Mat	Inns	NO	Runs	HS	Ave	100	50
VT Trumper (AUS)	43	80	7	2883	214*	39.49	7	12
C Hill (AUS)	38	70	2	2629	191	38.66	5	14
JB Hobbs** (ENG)	28	49	6	2465	187	57.32	5	16
WW Armstrong (AUS)	40	71	8	2247	159*	35.66	3	7
W Rhodes (ENG)	44	73	15	1947	179	33.56	2	10
GA Faulkner (SA)	24	45	4	1717	204	41.87	4	8
MA Noble (AUS)	33	59	4	1524	133	27.70	1	12
AW Nourse (SA)	32	60	7	1512	93*	28.52	0	11
W Bardsley (AUS)	20	33	0	1490	164	45.15	5	7
JT Tyldesley (ENG)	27	47	1	1452	138	31.56	3	9

**qualifies for the 1920s era   *not out

Most Test Wickets in Period

Player	Mat	Inns	Wkts	BBI	BBM	Ave	SR	5	10
SF Barnes (ENG)	27	50	189	9/103	17/159	16.43	41.6	24	7
C Blythe (ENG)	19	37	100	8/59	15/99	18.63	45.4	9	4
W Rhodes (ENG)	44	66	92	8/68	15/124	24.71	55.3	6	1
A Cotter (AUS)	21	38	89	7/148	9/221	28.64	52.0	7	0
MA Noble (AUS)	33	55	89	7/17	13/77	25.10	60.1	7	2
GA Faulkner (SA)	24	42	82	7/84	9/75	25.52	50.3	4	0
JV Saunders (AUS)	14	27	79	7/34	9/66	22.73	45.1	6	0
H Trumble* (AUS)	13	23	78	8/65	12/173	18.67	51.8	6	2
WW Armstrong (AUS)	40	64	70	6/35	7/166	35.81	94.9	3	0
WJ Whitty (AUS)	14	25	65	6/17	9/98	21.12	51.6	3	0

*qualifies for the 1800s era

Results

Team	Mat	Won	Lost	Tied	Draw	W/L
England	59	25	22	0	12	1.136
Australia	49	23	15	0	11	1.533
South Africa	32	8	19	0	5	0.421

1900 – World War One XI

1. Victor Trumper (AUS)
2. Wilf Rhodes (ENG)
3. Clem Hill (AUS)
4. C.B. Fry (ENG) vc
5. Aubrey Faulkner (SA)
6. Warwick Armstrong (AUS)
7. Monty Noble (AUS) c
8. Hanson Carter (AUS) wk
9. Sydney Barnes (ENG)
10. Tibby Cotter (AUS)
11. Colin Blythe (ENG)

1. Victor Trumper (AUS)

Test Record

Bat	M	Inn	NO	Runs	HS	Avg	100	50	Ct
	48	89	8	3163	214*	39.04	8	13	31

Bowl	M	Inn	Wkts	Avg	BBI	BBM	5i	10m	SR
	48	15	8	39.62	3/60	3/87	0	0	68.2

*not out

The embodiment of the Golden Age.

George Beldam's classic photograph of Trumper, 'Jumping Out', captures him in full flow, down the pitch, bat raised, eyes set, ready to artistically smite the ball to the boundary. It was not just the runs that Trumper made but the way he made them. Neville Cardus wrote that trying to judge Trumper's batsmanship by number of runs or his average would be like trying to judge Mozart by the number of notes he scribed. In the words of C.B Fry, 'He had no style and yet he was all style.'

The astute English captain Archie MacLaren said, 'You couldn't set a field for him. He was the most fascinating batsman I have ever seen. He had grace, ease, style and power.' The Englishman known for his own artistry and skill, Ranjitsinhji, said, 'Every stroke he made so fascinated me that I couldn't take my eyes off him.' However, his fragile health often affected his batting. Joe Darling wrote in his memoirs that, 'Owing to the fact he did not enjoy the best of health, Trumper had many bad days, but when he was well there was only one cricketer in it for champion of the world.'

Many who saw both Trumper and Bradman rated Trumper as the more brilliant batter. The difference was Bradman's insatiable appetite for runs and more runs, whereas Trumper would happily give it away once he had reached 100. In any event let's agree they are both legends of the sport.

Trumper's talent is acknowledged by being an inaugural inductee into both the Australian Cricket Hall of Fame and the ICC Hall of Fame.

Debuting as a teenager for New South Wales in 1894–95, it was several seasons later he found himself on the 1899 Ashes tour. Trumper made his Test debut in the first Test at Trent Bridge making a duck and 11. In his next Test on the hallowed turf at Lord's, he made his debut century with 135 not out. His tour also included a triple century against Sussex and *Wisden* noted that something phenomenal had come to life in Australian cricket.

Trumper underlined his brilliance on the next Ashes tour. On the first day of the fourth Test at Old Trafford, on a wet pitch, he hit a century before lunch (the first of six to have achieved the feat). Jumping ahead to the end of his career, in 1910–11 Trumper saved his best for last with 661 runs in five Tests at an average of 94.43 including his highest Test score, an undefeated 214 against the South Africans.

Trumper's death came too early, of Bright's disease, aged only 37 as the Gallipoli campaign raged in 1915. In the grip of wartime, over 20,000 Sydney-siders lined the streets to farewell Trumper as his funeral proceeded both sides of the harbour (before the Sydney Harbour Bridge was in place). In London, where the darkness of war was front page daily, placards appeared in newsstands proclaiming, 'Great Cricketer Dead'.

2. Wilf Rhodes (ENG)

Test Record

Bat	M	Inn	NO	Runs	HS	Avg	100	50	Ct
	58	98	21	2325	179	30.19	2	11	60

Bowl	M	Inn	Wkts	Avg	BBI	BBM	5i	10m	SR
	58	90	127	26.96	8/68	15/124	6	1	64.7

Another ICC Cricket Hall of Fame inductee, Yorkshireman Wilfred Rhodes was a complete all-rounder; batting right-handed and bowling with a left-arm orthodox spin. Over a 30-year career in all First Class cricket, Rhodes scored 39,802 runs and took 4187 wickets – the most by any bowler. Rhodes also completed the 1000 runs and 100 wickets double in a season a record 16 times. His 1110 First Class matches is also a record.

Rhodes was a genuine slow bowler, one who relied on flight and variations to capture his wickets. As a batter he was sometimes criticised for being too cautious, but after spending his first few Tests at number 10 or 11 he moved up the order to form a successful opening partnership with Jack Hobbs. They once put on 323 for the first wicket against Australia.

In 1899 Rhodes took 179 wickets in First Class cricket leading *Wisden* to describe him as 'head and shoulders above the rest' and he made his Test debut against the touring Australians. He took 4/58 opening the bowling in the first innings, including Monty Noble as his first Test scalp. Despite taking three wickets in the next Test, he was dropped until the final Test of the summer and he finished the series as equal leading wicket-taker for England with 13.

Rhodes topped England's wicket tally again in the 1902 Ashes as he collected 22 dismissals across the five Tests at 15.27, including 7/17 in the first innings of the first Test which was washed out. He repeated the dose in Australia in 1903–04 as he led the wicket table again with 31 at 15.74. In the second Test he nabbed 15/124 and had eight catches dropped off his bowling.

Gradually as Rhodes's batting improved, his bowling showed a slight decline and he was not the wicket-taking force he had been although he remained highly effective, especially on damp pitches. In 1909, *Wisden* judged that he had 'now become such an exceptionally good batsman that the regret one used to feel at his ever giving his mind to run getting has lost its force.'

In 1911–12 Rhodes made his third trip to Australia, this time as an opening batter alongside Hobbs. He finished the Test series with 463 runs at 57.88, second only to Hobbs. This included his maiden Test century, 179 in the fourth Test at the MCG. He bowled only 18 wicketless overs in the five Tests.

Rhodes spent the war working in a munitions factory in Huddersfield and was available for selection when cricket resumed. He took up bowling seriously once again and started to take wickets in the County Championship. However, after playing all five matches in Australia in 1920–21 with limited success, his appearances for England became irregular.

Playing his last Test against the West Indies in 1930, Rhodes was the oldest ever Test cricketer at 52 years and 165 days.

After his playing career, Rhodes coached Harrow School for a time but with limited success.

3. Clem Hill (AUS)

Test Record

Bat	M	Inn	NO	Runs	HS	Avg	100	50	Ct
	49	89	2	3412	191	39.21	7	19	33

Hill played in the same era as Trumper, in a few more Tests than Trumper, scored a few more runs than Trumper, at an average on par with Trumper, yet Hill is not held in the same reverential manner as Trumper. Certainly, he is regarded as a great of Australian cricket (he is inducted into the Australian Cricket Hall of Fame and the Sport Australia Hall of Fame), but perhaps Clem Hill should be held in even higher esteem than he is. Perhaps it was his propensity to bat in a crouched stance with a strong lower hand grip which was not conducive to the elegant stroke play of many left-handers.

Hill was a schoolboy prodigy, highlighted by 360 scored in an intercollege match when he was 16. He debuted for Australia on the 1896 England tour but disappointed. However, when England came back Down Under, Hill found his feet in Test cricket by averaging 56.5 across the five Tests including his maiden Test century, knocking up 188 in the fourth Test at the MCG.

After a few more series averaging over 50, Hill's series averages dropped back to a more consistent mid-30s level, until he averaged over 50 against the English in Australia in the 1901–02 series and was the leading run scorer (521) for either side over the five Tests. He failed to score a century but made 99, 98 and 97 in successive innings. Hill was also in top form when Australia visited South Africa for three Tests in 1902–03, and he topped the runs scored (327) and averages (81.75) for both sides.

In the second innings of the third Test in 1907–08 on his home ground, the Adelaide Oval, Hill played perhaps his finest innings. He was ill and throwing up but still came to the crease to join Roger

Hartigan at the fall of the seventh wicket. Australia, in their second innings, was in trouble and barely 100 ahead. Together, they added 243 which is still a record eighth wicket partnership for Australia. Hill made 160.

Hill had a running battle with administrators and refused to tour with the 1909 team. Despite this, Hill was made captain for the 1910–11 series against South Africa which Australia won 4–1. Hill averaged 53 for the series and made his highest Test score of 191.

He retained the captaincy for the 1911–12 English series which turned out to be his last. Australia lost the series 4–1 leaving Hill with a captaincy record of five wins and five losses. It was during this series he had his infamous fisticuffs with fellow selector and noted 'Board Man' Peter McAlister. Hill resigned as a selector mid-series.

These spats with administration may have ended Hill's career anyway but, regardless of that, cricket came to a stop due to the war and Hill's Test career was over. In 1912, when his career came to an end, Hill was the leading all-time run scorer in Test cricket. This was surpassed by Jack Hobbs 12 years later.

Perhaps not surprisingly, Hill turned his back on cricket and moved into administration in his other sporting love, horse racing. He was a stipendiary steward and then handicapper for the South Australian Jockey Club, then later moved to the post of handicapper for the Victorian Amateur Turf Club (which included the Caulfield Cup) before finishing in a lower profile role at Geelong.

4. C.B Fry (ENG) vc

Test Record

Bat	M	Inn	NO	Runs	HS	Avg	100	50	Ct
	26	41	3	1223	144	32.18	2	7	17

Bowl	M	Inn	Wkts	Avg	BBI	BBM	5i	10m	SR
	26	1	0	-	0/3	0/3	0	0	-

Charles Burgess Fry is one of the most accomplished all-round sportsmen to have come out of England. In addition to his cricketing feats, he played football for England and in a FA Cup final for Southampton, equalled the world long jump record, and played rugby for Oxford and the Barbarians. In First Class cricket, he manufactured over 30,000 runs at a touch above 50.

John Arlott described him with these words: 'Charles Fry could be autocratic, angry and self-willed: he was also magnanimous, extravagant, generous, elegant, brilliant – and fun ... he was probably the most variously gifted Englishman of any age'. Ranjitsinhji's opinion was that he was 'the greatest of all batsmen of his time on all wickets and against every type of bowling'.

Fry was not a classical batter but an analytical one, dissecting opposition attacks with a carefully crafted batting technique. He once said of his game 'I really only had one stroke but it went to ten different parts of the field'.

Making his Test debut in 1896 against South Africa, Fry was the top scorer in a low scoring match with 43 in the first innings. He followed this up with several scores over 50 but couldn't convert his starts into big scores.

Fry was probably at his peak in county cricket at the start of the twentieth century when he scored 3147 runs, average 78.67 in 1901, and in 1903 when he scored 2683 runs, average 81.30. His 1901 effort included six centuries in succession.

In 1905 Fry finally broke through for his first Test hundred – 144 against Australia at The Oval in a dead rubber. It was two years later he made his second century, this time against South Africa also at The Oval.

Fry was appointed captain for the 1912 Triangular Tournament with an understrength Australia and South Africa in England. Fry led the English XI to a 3–0 sweep against South Africa and a 1–0 win with two draws against Australia, leaving him undefeated as captain.

He dabbled in many things after his cricket career ended, including writing. He published several books and wrote for the press of the day. Fry also represented India at the League of Nations with Ranjitsinhji and was purportedly offered the throne of Albania. Fry's main passion was commanding the training ship *Mercy* where he educated young boys. For his efforts, he was made an honorary captain.

5. Aubrey Faulkner (SA)

Test Record

Bat	M	Inn	NO	Runs	HS	Avg	100	50	Ct
	25	47	4	1754	204	40.79	4	8	20

Bowl	M	Inn	Wkts	Avg	BBI	BBM	5i	10m	SR
	25	43	82	26.58	7/84	9/75	4	0	51.5

Another of the many all-rounders in this XI, Faulkner was among the best batters of his era and bowled leg-spin, being one of the first to use the googly to any extent. Faulkner is an inductee into the ICC Cricket Hall of Fame (2021).

Faulkner debuted for South Africa in 1906 against England, and managed just four and six with the bat, but picked up six wickets.

In the second Test of the 1907 series against England, he picked up 6/17 in 11 overs in one of his best bowling performances. However, it wasn't until 1910 that he scored his maiden Test century – 123 versus England at Johannesburg. He came close again in the same series being dismissed for 99 at Durban.

On the 1910–11 tour of Australia, Faulkner became the first South African to score a double century with 204 at Melbourne. He added a second century on the same tour to lead the Test averages with 732 runs at 73.20. He added a useful ten wickets to his tally as well.

In the 1912 Tri-Series with England and Australia, Faulkner added another hundred against Australia and then had his best Test bowling of 7/84 versus the English.

During the Great War he served with distinction in Egypt and Palestine (he was awarded a DSO) and returned to the South African side for a single Test at Lord's on the resumption of Test cricket, bowing out with 25 and 12.

After his playing career, Faulkner established a highly successful coaching operation in London. This was despite his own technique being somewhat unorthodox. Sadly, Faulkner battled with what was known at the time as melancholia and took his own life in 1930, aged 48.

Despite the brevity of his international career, Aubrey Faulkner remains an important figure in the history of South African cricket. His contributions during the early years of South Africa's Test cricket helped establish a foundation for the country's future successes in the sport.

6. Warwick Armstrong (AUS)

Test Record

Bat	M	Inn	NO	Runs	HS	Avg	100	50	Ct
	50	84	10	2863	159*	38.68	6	8	44
Bowl	**M**	**Inn**	**Wkts**	**Avg**	**BBI**	**BBM**	**5i**	**10m**	**SR**
	50	80	87	33.59	6/35	7/166	3	0	92.2

*not out

Warwick Armstrong was tall and slim when first chosen for Australia in 1902. By the time he went to England in 1921, he was trying to keep his weight under 20 stone (127 kilograms) by stoking the ship for two hours a day. He failed and went into the tour at 22 stone (140 kilograms). There is little wonder then that he earned the moniker 'The Big Ship'.

Another all-rounder, Armstrong was stronger with the bat but was a very effective leg-spin bowler who relied more on flight than spin to deceive batters. Statistics don't always tell the full story but in Armstrong's case, they reveal a pretty good one. Along with his Test career, he represented Victoria from 1899-1922 and scored 6615 runs at 51.7 and took 244 wickets at just 22.68.

An all-round sportsman, Armstrong also played for South Melbourne in the 1899 VFL grand final against Fitzroy (losing by a single point). Clearly, he was athletic at this point of his life.

Armstrong debuted for Australia in the second Test of the 1901–02 series against England. His average for his first series was 53 in the four Tests he played (although this was inflated by four not outs). In England in 1905, Armstrong was at his all-round best, topping the tour averages for both batting and bowling including a 303 against Somerset. His Test results were solid too, knocking up 252 runs at 31.5 and picking up 16 wickets (the most for either side, tied with Frank Laver).

By this stage Armstrong was being drawn into the players' running battle with the administrators. He played in the 1911–12 England series but was then one of the 'Big Six' who refused to tour England in 1912 due to the Board appointing their own manager and the treatment of the players by the Board. This put a pause on Armstrong's career until after World War One.

On resuming cricket for the 1920–21 season, it appeared Armstrong had been forgiven for the 1912 spat and he was appointed captain. Australia dominated the English completely, winning the Ashes 5–0. Armstrong, aged over 40, also dominated scoring 464 runs at 77.33 and chipping in with nine wickets. This included 123 not out in the fourth Test where Armstrong played despite a recurrence of malaria. In all, he captained Australia to eight wins from ten Tests with two draws.

Variously described as cantankerous, a man of strong opinions and a strong disciplinarian, it is also said the men who played for him loved him. In his obituary, *Wisden* noted, 'After retiring from active participation in the game, Armstrong wrote for the Press, and his caustic Test criticisms created ill-feeling of a kind which should not be associated with cricket.'

In the 1930s he moved to Sydney to take up a position of general manager for a whisky distiller. He died a wealthy man in 1947, his estate worth £105,813.

Armstrong was inducted into the Australian Cricket Hall of Fame in 2000 and is a member of the Sports Australia Hall of Fame.

7. Monty Noble (AUS) c

Test Record

Bat	M	Inn	NO	Runs	HS	Avg	100	50	Ct
	42	73	7	1997	133	30.25	1	16	26

Bowl	M	Inn	Wkts	Avg	BBI	BBM	5i	10m	SR
	42	71	121	25.00	7/17	13/77	9	2	59.1

One of Australia's all-time great all-rounders, Noble provides a genuine fourth bowling option (plus Armstrong, Rhodes and Faulkner's better than part time trundles) which means this team is very well balanced.

A well-respected commentator – who had seen all of Warwick Armstrong, Jack Gregory and Keith Miller and knew of George Giffen – wrote in 1959 that Monty Noble was the most accomplished all-round cricketer that Australia had produced. The fact he is an inductee in both the Australian Cricket and ICC Halls of Fame and the Sports Australia Hall of Fame is evidence of his outstanding ability.

It is said Noble learnt his bowling technique from baseball, holding the ball between thumb and forefinger, imparting both swing and spin on the ball. On worn and wet pitches, he was a very frightening proposition. As a batter he was considered orthodox and equally capable of solid defence or hitting out as the situation dictated.

Noble was born in Sydney in 1873. He excelled in junior cricket, learning his craft in Paddington. Chosen for his Test debut in the second Test of the 1897–98 summer, Noble took 6/49 in England's second innings, bowling Australia to an innings victory and his career was underway.

One of the features of Noble's career was he never seemed to be out of form with both bat and ball at the same time. 1901–02 versus England proved this, as he averaged only 15.33 with the bat but topped the wicket-taking for both teams with 32 wickets at 19.

Noble was made captain in the 1903–04 series. He led from the front, getting his batting and bowling right, averaging 59.57 with the bat, including his only Test century of 133, and 14 wickets at just 20.50 each.

Noble was a master tactician on the field, setting carefully planned fields for each batter. He was also an excellent man manager, preferring to quietly talk to each individual rather than pick on an individual in a group. He also stood up to the Board on behalf of his players. His overall captaincy record was eight wins, five losses and two draws. For these reasons, Noble has been selected as captain of the 1900–World War One team.

Noble wasn't immune from the ill will that existed between the administrators and the players. When Noble retired in 1910, he wrote to the Board that it was due to the demands of his business (he had qualified as a dentist and ran a growing practice in Macquarie Street), however it was well known that he was sick and tired of the machinations of the Board of Control, in particular the appointment of McAlister as manager on the 1909 tour where Noble was reported upon and second guessed.

Noble was granted a testimonial match in 1908 where in excess of £2000 was raised.

8. Hanson Carter (AUS) wk

Test Record

Bat	Mat	Inn	NO	Runs	HS	Avg	100	50	Ct	St
	28	47	9	873	72	22.97	0	4	44	21

Hanson 'Sammy' Carter was born in Yorkshire in 1878. His Test career straddled World War One, with 20 pre-War Tests and a further eight in 1921, when aged in his forties. As such, he qualifies for selection in the 1900–World War One.

It was a tight selection choice, with Australian Jim Kelly also worthy of consideration. Kelly's Test career ran from 1896 to 1905 and he qualified for selection in this era, however Carter's keeping was so highly regarded that when he toured England in 1909 he was regarded as second only to the Prince of Wicketkeepers, the great Jack Blackham.

Carter is also credited as being the first keeper to squat on his haunches rather than simply bending from the waist. His batting was solid at best, but not spectacular, and he was known for playing the hook shot by shovelling the ball over his shoulder 'like a labourer throwing dirt', a precursor to some of the Twenty20 shot-making.

He was also known as 'The Undertaker' due to his involvement in the family funeral business. Carter would show up to cricket fields in a hearse on occasions. He was an astute businessman and ran the undertaking business for the family before taking ownership on his father's death in 1914. Carter also dabbled in real estate development and co-owned a sports store with Victor Trumper, his cool business head countering the generosity of Trumper at the store's cash register. He was a pallbearer at Trumper's funeral in 1916.

Carter was chosen to make his Test debut against England at the Sydney Cricket Ground in the first Test of the 1907–08 series after Kelly retired. All up in the series, he made 300 runs at 42.86, took eight catches and made three stumpings over the five Tests. He made three fifties in the series.

An automatic selection for the 1909 English tour, Carter did not handle the wet summer with the bat making just 30 runs in eight innings (over five Tests). His keeping was solid, however, and he took six catches and four stumpings.

His batting did not improve when South Africa visited in 1910–11, but he maintained his dismissal rate with the gloves. Carter regained some form in 1911–12 against England and included his Test best of 72 in the series.

While probably not a central operative, he was caught up as one of the 'Big Six' who did not tour England in 1912 due to the ongoing bickering over who would manage the tour. It was assumed Carter's international career was over, especially given his burgeoning business interests. However, on resumption of cricket after the war, Carter played in two Tests in 1920–21 against England and then toured England in 1921 playing in four of the five Tests. In the latter series Carter averaged 32 with the bat and took eight catches and three stumpings, showing even in his 40s he still had it.

Carter added a further two Tests in South Africa before time was called and he returned to his business pursuits.

9. Sydney Barnes (ENG)

Test Record

Bat	M	Inn	NO	Runs	HS	Avg	100	50	Ct
	27	39	9	242	38*	8.06	0	0	12

Bowl	M	Inn	Wkts	Avg	BBI	BBM	5i	10m	SR
	27	50	189	16.43	9/103	17/159	24	7	41.6

*not out

There is more than one respected judge who rates Syd Barnes as the greatest Test bowler of all time. His statistics of a wicket every 41 balls and an average of 16.43 certainly indicate he is in the discussion. Well before Shane Warne's ball of the century pitched outside Gatting's leg stump and took off stump, Barnes was doing the same on a regular basis. Not only that, but he had it moving back in from outside off stump and when the ball was new, swinging it late both ways.

Barnes was not a fast bowler, more medium pace, but he was relentless, never giving the batter a moment's peace. As Neville Cardus wrote, 'A chill wind of antagonism blew from him even on the sunniest day.'

He was a professional with Lancashire when he bowled to English captain Archie MacLaren in the nets and impressed him so much Barnes was chosen for the 1901–02 tour of Australia. In his first Test outing Barnes collected 5/65 in 35.1 overs. In the second Test he took 6/42 and 7/121 before breaking down in the third and missing the rest of the series.

Barnes was a difficult man to manage, and accordingly he wasn't always selected for England even where his talents would have made a significant difference. For much of his career he measured cricket in terms of what it could bring him in cash terms and not in terms of traditions of the game or what his legacy might be. Thus, he missed several Tests and even whole series.

He did play on the Ashes tour of 1911–12 and was the leading wicket-taker with 34 in the five Tests.

On the matting wickets in South Africa in 1913–14, Barnes was unplayable with 49 wickets in four Tests at 10.93. This included his best bowling in a Test of 17/159 which remained a Test record until Jim Laker's 19 wickets in 1956.

Barnes continued to play professional cricket well into his 50s, turning out for Staffordshire. Neville Cardus tells the story that when Barnes was 56 he turned out against the Lancashire Second XI where a young professional was due to bat at six and was heading off to watch Barnes bowl. His captain asked him where he was going and told him to pad up. The youngster queried the need to be padded up so early but within half an hour was back in the pavilion having had his brief turn at facing Barnes.

10. Tibby Cotter (AUS)

Test Record

Bat	M	Inn	NO	Runs	HS	Avg	100	50	Ct
	21	37	2	457	45	13.05	0	0	8
Bowl	M	Inn	Wkts	Avg	BBI	BBM	5i	10m	SR
	21	38	89	28.64	7/148	9/221	7	0	52.0

Albert 'Tibby' Cotter was a fast bowler who it was said generated extreme pace from a 'spear-throwing' action using powerful shoulders and chest. He could make the ball rear dangerously from a good length and was known to have shattered either the bails or the stumps on at least 20 occasions, such was the ferocity of his delivery. Cotter's strike rate of 52 exactly matches that of the great Dennis Lillee. On the downside he could often be erratic, even hitting WG Grace with a full toss on his first English tour. He was also said to be a useful hard-hitting batter, especially at district level, although he never really converted that to Tests.

Early success against the English in 1903–04 saw him selected for his Test debut that same summer as he played in the fourth and fifth Tests. He went wicketless in his first attempt but then grabbed three in the second innings of his first Test and then 6/40 and 2/25 in the final Test of the series. Australia had unearthed a genuine fast bowler to strike some fear into the hearts of opponents, picking up the mantle from Ernie Jones.

On the 1905 English tour, in the drawn fourth Test at The Oval, Cotter nabbed his best Test figures in an innings as he sent down 40 overs for 7/148. He also chipped in with his highest Test score during the series, 45 in a losing effort at Trent Bridge

Cotter played only two of the five Tests back in Australia in 1907–08 but still managed 14 wickets including a six-for and a five-for in the first innings of the first and second Tests respectively. In one of his better outings as a batter he made 33 not out as Australia chased 274 to win the first Test. He added 56 with for the eighth wicket with Hazlitt to see Australia home.

He was productive in England in 1909 taking 17 wickets in the five Tests, including 5/38 and 6/95 in the third and fifth Tests respectively. Cotter powered on against the South Africans back home in 1910–11 grabbing 22 wickets in the five Tests. However, in what turned out to be his final series in 1911–12 against England, Cotter managed only 12 wickets in the four Tests he played in.

The final member of this team who was part of the 'Big Six', Cotter finished his Test career after the 1911–12 series as he stood out of, or was not selected (depending how you look at it), for the 1912 tour of England.

It is unlikely that Cotter, in his late thirties, would have resumed his Test career after the war, but tragically he was killed in battle while acting as a stretcher bearer at Beersheba in 1917. There are several stories around how Cotter actually died, all suggesting his foresight of his impending doom. One has him peeping over the top of the trenches and being shot dead by a sniper. Shortly before doing so, he is said to have tossed a ball of mud in the air and said to a mate, 'That's my last bowl, something's going to happen.' He was only 33 when he was killed.

11. Colin Blythe (ENG)

Test Record

Bat	M	Inn	NO	Runs	HS	Avg	100	50	Ct
	19	31	12	183	27	9.63	0	0	6
Bowl	M	Inn	Wkts	Avg	BBI	BBM	5i	10m	SR
	19	37	100	18.63	8/59	15/99	9	4	45.4

Blythe would probably have played more Test matches if it were not for the fact Wilf Rhodes bowled similar left-arm spin and held down a regular spot in the English XI.

As it is, 100 wickets in just 19 matches is not a bad Test record. On top of that, Blythe took 2502 First Class wickets in all at an impressive average of 16.81, including a 10/30 bowling for Kent against Northants.

The first real record of Blythe the cricketer is his attendance at a county match as a spectator. There were few at the ground that day and Blythe found himself bowling in the nets. He impressed, and before too long found himself attending the Kent cricket nursery designed to develop young cricketers.

Blythe debuted for Kent in 1899 and took a wicket with his first ball against Yorkshire. During the course of the season *The Times* wrote that 'Blythe, the new Kent left-hand slow bowler, seems a very promising man'. The following year he picked up over 100 wickets in county cricket.

Chosen to tour Australia in 1901–02 with Archie MacLaren's side, Blythe made his Test debut in the first Test taking three wickets in the first innings and four in the second. In all, he ended up with 18 wickets at 26.11 even after he split his bowling hand on tour.

Blythe missed out when Australia toured in 1902 and played a single Test in 1905, filling in for Rhodes despite the opinion of *The Times* that he was 'very likely a better bowler'.

Selected to tour South Africa in 1905–06 Blythe took 21 wickets at 26.09 including his best figures to date of 6/68 and 5/50. He was also selected when South Africa toured England in 1907 and in the second Test ran through the South Africans with match figure of 15/99.

It wasn't enough to cement his place in the England XI and he played just once on the Australian tour in 1907–08, then twice when Australia visited in 1909. Despite just playing the couple of Tests out of the five, he topped the wickets tally for both teams with 18 at 13.44.

Blythe's final tour was to South Africa in 1910 and in his final Test at Cape Town took 10/104. Despite continuing to take county wickets and helping Kent to a couple of championships, Blythe did not play for England again.

He served during the Great War and he died tragically, killed in action at Passchendaele. A memorial stands on the St. Lawrence Ground in Canterbury.

1900–World War One Second XI

1. Archie MacLaren (ENG) c
2. Johnny Tyldesley (ENG)
3. Dave Nourse (SA)
4. Charles Macartney (AUS) vc
5. Reg Duff (AUS)
6. Vernon Ransford (AUS)
7. George Hirst (ENG)
8. Jim Kelly (AUS) wk
9. Bill Whitty (AUS)
10. Bert Vogler (SA)
11. Herbert Hordern (AUS)

1920s

After the horrors of World War One it was sweet relief to return to normalcy, and Test cricket was a large part of that. To get things underway England toured Australia in 1920–21. Australia set the tone for the series with a 377 run win in the first Test. They went on to easily win every Test in the five match series, the first time this had been achieved. The margins after the first Test were an innings and 91 runs, 119 runs, eight wickets and nine wickets. However, by the end of the decade the Ashes were back in England's hands after they won the 1928–29 series 4–1.

England played by far the most Tests at 48 and won 37.5% of them with Australia having the best win rate with a 50% record from 28 Tests. South Africa won a handful of Tests, all at home against England.

The West Indies played their first Tests in 1928 as part of a three Test tour of England. They were resoundingly thrashed by an innings in each of the Tests. The first batter to face up for the West Indies was George Challenor who ended up making 29. The first bowler to snare a wicket was Baron Constantine.

Herbert Sutcliffe and Jack Hobbs topped the runs scoring for the decade at the top of the English batting order. Batting averages as a whole took a leap forward; Sutcliffe and Hobbs averaged in the 60s compared to in the high 30s for the openers of the 1900s side. This occurred as better batting conditions were provided, including covered wickets. In fact, the batting averages for this 1920s XI could be said to be superior to the bowling averages for the decade. In other words: bat dominated ball for the era.

The unlucky player to have been left out of this XI was England's Patsy Hendren, who averaged 47.63 with the bat but didn't fit in the middle order: Australia's Herbie Collins's tenacity was preferred. Warren Bardsley of Australia also averaged over 40, but could not be squeezed into the team.

The opening bowling for the 1920s team would be a joy to watch for anyone but the opening batters as Harold Larwood and Jack Gregory steamed in. Gregory's ability as an all-rounder is an added benefit to the side. Maurice Tate, the leading wicket-taker for the decade, would provide an excellent first change option as well as some overs of off-spin, complemented by Arthur Mailley's leg-spin. Tich Freeman of England was closely considered for the leg-spinner's spot, but Mailley performed at a high level for a longer period of time than Freeman's 12 Tests and was chosen ahead of him.

A fine keeper he may have been, but Bert Strudwick almost gets the wicketkeeping spot by default as no Australian keeper qualified to be selected in this decade. Only two keepers played for Australia in the 1920s, and Sammy Carter belonged to the 1900s while Bert Oldfield qualified for selection in the 1930s.

Captain of the XI was also a close call with Australia's Herbie Collins laying a claim to the position. But, with his overall record, knowledge and experience, the honour went to Jack Hobbs.

Another cricketing event of note in the decade was the Test debut of Donald Bradman in 1928, signalling the start of a colossal career.

Most Test Runs in Period

Player	Mat	Inns	NO	Runs	HS	Ave	100	50	0
H Sutcliffe (ENG)	32	50	4	2960	176	64.34	12	13	1
JB Hobbs (ENG)	28	44	1	2644	211	61.48	10	10	1
FE Woolley (ENG)	33	50	3	2003	154	42.61	4	13	8
EH Hendren (ENG)	32	50	6	1869	169	42.47	4	11	4
WR Hammond** (ENG)	17	29	4	1689	251	67.56	6	5	1
HW Taylor (SA)	21	37	2	1612	176	46.05	5	9	0
J Ryder (AUS)	20	32	5	1394	201*	51.62	3	9	1
RH Catterall (SA)	20	36	2	1378	120	40.52	3	9	3
HL Collins (AUS)	19	31	1	1352	203	45.06	4	6	0
CG Macartney*** (AUS)	14	21	3	1252	170	69.55	6	3	0

*not out **qualifies for the 1930s *** qualifies for 1900–World War One

Most Test Wickets in Period

Player	Mat	Inns	Wkts	BBI	BBM	Ave	SR	5	10
MW Tate (ENG)	26	46	118	6/42	11/228	25.16	76.6	6	1
AA Mailey (AUS)	21	34	99	9/121	13/236	33.91	61.8	6	2
JM Gregory (AUS)	24	42	85	7/69	8/101	31.15	65.6	4	0
AP Freeman (ENG)	12	22	66	7/71	12/171	25.86	56.5	5	3
CV Grimmett* (AUS)	9	16	47	6/37	11/82	32.34	80.9	5	1
EA McDonald (AUS)	11	21	43	5/32	8/74	33.27	67.0	2	0
JM Blanckenberg (SA)	13	18	41	6/76	9/135	33.87	69.7	3	0
G Geary (ENG)	11	18	41	7/70	12/130	25.73	74.9	4	1
H Larwood (ENG)	12	22	41	6/32	8/62	31.12	74.1	2	0
AER Gilligan (ENG)	11	20	36	6/7	11/90	29.05	66.7	2	1

*qualifies for the 1930s

Results

Team	Span	Mat	Won	Lost	Tied	Draw	W/L
England	1920–29	48	18	16	0	14	1.125
Australia	1920–29	28	14	6	0	8	2.333
South Africa	1921–29	23	3	10	0	10	0.300
West Indies	1928–28	3	0	3	0	0	0.000

1920s XI

1. Jack Hobbs (ENG) c
2. Herbert Sutcliffe (ENG)
3. Jack Ryder (AUS)
4. Frank Woolley (ENG)
5. Herbie Taylor (SA)
6. Herbie Collins (AUS) vc
7. Jack Gregory (AUS)
8. Maurice Tate (ENG)
9. Harold Larwood (ENG)
10. Arthur Mailey (AUS)
11. Bert Strudwick (ENG) wk

1. Jack Hobbs (ENG) c

Test Record

Bat	M	Inn	NO	Runs	HS	Avg	100	50	Ct
	61	102	7	5410	211	56.94	15	28	17

Bowl	M	Inn	Wkts	Avg	BBI	BBM	5i	10m	SR
	61	11	1	165	1/19	1/30	0	0	376.0

Jack Hobbs is one of the all-time greats and was voted one of the five best cricketers of the twentieth century by *Wisden*. Naturally he is also an inductee in the ICC Cricket Hall of Fame.

'The Master', as he was known, is the oldest player to score a Test century at 46 years old. Hobbs's record would be even greater if the Great War had not intervened, but his First Class record of 197 hundreds is unlikely to be beaten. Over half his centuries were scored in his forties and in all he knocked up over 60,000 First Class runs. His record would likely be higher if he did not have the habit of giving up his wicket on reaching a century to give others a go.

Hobbs played for Surrey and made his English debut in 1908 versus Australia at Melbourne, where he made 83 at his first bat. He played in four of the five Tests and scored 302 runs at an average of 43.44. In 1908 Hobbs was chosen as one of the five *Wisden* Cricketers of the Year.

When Australia visited in 1909, Hobbs retained his place at the top of the order and scored 62 not out in the second innings of the first Test as England chased down 105 to win. He later injured his finger and missed the last couple of Tests.

In early 1910 Hobbs played his first Tests on the difficult matting pitches in South Africa and performed admirably with 539 runs at 67.37, including his maiden Test century of 187. Lacking in fast-bowling depth, Hobbs also opened the bowling on a couple of occasions but took just a single wicket.

Hobbs continued his success in Australia in 1911–12 amassing 662 runs at 82.75. His opening partnership with Wilf Rhodes was flourishing and they added 323 together in the fourth Test. In a wet 1912 in the triangular series, Hobbs topped the averages for all three teams averaging 40 against South Africa and 56 against Australia.

During the war, Hobbs worked first in a munitions factory then as an air mechanic, and returned to cricket with a less attacking frame of mind, becoming more a ruthless accumulator of runs. He averaged 50, topping the English averages, on the disastrous 1920–21 Ashes tour which saw the resumption of Test cricket.

In 1924 Hobbs began his successful opening partnership with Herbert Sutcliffe, one of the great opening partnerships in history. That year, Hobbs added 355 runs at 71 to his career tally against South Africa. He backed this up with 573 runs at 63.67 on the 1924–25 tour of Australia.

Hobbs continued to score heavily until his final series in 1930 against the Australians. He was below his best with 301 runs at 33.44, but was given a rousing reception by the crowd and three cheers from the opposition in his final Test where he made 47 and nine. He retired from Test cricket as the leading run scorer in Test history.

2. Herbert Sutcliffe (ENG)

Test Record

Bat	M	Inn	NO	Runs	HS	Avg	100	50	Ct
	54	84	9	4555	194	60.73	16	23	23

Yorkshireman Sutcliffe sits fifth on the all-time batting averages table (minimum 20 Tests) and leads the averages for Test openers, which demonstrates his quality as a player. In all First Class cricket he scored in excess of 50,000 runs at an average over 50 with 149 centuries.

His *Wisden* obituary noted: 'Courage and concentration were his basic attributes. No prospect daunted him, no difficulty dismayed him, no crisis upset him. He was an artist of the dead bat and an uncompromising hooker of fast bowling. He sought solution to his batting problems by taking them as they came, one at a time. He never allowed the present to be influenced by the alarms of the past or fears for the future. In the means and manner of his performances he raised enormous prestige for himself throughout the cricketing world. He was admired and respected wherever he played and by his refusal to depreciate his own value he raised the status of his profession'.

Due to the Great War, Sutcliffe was 24 before he played county cricket and thus delayed his Test debut which came against South Africa at Birmingham in 1924. There, he compiled 54 at his only bat as England won by an innings. It was also the debut of the famed Sutcliffe and Hobbs opening partnership and they kicked off with a century stand (136).

Sutcliffe was renowned as a master on all pitches, even on a rain affected 'sticky' such as his hundreds against Australia at The Oval in 1926 (161) and Melbourne in 1929 (135). He could also accelerate the scoring tempo should the situation dictate – his 113 against NHS on a 'sticky', for example, included ten sixes, and he made his hundredth hundred of 132 in under two hours while playing Gloucestershire.

He was offered the captaincy of Yorkshire as a professional which was unheard of in the 1920s and, sensing the disquiet his appointment may cause, he politely declined the offer.

Sutcliffe's final Test came in South Africa in 1935 where he managed only three and 38.

Post-cricket, Sutcliffe tended to his sports outfitters store he had started while playing and took a managerial appointment in the paper trade.

3. Jack Ryder (AUS)

Test Record

Bat	M	Inn	NO	Runs	HS	Avg	100	50	Ct
	20	32	5	1394	201*	51.62	3	9	17

Bowl	M	Inn	Wkts	Avg	BBI	BBM	5i	10m	SR
	20	28	17	43.70	2/20	2/29	0	0	111.5

*not out

In any era, a batter who plays at least 20 Tests and averages over 50 is regarded as a class batter. Ryder was the first Australian to meet these criteria at the end of their career. Further, he sits just below Ricky Ponting and above Alan Border and Steve Waugh on the averages chart, so he demands respect. Nonetheless, despite being admitted to the Australian Cricket Hall of Fame with Adam Gilchrist in 2015, Ryder does not seem to be remembered with the same reverence as some of his contemporaries.

Perhaps his style of play didn't endear him to spectators back in the 1920s. Jack Fingleton described him as 'a plucky, competent player who made up for technical difficulties with an indomitable spirit'. However, Australians have always admired an indomitable spirit. He was tall – 6 foot 2 inches in the old scale (188 centimetres) – and a powerful front-foot player who once notched 295 in 245 minutes against New South Wales in a Sheffield Shield match. Monty Noble described him as 'a master of the forcing game'.

Debuting for Victoria in the 1912–13 season, Johnny Moyes noted, 'He ranked high among the all-rounders.' On resumption of 'Big' cricket after the war, Ryder was selected in the first Test team in 1920 against the English. He had the ignominy of being run out in both innings for not many and remains the only debutant to be run out in both innings of a Test.

Ryder found his feet in Test cricket on the way home from the Ashes in 1921, where the South African bowling was to his liking as he thrashed them for 334 runs at 111. Here, he crafted his first Test century (142) in the third Test to go with three fifties from three at bats in the other Tests. In the third Test of the 1924–25 Ashes series, he came to the wicket at 5–118 and made 201 not out taking Australia to 489. He added 88 in the second innings, giving him a match aggregate of 289 – the highest in Test history at the time.

Ryder was made captain of the Australian team for the 1928–29 summer against England. This series was an unfortunate one to be called upon to lead, as a draft of experienced players had retired and young stars, like Bradman, were just starting out. It was his only series in charge as Australia lost 1–4. He did gain the admiration of his teammates and gradually gelled the side into one that could bounce back in the future. It wasn't that Ryder's batting that let the side down either, as he averaged 54.67 for the series. Ryder was unceremoniously dumped as captain for the 1930 tour of England (to be replaced by Bill Woodfull) and left out of the team altogether and then forever.

The Jack Ryder medal was instituted in 1973 by the Victorian Cricket Association for the best district cricketer. He was an Australian selector from 1946 to 1970 and awarded an MBE in 1958. Ryder also played seconds football for Collingwood and was associated with the Collingwood Cricket Club as player, selector, coach and official for 71 years. He became known as the 'King of Collingwood' – not bad for a non-footy player in the football-mad suburb. And in a final notable point, Ryder was the oldest Ashes player in attendance at the Centenary Test in March 1977 and led the players' parade.

4. Frank Woolley (ENG)

Test Record

Bat	M	Inn	NO	Runs	HS	Avg	100	50	Ct
	64	98	7	3283	154	36.07	5	23	64

Bowl	M	Inn	Wkts	Avg	BBI	BBM	5i	10m	SR
	64	87	83	33.91	7/76	10/49	4	1	78.2

Like many of his contemporaries, Woolley had an outstanding First Class career which his Test record does not quite match. He scored 58,969 runs (still second only to the great Jack Hobbs) at 40.75, mostly for England and Kent. Woolley could also be considered an all-rounder as his slow left-arm orthodox took over 2000 wickets at less than 20 each. Woolley also held over 1000 catches, mainly at slip, the only non-wicketkeeper in the history of First Class cricket to have achieved this. His Test career lasted over 25 years – the third longest in terms of time – although he lost several years to the war. He was known as the Pride of Kent.

Woolley's *Wisden* obituary, published in 1978, stated: 'Even more impressive than the number of runs Woolley amassed was the manner in which he made them. Standing well over 6 foot, he was a joy to watch. He played an eminently straight bat, employed his long reach to full advantage, and used his feet in a manner nowadays rarely seen. His timing of the ball approached perfection and he generally dealt surely with all types of bowling. Master of all the strokes, he was at his best driving, cutting, and turning the ball off his legs.'

Australian captain Bill Woodfull described him thus: 'He made the game look so untidy. It appeared as if the wrong bowlers were on and the fieldsmen all in the wrong places.'

Debuting against Australia at The Oval in 1909, Woolley began inauspiciously scoring only six and going wicketless. He was soon into his stride with several fifties in South Africa before his maiden

Test ton in 1911–12 in Australia, where he averaged just under 50 for the five Tests.

Woolley was initially declined service during the war on medical grounds, but was later accepted into the Royal Naval Air Service. He also played some exhibition matches.

On the resumption of cricket, he was back in the English side for the 1921 Australian tour of England. He had a solid series again averaging just under 50, narrowly missing hundreds in the second Test. In his words: 'As a matter of fact I consider the two finest innings I ever played were in the second Test against Australia in 1921 when I was out for 95 and 93. I don't think I ever worked harder at any match during my career to get runs as I did then, nor did I ever have to face in one game such consistently fast bowlers as the Australian pair, Gregory and McDonald. Square cuts which ordinarily would have flashed to the boundary earned only two, and I believe that those two innings would have been worth 150 apiece in a county match.'

Woolley played Test cricket until 1934 when he was 47 (failing in his last Test with four and a duck).

Elected as a life member of the MCC and of course Kent, he remarried later in life to an American widow and settled in Canada, where he died in 1978 aged 91.

5. Herbie Taylor (SA)

Test Record

Bat	M	Inn	NO	Runs	HS	Avg	100	50	Ct
	42	76	4	2936	176	40.77	7	17	19

Bowl	M	Inn	Wkts	Avg	BBI	BBM	5i	10m	SR
	42	11	5	31.20	3/15	4/53	0	0	68.4

Herbie Taylor is one of the greats of South African cricket. Playing much of his cricket on the matting used during his career in South Africa, he mastered all that England and Australia could throw at him, including the deadly Syd Barnes. EW Swanton wrote of Taylor: 'The basis of his play was the straightest of straight bats, nimble footwork, and an almost unfailing judgment of length. His method was so sound that he remained a beautiful player when nearer 50 than 40.' Taylor so mastered the matting that he averaged just under 50 at home and around 30 away from home.

Taylor debuted in the 1912 triangular series with England and Australia, beginning slowly but showing promise with a 93 in the second Test against Australia (which remained his highest score against Australia).

At age 24 he was made captain of his country for the 1913–14 tour by England. As Barnes destroyed his team, Taylor emerged unscathed as the leading run scorer for the series with 508 runs at 50.80 including his maiden Test ton in the first Test at Durban. The cricket historian HS Altham wrote: 'The English cricketers were unanimous that finer batting than his against Barnes at his best they never hoped to see.'

He spent the war in the Royal Flying Corps (later the Royal Air Force) and was awarded the Military Cross.

Taylor returned to Test cricket in 1921 against the Australians in South Africa with moderate success. However, in 1922–23 he had another run-leading series against England at home with 582 runs at 64.66 (he also topped the averages) including two centuries.

Once again showing his liking for the English at home, Taylor added a further 412 runs (topping the South Africans' run list) at 41.20 in 1927–28, and 299 runs at 49.83 in 1931.

Taylor played his final Test against New Zealand in 1932 but made only nine in his only bat.

His captaincy record was disappointing with just a single win from 18 matches in charge, although this is more a reflection of the relative standard of South African cricket at the time than it is commentary on Taylor's captaincy.

In Currie Cup (South Africa's domestic competition) matches, he scored 3226 runs at an average of 58.65 and was part of seven championship-winning teams, four with Natal and three with Transvaal.

After his Test career, Taylor stayed involved in cricket, coaching boys in Cape Town most Sunday mornings for the rest of his life.

6. Herbie Collins (AUS) vc

Test Record

Bat	M	Inn	NO	Runs	HS	Avg	100	50	Ct
	19	31	1	1352	203	45.06	4	6	13

Bowl	M	Inn	Wkts	Avg	BBI	BBM	5i	10m	SR
	19	12	4	63.00	2/47	2/84	0	0	163.5

Herbert Collins was more a nudger and deflector than a dasher, whose Test debut was likely delayed by World War One.

During the war, Collins served in the AIF in Palestine and then as a driver in France with the unenviable role of delivering artillery to the front lines. He finished the war as a lance corporal and was selected as captain of the AIF team at the conclusion of the war, despite it comprising several more senior officers.

Collins was then selected to debut for Australia in the first Test on resumption of cricket. He performed beyond expectation, making 70 in the first dig and completing a century on debut in the second. He added another century (162) in the third Test and finished as the leading Australian run scorer for the series.

Collins was appointed captain in Armstrong's absence for the stopover in South Africa on the way home from England in 1921. He led from the front with a double century in the second Test and captained the team to 1–0 series victory. He retained the captaincy when England next visited Australia in 1924–25, this time leading his country to a 4–1 series victory.

As a noted gambler, Arthur Mailey said of him, 'Collins' hunting grounds are the race-track, the dog-track, Monte Carlo, a baccarat joint at King's Cross, a two-up school in the Flanders trenches and anywhere a quiet game of poker was played.' In fact, it was in the 1924–45 series, with England needing 27 to win with two wickets in hand, that Collins was approached by a well-dressed man at the hotel before they departed for the day's play. Collins was offered £100 to lose the match and he immediately went to Mailey to inform him of the offer and suggested they throw the guy down the stairs. Given his size they thought better of it. Australia went on to win by 11 runs.

Collins's last hurrah with the Australian team was captaining them to England in 1926. Unfortunately, he suffered from neuritis and he missed the third and fourth Tests (which were drawn) due to an injury, but England regained the Ashes 1–0. Again, Collins had an ordinary tour with the bat and he retired after the last Test, the pain from his condition proving too great to carry on.

As a captain, Collins was in stark contrast to Armstrong, the man he took over from. Collins was a quieter, more controlled captain who won the respect of his teammates as well as the opposition. Mailey said, 'I learnt more from him of the psychology of cricket than all the hundreds of cricketers I met, he would carry the burden of responsibility yet transfer the credit to those he thought deserved it most.' With a record of 11 matches, five wins, two losses and four draws, Collins is the choice to vice-captain the 1920s XI.

Collins was also an outstanding rugby league player who turned out for Eastern Suburbs (now the Sydney Roosters) playing at five-eighth alongside the great Dally Messenger, and figured in their first New South Wales Rugby League premiership in 1911.

7. Jack Gregory (AUS)

Test Record

Bat	M	Inn	NO	Runs	HS	Avg	100	50	Ct
	24	34	3	1146	119	36.96	2	7	37
Bowl	M	Inn	Wkts	Avg	BBI	BBM	5i	10m	SR
	24	42	85	31.15	7/69	8/101	4	0	65.6

Jack Gregory was of the famed Gregory cricketing family. His uncle Dave was Australia's first Test captain, and his cousin Syd played 58 Tests around the turn of last century. Jack was perhaps the most famous of them all.

An explosive all-rounder, he bowled right-handed with fearsomeness and batted left-handed without gloves or a box for protection, and with equal venom. His slip-fielding was said to round out his brilliance. Neville Cardus wrote of him, 'A giant of superb physique, ran some twenty yards to release the ball with a high step at gallop, then, at the moment of delivery, a huge leap, a great wave of energy breaking at the crest, and a follow-through nearly to the batsman's doorstep.' His high action meant plenty of bounce at pace, which spelt trouble for batters.

Gregory volunteered as an artillery gunner with the AIF and did two tours of duty in France, rising to the rank of lieutenant by the end of the war. In 1919, Gregory was selected to take part in the AIF matches and made an impact with bat and ball.

Gregory made his Test debut on the resumption of Test cricket in 1920–21. He had an outstanding series and contributed greatly to Australia's 5–0 drubbing of the old enemy, scoring 442 runs at 73.67 including his maiden hundred and taking 23 wickets at 24. Gregory also took 15 catches, the most for any player in the series including the wicketkeepers. In fact, it remains a record for the most catches taken in a series by a fielder who was not a wicketkeeper.

For the 1921 tour of England Gregory was joined by Ted McDonald, and together they formed a fearsome opening bowling partnership, probably the first of the great truly fast ones. Between them they took 46 of 71 wickets to fall to bowlers in the series. Gregory was not as productive with the bat, averaging just 21, but took 19 wickets as the English were again tamed.

Gregory would be forever remembered for this innings in the second Test on the stopover in South Africa, where he brought up his hundred in only 70 minutes. A hundred years later, this remains the all-time record for the fastest Test century in terms of minutes taken.

By the late '20s, Gregory's ferocious approach to his craft was catching up with him, and in the first Test of the 1928–29 season he broke down with a knee injury and his career was over. It was Bradman's first Test, and he recalls Gregory limping in to the dressing rooms and saying, 'Boys I'm through, I've played my last game.'

Gregory died in 1973 and Bill O'Reilly wrote, 'Gregory assumed a cricket stature of such magnetic appeal that one can truthfully say that Don Bradman has been the only Australian to reach the same plane.'

8. Maurice Tate (ENG)

Test Record

Bat	M	Inn	NO	Runs	HS	Avg	100	50	Ct
	39	52	5	1198	100*	25.48	1	5	11

Bowl	M	Inn	Wkts	Avg	BBI	BBM	5i	10m	SR
	39	68	155	26.16	6/42	11/228	7	1	80.7

*not out

Tate's versatility with the ball, bowling medium-fast or orthodox spin, won his place in the 1920s XI over the express Ted McDonald. His batting is also a useful addition lower down the order.

His old English captain Arthur Gilligan wrote in 1954 of his conversion from slow to fast bowler: 'Tate, I must say at once, was the greatest bowler our county has produced. Curiously, when I first played for Sussex, Maurice used the same run-up and style of delivery as his father – a slow bowler! A sheer piece of luck caused Maurice to change his methods. Sussex had batted very badly in 1922, and when we had a day off the whole team practised at the nets. Maurice Tate bowled me several of his slow deliveries, then down came a quick one which spreadeagled my stumps. He did this three times. I went up to him and said: "Maurice, you must change your style of bowling immediately." My hunch paid. In the next match against Kent at Tunbridge Wells, Maurice, in his new style as a quick bowler, was unplayable. He took three wickets in four balls and eight in the innings for 67. That was the turning-point in his career.'

C.B Fry wrote: 'Tate was a very great cricketer indeed. He could make the ball swing away very late outside the off-stump, and even the best batsmen were often beaten by him. He could make the ball rear off the pitch like a snake striking. He was even more successful in Australia than in this country – in fact, he ranks with S.F Barnes as the most successful bowler England has ever sent there.'

Bert Strudwick said: 'He was the best length bowler I ever kept wicket to and the best bowler of his pace I ever knew. There was not a quicker bowler off the wicket. I class him with Sidney Barnes and F.R Foster as the three best bowlers I ever kept to.'

Tate debuted against South Africa in England in 1924 and took 4/12 as South Africa were bowled out for 30. He also picked up four in the second innings and 27 for the series.

He then dominated the bowling on the 1924–25 Ashes tour as he took 38 wickets in five Tests. In the 1926 Ashes series, Tate again led the English wickets tally with 13 and took a further 17 on the 1928–29 tour of Australia. In all Tate took 83 Ashes wickets at an average of around 30.

Tate took 53 wickets against the South Africans and a handful as the West Indies and New Zealand entered the Test cricket arena.

When he retired from First Class cricket, Tate took over the licences of several Sussex inns and for a number of years coached the boys of Tonbridge School.

9. Harold Larwood (ENG)

Test Record

Bat	M	Inn	NO	Runs	HS	Avg	100	50	Ct
	21	28	3	485	98	19.40	0	2	15 |//

Bowl	M	Inn	Wkts	Avg	BBI	BBM	5i	10m	SR
	21	36	78	28.35	6/32	10/124	4	1	63.7

A genuine fast bowler who struck fear into the hearts of opposition batters, especially during the infamous bodyline series of 1932–33 against Australia. Standing at just 173 centimetres (5 foot 8 inches) Larwood was powerfully built and had a smooth, rhythmic approach and a high action. Larwood's stock ball cut back from the off and his bouncer tended to skid onto the batter, making evasion difficult.

Larwood debuted at Lord's in 1926 against the Australians and dismissed Charlie Macartney, Jack Gregory and Herbie Collins. He toured Australia in 1928–29 and took 6/32 in the first innings of the first Test. He also played in the 1930 Ashes series, but took only four wickets from three Tests and got Bradman out only once after he had reached a double century.

Douglas Jardine was selected as captain for the 1932–33 Ashes tour and he adopted 'leg theory' – bowl fast and short at the body of the batter and have a ring of close in fielders on the leg side. Australia called it bodyline. Larwood was selected to be Jardine's chief henchman in executing the plan, primarily to stop Bradman.

Larwood executed the plan to perfection and dismissed Bradman four times in eight innings. The crowd and the Australian public were incensed, and while Jardine was public enemy number one Larwood was not far behind, especially after he hit Woodfull above the heart and knocked Bert Oldfield out cold with a bouncer (which Oldfield did edge into his own head).

The Australian Cricket Board shot off a cable to their England counterparts complaining but to no avail. Strangely though, when Larwood scored 98 as nightwatchman he was cheered from the ground. Larwood took 33 wickets in the series at an average of just under 20.

However, this would be the end of Larwood's Test career. While Jardine was the architect of bodyline, Larwood seemed to carry the blame once English authorities realised what was going on. A letter of apology was drawn up for Larwood to sign – which he refused – and he was not selected again.

Larwood was injured for the 1933 season but was fit again for the first Test of the 1934 Ashes series, only to be omitted. Larwood said, 'I refuse to play in any more Tests. Politicians are trying to hound me out of cricket. I was fit for the last Test. They feared I would burst the Empire.'

He took 82 cheap wickets for Nottinghamshire that summer, and over 100 in 1935 and 1936, topping the national bowling averages in 1936 for the fifth time in his life.

After cricket Larwood grew flowers and vegetables, and then for a time owned a confectionary store before uprooting the family and moving, of all places, to Australia. He was readily accepted by his new country and was happy to give interviews and receive visitors, and was eventually elected to life membership of the SCG.

10. Arthur Mailey (AUS)

Test Record

Bat	M	Inn	NO	Runs	HS	Avg	100	50	Ct
	21	29	9	222	46*	11.10	0	0	14
Bowl	M	Inn	Wkts	Avg	BBI	BBM	5i	10m	SR
	21	34	99	33.91	9/121	13/236	6	2	61.8

*not out

One of Australia's great all-time leg-spinners along with Warne, O'Reilly, Grimmett and Benaud, Mailey was prepared to give the ball a real rip as well as use flight in deceiving the batter. Occasionally this meant he was a little erratic especially in length, and thus expensive, which is where he falls down in comparison with the others, as he averaged in the 30s while the other greats were in the low to mid-20s. However, his strike rate of 61.8 was better than O'Reilly, Grimmett and Benaud, and just behind the legendary Warne on 57.4. As Wilfred Rhodes said of him: 'He never gave up. He would have nought for 100 and might finish with six for 130.'

Christened Alfred Arthur Mailey, he was born in Waterloo – one of Sydney's worst slums – in 1886. Mailey did well to survive infancy, as mortality rates were high in areas such as Waterloo and two of his siblings did not make it past the age of two.

Another whose Test debut was pushed back by World War One, Mailey was nearing his 35th birthday when he was finally able to make his Test debut in the first Test of the 1920–21 Ashes. He began well, claiming three wickets in each innings and finished the series as the leading wicket-taker for either side with 36. This was also an Australian record for any series and the record stood for 57 years. Mailey also set another record as he took 9/121 in the second innings of the fourth Test – this remains the best bowling in an innings by any Australian in the history of Test cricket.

On the 1921 England tour playing in four of the five Tests, Mailey again tormented the English by bagging 27 wickets, also the most for either team. While on tour, Mailey also took all ten wickets in an innings (10/66) versus Gloucestershire. He took inspiration from this when he named his autobiography *10 for 66 and All That*. For good measure, he added another 13 wickets in the three Tests against South Africa on the way home from England.

Mailey again led the Australian wicket tally with 24 when England visited Australia in 1924–25, although he was becoming a little more expensive as he averaged 40 runs per wicket. While we're on the number 40, he was aged 40 when he was selected on the 1926 Ashes tour. He wasn't as productive as he had been on the previous trip but once again led Australia's wicket-taking with 14 wickets in five Tests. The fifth Test of the 1926 tour was to be Mailey's swansong, and he retired from international cricket.

Post-cricket, Mailey became a talented cartoonist and journalist and worked as a sporting cartoonist and a cricket writer, as well as composing several booklets of anecdotes and sketches and, of course, his autobiography. Mailey also led cricket tours within Australia and one to North America in 1932.

Mailey was beloved by his teammates and the public alike. He enjoyed his cricket; it was not something to be taken too seriously and matters such as statistics meant little to him. Having a go was the important thing.

11. Bert Strudwick (ENG) wk

Test Record

Bat	Mat	Inn	NO	Runs	HS	Avg	100	50	Ct	St
	28	42	13	230	24	7.93	0	0	61	12

Bert Strudwick still sits third on the all-time list of catches in First Class cricket with 1237. Add to that 258 stumpings and it makes for a pretty good career.

Tributes to Strudwick included the comment from Arthur Gilligan that, 'Not only was he a magnificent wicketkeeper, but he set a fine example to the rest of the side, always being first to be ready to play. He was 100 per cent in every way.'

Herbert Sutcliffe noted, 'He was first of all a gentleman and a sportsman and in his capabilities as fine a player as Bertie Oldfield, the great Australian wicketkeeper. I played both with and against Struddy and rated him absolutely first-class in every way.'

Strudwick's *Wisden* obituary notes that he became a wicketkeeper at a young age: 'It is of interest to note that a lady set Struddy on the path to becoming the world's most celebrated wicketkeeper. As a choir-boy at Mitcham, his birth-place, he took part in matches under the supervision of the daughter of the vicar, a Miss Wilson. Then about 10 years old, Strudwick habitually ran in from cover to the wicket to take returns from the field. Observing how efficiently he did this, Miss Wilson once said: You ought to be a wicketkeeper. From that point, Strudwick became one.'

Debuting against South Africa in Johannesburg in 1910, Strudwick took three catches and made seven, on par with his somewhat meagre Test average.

In his early Test career Strudwick showed his skill in keeping to the great Syd Barnes, particularly on the matting pitches of South Africa in 1913–14 when Barnes was at his best.

After the war, he maintained his place in the England XI, except for a couple of Tests in 1920–21 when he was dropped to try and improve the batting in that disastrous series for England.

Strudwick retired after the fifth Test of the 1926 Ashes series at The Oval. He turned to coaching and became scorer for Surrey for many years and wrote articles for *Wisden*.

1920s Second XI

1. Warren Bardsley (AUS) vc
2. Bob Catterall (SA)
3. Patsy Hendren (ENG) c
4. Charles Russell (ENG)
5. Johnny Taylor (AUS)
6. Charles Kelleway (AUS)
7. Horace Ward (SA) wk
8. Ted McDonald (AUS)
9. Arthur Gilligan (ENG)
10. Alfred Hall (SA)
11. Tich Freeman (ENG)

1930s

The 1930s was the Bradman decade. He may not have scored the most runs, but he averaged over a hundred over the course of the decade. West Indian George Headley also excelled and averaged 66 while Hammond, Ponsford and Paynter finished in the 50s and were all automatic selections. Some very good batters were left out including Australia's Stan McCabe and Bill Brown, and England's Maurice Leyland, all of whom averaged in the high 40s.

Spinners filled the top-three bowling spots (and four of the top-six) with Kiwi-born Australian leg-spinner Clarrie Grimmett taking pole position. It was not possible to fit all three in the 1930s XI, and Englishman Hedley Verity was the unlucky omission. Bill Voce and Gubby Allen were the standout pace bowlers of the decade with Hammond to provide back up with his medium pacers.

Perhaps Australia's Bert Oldfield was the best keeper of the decade, but Englishman Les Ames's ability with the bat saw him get the nod.

Australia was statistically the most successful nation with a win rate of 56%, followed by England on 32% and the West Indies on 21%.

New Zealand and India played Test cricket for the first time, but neither country tasted success during the decade. New Zealand did manage to draw nine of their 14 Tests after losing their first Test by eight wickets. India lost five of their seven Tests after debuting at Lord's in 1932 and losing by 158 runs.

The West Indies recorded their first Test wins over England and Australia, at Georgetown and Sydney respectively, and to prove it was no fluke they defeated England twice more.

Then there was the drama of 1932–33. The infamous bodyline series with Douglas Jardine and Harold Larwood front and centre. The idea of course was to bowl fast into the body with a very heavily weighted close in leg side field. Jardine believed this was the way to curb Bradman after he thought Bradman drew away from Larwood while racking up a mere 232 in the fifth Test in 1930. 'Leg theory' as it was known was not a new concept, it had been around before in county cricket and Jardine was simply adopting it for the English.

England beat a Bradman-less Australia by ten wickets in the first Test but Australia bounced back to win the second. Things really threatened to boil over in the third Test at Adelaide when Australian captain Bill Woodfull was hit above the heart by Larwood on an orthodox-set field. Once Woodfull had recovered, Jardine ordered his players to take up their leg theory positions. The crowd of 50,962 went berserk. That evening Woodfull made his famous statement that, 'There are two teams out there on The Oval. One is playing cricket, the other is not.' Matters weren't helped when, the next day, Bert Oldfield deflected a ball from Larwood onto his head, fracturing his skull. Oldfield, however, has always claimed that it was his own fault. England won the Test.

During the series, in response to bodyline, the Australian Board of Control sent a cable to the MCC stating, amongst other things, that bodyline was unsportsmanlike. The MCC wrote back saying, 'We deplore your cable', denying anything unsportsmanlike was taking place and threatening to cancel the balance of the tour unless the Board withdrew the perceived slur. However, after to and fro – including the intervention of Australian Prime Minister Joseph Lyons – the tour was not cancelled. Perhaps the financial realities were a consideration too?

Most Test Runs in Period

Player	Mat	Inns	NO	Runs	HS	Ave	100	50
WR Hammond (ENG)	60	98	11	5194	336*	59.70	16	17
DG Bradman (AUS)	33	49	4	4625	334	102.77	19	6
SJ McCabe (AUS)	39	62	5	2748	232	48.21	6	13
LEG Ames (ENG)	46	71	12	2434	149	41.25	8	7
M Leyland (ENG)	34	55	4	2280	187	44.70	7	7
B Mitchell (SA)	27	51	6	2148	164*	47.73	5	13
GA Headley (WI)	19	35	3	2135	270*	66.71	10	5
EH Hendren (ENG)	19	33	3	1656	205*	55.20	3	10
WH Ponsford (AUS)	20	32	3	1604	266	55.31	5	5
H Sutcliffe** (ENG)	22	34	5	1595	194	55.00	4	10

**qualifies for the 1920s era   *not out

Most Test Wickets in Period

Player	Mat	Inns	Wkts	BBI	BBM	Ave	SR	5	10
CV Grimmett (AUS)	28	51	169	7/40	14/199	21.95	63.3	16	6
H Verity (ENG)	40	73	144	8/43	15/104	24.37	77.5	5	2
WJ O'Reilly (AUS)	26	46	136	7/54	11/129	23.68	72.8	10	3
W Voce (ENG)	24	46	97	7/70	11/149	26.04	60.3	3	2
GOB Allen (ENG)	22	40	76	7/80	10/78	28.60	54.1	5	1
H Ironmonger (AUS)	12	24	68	7/23	11/24	15.05	54.7	4	2
WE Bowes (ENG)	14	27	67	6/33	9/219	21.58	51.9	6	0
K Farnes (ENG)	15	27	60	6/96	10/179	28.65	65.5	3	1
WR Hammond (ENG)	60	79	59	5/57	7/87	38.15	97.6	1	0
RWV Robins (ENG)	18	32	59	6/32	7/68	28.45	51.8	1	0

Results

Team	Mat	Won	Lost	Tied	Draw	W/L
England	72	23	14	0	35	1.642
Australia	39	22	10	0	7	2.200
South Africa	27	4	10	0	13	0.400
West Indies	19	4	9	0	6	0.444
India	7	0	5	0	2	0.000
New Zealand	14	0	5	0	9	0.000

1930s XI

1. Bill Ponsford (AUS)
2. Bruce Mitchell (SA)
3. Don Bradman (AUS) c
4. Wally Hammond (ENG) vc
5. George Headley (WI)
6. Eddie Paynter (ENG)
7. Les Ames (ENG) wk
8. Gubby Allen (ENG)
9. Clarrie Grimmett (AUS)
10. Bill Voce (ENG)
11. Bill O'Reilly (AUS)

1. Bill Ponsford (AUS)

Test Record

Bat	M	Inn	NO	Runs	HS	Avg	100	50	Ct
	29	48	4	2122	266	48.22	7	6	21

Ponsford had an insatiable appetite for building huge scores and with them huge partnerships. Johnny Moyes described Ponsford thus: '[he] accumulated runs like a miser hoards wealth. Almost infallible against spin. He sidled down the pitch like a crab, was always in the right place, seemed to know just what spin had been imparted.' Arthur Mailey took the view, perhaps a little unkindly, that Ponsford was 'dour, sullen, determined, breaker of batting records and bowlers' hearts.' Quiet and standoffish, he let his 'Big Bertha' bat (weighing in at 2.4 kilograms; heavy for the day but comparable to many bats these days) do the talking.

Not overly tall at 175 centimetres (5 foot 9 inches) he was an excellent front-foot player, driving through the covers and to the on side. He possessed a fierce cut-shot and was an outstanding hooker of the ball if in the mood. Ponsford's biggest strength was his concentration over long periods that drove opposing teams to distraction. Interestingly when Ponsford volunteered for the Royal Australian Air Force for World War Two, it was discovered he had acute red-green colour blindness.

Before getting to Ponsford's Test career, it is worth considering his First Class average was 65.18 with 47 hundreds, 13 double hundreds, two triple centuries and two quadruple hundreds. He scored centuries in 20% of his innings. In Sheffield Shield he averaged 83.27.

In the first Test of the 1924–25 Ashes series, Ponsford debuted with a century (110) and followed this up with another century (128) in the second.

From early December 1926 he strung together a torrent of First Class runs – 11 centuries in consecutive matches including a 437 and two other triples. Thus, he was considered to be in form when the English arrived in 1928–29. However, his little finger was shattered by a Larwood delivery in the first innings of the second Test and the series was cruelled. It was in the first Test he struck up his opening partnership with fellow Victorian Bill Woodfull in what was to become one of Australia's most successful opening duos. In 30 innings together, they amassed 1173 runs at 41.89 per innings.

Averages of 55 and 77 followed in series against England and the West Indies respectively. Ponsford played the first Test of the bodyline series but struggled against the pace of Larwood.

His final tour of England in 1934 showed his class. He played in four of the five Tests and topped the averages for both sides with a Bradmanesque 94.83, beating Bradman himself by the slightest of margins (0.08). Ponsford's tour was highlighted by 181 in the fourth Test and his highest Test score of 266 in the fifth, where he shared a then-world record partnership of 451 with Bradman (the record stood until 1991).

Ponsford was awarded an MBE and was an inaugural inductee into the Australian Cricket Hall of Fame in 1996. He has a grandstand named after him at the MCG together with a bronze statue of him in full cover drive.

2. Bruce Mitchell (SA)

Test Record

Bat	M	Inn	NO	Runs	HS	Avg	100	50	Ct
	42	80	9	3471	189*	48.88	8	21	56

Bowl	M	Inn	Wkts	Avg	BBI	BBM	5i	10m	SR
	42	39	27	51.11	5/87	5/87	1	0	93.5

*not out

Bruce Mitchell appeared in all 42 of South Africa's Test matches from 1929 to 1948. His country lacked batting depth during this period and Mitchell carried the batting, resulting in him often playing more defensively than he otherwise might have. With a full range of shots and more support, perhaps his career statistics would have been even better.

Mitchell started his Test career at Edgbaston in 1929 and he contributed 88 and 61 not out, sharing in two first wicket century partnerships with Bob Catterall. He finished the series with 251 runs at 31.37.

England visited South Africa in 1930–31 and Mitchell excelled, topping the South African averages with 455 runs at 50.55 including his maiden ton of 123 in the second Test. He was affected by ill health on the Australian tour of 1931–32 but still topped the batting on a rain affected tour with 322 runs at 32.20. Mitchell struck form in New Zealand however and added a second century in the first Test.

Mitchell's leg-spin bowling was also very useful, and he topped the wickets tally for the Currie Cup in 1933–34 with 32 wickets at 14.87.

The 1935 South African tour of England was a triumph for Mitchell as he led the Test batting averages, scoring 488 runs with an average of 69.71. He also led the tour bowling figures with 35 wickets at 19.02. He put himself on the honour board at Lord's with an outstanding 164 not out in the second innings and set up the Proteas' first win in England. A century in the final Test ensured a series win for the South Africans.

Mitchell continued his rich vein of form against the English at home in 1938–39, knocking up 466 runs at 58.25 including a superb century in the third Test.

During World War Two Mitchell served with the Transvaal Scottish Regiment in East Africa, El Alamein and Italy.

He returned to Test cricket on the 1947 tour of England where he made 597 runs at an average of 66.33. This included twin centuries (120 and 189 not out) in the final Test at The Oval where he batted for more than 13 hours. He spent all but eight minutes on the field in the four days.

England toured in 1947–48 and Mitchell was as productive as ever with 475 runs at 52.77 including a century (120) at Newlands in the third Test. In what turned out to be his final Test, Mitchell ended his career as it began with a pair of fifties.

Australia visited the following summer and the selectors decided Mitchell, being 40, was not up to facing the pace barrage of Ray Lindwall and Keith Miller. He was thus omitted from the South African XI and his Test career was over with an average of just under 50.

3. Don Bradman (AUS) c

Test Record

Bat	M	Inn	NO	Runs	HS	Avg	100	50	Ct
	52	80	10	6996	334	99.94	29	13	32
Bowl	M	Inn	Wkts	Avg	BBI	BBM	5i	10m	SR
	52	9	2	36.00	1/8	1/15	0	0	80.0

Wisden's Cricketers' Almanack stated, 'Sir Donald George Bradman was, without any question, the greatest phenomenon in the history of cricket, indeed in the history of all ball games.' Maybe that's all that needs to be said, but perhaps it would be interesting to add a little more.

As he famously noted in his book *Farewell to Cricket,* 'Armed with a cricket stump as a bat, I would throw a golf ball at this [tank] brick stand and try to hit the ball on the rebound. The ball came back at great speed and to hit it was no easy task.' Bradman believed this helped sharpen his eye and reflexes later reflected in his batting.

In 1927, at the age of 19, Bradman was called up to the New South Wales side and made a hundred on debut. He was selected in the Australian team at the age of 20 for the first Test of the 1928–29 Ashes series. It wasn't a memorable beginning, as he made 18 and one and was dropped to twelfth man for the second Test. He returned for the third and began his relentless run-making with 79 and a maiden Test hundred of 112, the youngest Test centurion to that point.

England had got a taste of Bradman in the 1928–29 summer but they had no idea of the deluge of runs about to engulf them at home in 1930. Bradman began in the first Test with a warm up 131 and followed it up in the second Test with 254, an innings he often described as his finest. These were only appetisers for the third Test when he went to the wicket on the first day at one for two. By lunch he had brought up a century, by tea a double century and his triple, the first in Test cricket, was achieved by stumps. He ended his innings on the second day at 334. All up he had scored an unbelievable record of 974 runs for the series, averaging 139.

Not a lot needs to be written about the bodyline series. It was instigated to stop Bradman and to a certain extent it did that. Bradman missed the first Test but crafted a not out century in the second innings of the second Test. He made scores between 50 and 100 in the remaining three Tests but didn't go on with it. An average of 56.57 was pretty good in any series but especially in these circumstances.

Bradman's run-scoring spree continued unabated up until and after World War Two until his final ball in Test cricket on the 1948 Ashes tour. Needing only four runs to average 100 in Test cricket, Bradman was bowled second ball by a Hollies googly for a duck.

Bradman was also captain of Australia in five series and did not lose any of them. He was a shrewd tactician and was prepared to do things a little differently if the occasion demanded it.

He was knighted for his services to cricket, the only Australian cricketer to be acknowledged accordingly. Naturally he was also an inaugural inductee to the Australian Cricket Hall of Fame and ICC Hall of Fame, and is a 'Legend' (the exclusive club of the very top echelon of Australian sporting royalty) in the Australian Sporting Hall of Fame (perhaps a category above this is needed known simply as 'Bradman').

4. Wally Hammond (ENG) vc

Test Record

Bat	M	Inn	NO	Runs	HS	Avg	100	50	Ct
	85	140	16	7249	336*	58.45	22	24	110
Bowl	M	Inn	Wkts	Avg	BBI	BBM	5i	10m	SR
	85	110	83	37.80	5/36	7/87	2	0	96.0

*not out

Hammond is one of the all-time great batters and made more than a fair all-rounder with his medium-fast bowling and superb ability in the slips. In First Class cricket between 1920 and 1950 he made 50,493 runs at 56.10 with 167 centuries and took 732 wickets at an average of 30.58. He also held 820 catches.

Wisden described him as, 'A natural player, he was virtually never coached until he had become a county player, when George Dennett used sometimes to advise him. Instinctively basically correct, he was sound in defence, but never defensively minded. Like most outstanding batsmen, he was primarily a front-foot player who, with the years, operated more off the back. His great power lay in his driving, which was pure textbook in style, clean, apparently effortless but, through the combination of innate timing and immense strength, often achieving huge velocity.'

Hammond debuted against South Africa at Johannesburg in 1927 and brought up a half-century in his only bat, as England won by 10 wickets. He also reached a half-century in five of his next seven Tests without going on to a hundred.

It was on the 1928–29 tour of Australia that Hammond really blossomed. He scored 905 runs at 113.12 in the five Tests which is still the second best aggregate for a series (behind Donald Bradman). His output included three double centuries (251, 232, 296) as well as another hundred (177).

Hammond followed this up with two centuries against South Africa at home in mid-1929, scoring 352 runs at 58.66 in the four Test series. He had a quieter series versus Australia in 1930 and averaged just 34, although he did add another century to his tally.

Returning to form in South Africa in 1930–31, he scored 517 runs at 64.62 to lead the runs aggregate for the series. Hammond again performed well on the bodyline tour of Australia in 1932–33, and he equal-top scored (with Herbert Sutcliffe) with 440 runs at 55.00.

In 1936, Hammond put India to the sword in England, as he scored 167 and 217 in two Tests. He wasn't as successful Down Under in 1936–37 but scored a magnificent double ton against Australia at Lord's in 1938. He followed this up with 609 runs at 87 on the South African tour of 1938–39. His last innings before the war was 138 against the West Indies at The Oval.

While he topped the First Class averages in 1946 he was not the same Test player after the war, and played eight Tests but averaged just 30 with no centuries. He played his last Test against New Zealand in 1947 and made 79.

Hammond captained England 20 times for just four wins, three losses and 13 draws. His medium-fast bowling is also necessary in this XI that contains two spinners.

Post-cricket, Hammond moved to South Africa where he died in 1965. One of cricket's immortals, he is an inductee in the ICC Cricket Hall of Fame.

5. George Headley (WI)

Test Record

Bat	M	Inn	NO	Runs	HS	Avg	100	50	Ct
	22	40	4	2190	270*	60.83	10	5	14

Bowl	M	Inn	Wkts	Avg	BBI	BBM	5i	10m	SR
	22	14	0	-			0	0	-

*not out

Headley was the first of the great batters to come out of the West Indies. At a time when the West Indies' batting line-up was vulnerable, Headley carried more than his share of the load. Although he was a naturally attacking player, Headley felt the need to play cautiously owing to the way his team depended on him.

Born in Panama where his father was working on the canal, Headley moved with his family to Jamaica at the age of 10 in the hopes that that he could improve his English and eventually move to America to study dentistry. However, he took up cricket and, though not yet 19, was chosen to play against a touring English side. He made 78 in the first match and 211 in the second, and dentistry was forgotten.

Headley debuted for the West Indies against England at Bridgetown in 1930 and struck a century on debut, 176 in the second innings. He added a century in each innings in the third Test and ended the series with 703 runs at 87.87.

A moderate series in Australia followed where he knocked up 336 runs in the five Tests at 37.33, but still managed a hundred in the third Test at Brisbane (102 not out) and in the final Test in Sydney (105).

In 1933, the West Indies toured England for a three Test series, where Headley contributed 277 runs at an average of 55.40 with a high score of 169 not out at Old Trafford in Manchester.

Headley anchored the West Indies' batting as they won their first series against England in 1935, including 270 not out at Kingston, as the West Indies won by an innings to secure the series 2–1. All up, Headley scored 485 runs at 97.

The 1939 series against England in England was another success for Headley, as he added 334 runs at an average of 66.80. This included a century in each innings (106 and 107) at Lord's in the first Test.

After the war, Headley played a further three Tests but added only 55 runs with a top score of 29. He captained the West Indies once, drawing with England in 1948. His final Test came in 1954 against England at Kingston where he managed just 16 and one.

Headley was an inaugural inductee into the ICC Cricket Hall of Fame in 2009.

6. Eddie Paynter (ENG)

Test Record

Bat	M	Inn	NO	Runs	HS	Avg	100	50	Ct
	20	31	5	1540	243	59.23	4	7	7

The final batting spot in the 1930s XI was a toss-up between Eddie Paynter of England and Stan McCabe of Australia. Paynter had the better average but much of his success came in two series near the end of his career. McCabe played nearly twice as many Tests and averaged 48.21 (11 less than Paynter) and was probably more consistent than Paynter. However, the coin came down on the side of Paynter.

In 1980, *Wisden* wrote of Paynter: 'A small man, Paynter was by instinct an attacking batsman, particularly effective against slow spin, but also a fine hooker and cutter who did not spare the fast bowler if he pitched short. He was one of the great outfields of his day and almost equally good at cover – a beautiful thrower with a safe pair of hands. This was the more remarkable as early in life he had lost the top joints of two fingers in an accident. At Lord's in 1938, when Ames had broken a finger, Paynter kept wicket through the Australian second innings of 204, and though he had little or no experience of wicketkeeping conceded only 5 byes and held a catch. A wonderful cricketer.'

Paynter's Test career began slowly, scoring just three against New Zealand at Old Trafford in 1931. Nearly a year later he played against India at Lord's and managed a half-century.

Selected for the Australian tour of 1932–33, Paynter played in three of the five Tests and made 184 runs at 61.33 with a top score of 83, which was scored under duress as he had been admitted to hospital with tonsillitis, and had to leave his hospital bed to bat before returning to hospital at the close of play. In a brief second innings he finished the match with a six.

It was four years after this tour before Paynter again played for England. He had scored heavily in the County Championship and his claim could no longer be ignored. He played in two Tests against New Zealand, scoring a 74.

Australia visited England in 1938 and Paynter had a breakthrough series. He scored 407 runs at an average of 101.75 and a top score of 216 not out at Trent Bridge, his maiden Test century.

Paynter continued his good form when England toured South Africa in 1938–39, scoring a further 653 runs in the five Tests at 81.62 with three centuries including his highest Test score of 243 at Durban.

He played just two more Tests in 1939, both versus the West Indies in England, before the war brought down the curtain on his brief but successful Test career.

7. Les Ames (ENG) wk

Test Record

Bat	Mat	Inn	NO	Runs	HS	Avg	100	50	Ct	St
	47	72	12	2434	149	40.56	8	7	74	23

The wicketkeeping spot in the 1930s side came down to Les Ames of England and Bert Oldfield of Australia. Oldfield may well have been the better keeper – *Wisden* suggested of Oldfield, 'The game has produced some great wicketkeepers, especially from England and Australia; there is little doubt that pride of place should go to the quiet Australian.' However, Ames's batting was far superior (40.56 average versus 22.65) and thus Ames was preferred. Ames also still holds the record for most stumpings in First Class cricket with 418.

Ames was the original keeper-batter in the mould of Adam Gilchrist or M.S Dhoni. It is estimated he scored his runs at around 50 per hour, which is a pretty decent rate.

He made an inauspicious debut with a duck in his only bat against South Africa at The Oval in 1929. The tour of the West Indies in 1929–30 was far more successful, as he scored 419 runs at 59.57 with two Test hundreds of 105 and 147, plus he collected 12 keeping dismissals.

Things went even better for Ames when New Zealand visited England in 1931 as he racked up 195 runs in the three Tests at 97.50 with another ton (137), four catches and a stumping.

Ames did not fare well on the Australian tour of 1932–33, averaging just 16, but kept well to the hostility of Larwood and Voce. He fared better in New Zealand in 1933, scoring another hundred and averaging 64 across the two Tests. Later in 1933 he also batted well against the West Indies in England, scoring 167 runs at 83.50 in the three Tests. Ames also grabbed 11 dismissals.

The 1934 tour of England by Australia produced the innings Ames was proudest of. He contributed 120 at Lord's in difficult conditions after coming in at 5/182. All up in the series, he made 261 runs at 43.50.

A string of mediocre batting series ensued for Ames, although he added two more centuries and kept picking up catches and stumpings at regular intervals. It was not until Australia were back in England in 1938 that Ames again averaged in the 40s with the bat.

Ames's final series was against South Africa away and he had an excellent series, scoring 339 runs at 67.80 including his eighth and final Test hundred in the first Test.

During World War Two, Ames served with the RAF and rose to the rank of squadron leader.

Post-war, Ames continued to plunder runs in First Class cricket – he added over 10,000 runs to his tally but never again played for England. Back troubles brought an end to his career.

After he retired from cricket Ames managed a number of overseas tours for the MCC, and from 1960–74 was manager of Kent, culminating in Championship success in 1970.

Ames died in 1990 aged 84 and the attendance of a thousand people at his memorial service in Canterbury Cathedral was a worthy tribute to him.

8. Gubby Allen (ENG)

Test Record

Bat	M	Inn	NO	Runs	HS	Avg	100	50	Ct
	25	33	2	750	122	24.19	1	3	20

Bowl	M	Inn	Wkts	Avg	BBI	BBM	5i	10m	SR
	25	45	81	29.37	7/80	10/78	5	1	54.1

Sir George Oswald Browning 'Gubby' Allen was actually born in Australia and moved to England aged six. His uncle played a Test for Australia in the 1886–87 summer. Allen was an all-rounder who bowled at genuine pace with the outswinger his stock delivery, his batting was tenacious and he was a sure close infielder. He was a genuine amateur and his business career often limited his playing career, especially at county level.

For much of his life Allen lived next door to Lord's and had a private gate into the grounds. He also wielded influence over the affairs of Middlesex and the MCC.

Allen was blooded in Test cricket in 1930 against Australia and scored a half-century but did not impress at the bowling crease and was dropped. He was back in the XI for the New Zealand tour the following year and scored a century batting at number nine at Lord's. He added 246 with Les Ames which stood as a record for the eighth wicket for many years. In the next match he picked up 5/14 but was not required to bat.

Selected for the 1932–33 bodyline tour of Australia, Allen refused to partake in the leg theory attack and captain Jardine was not inclined to argue with his strong willed amateur. He took 21 wickets in the series, the second most by the English bowlers after Larwood.

Back home in 1933 he played just the one Test against the West Indies and collected three dismissals. The next year, illness restricted him to two Tests versus Australia and he was useful with a half-century and five wickets.

Allen was made England's captain for the 1936 three Test home series against the Indians. England won the series 2–1 and Allen took 20 wickets including match figures of 10/78 in the first Test at Lord's (thus ensuring he is one of the few on both the batting and bowling honour boards). Allen captained England 11 times for four wins and five losses.

As captain for the Ashes tour in 1936–37, Allen started the series well both personally and as captain as England took a 2–0 series lead. However, a Bradman-inspired comeback saw Australia claim the series three Tests to two. Allen finished the tour with 17 wickets at 30.94 and scored 150 runs after his batting fell away after a half-century in the first Test.

Allen did not play Test cricket again until after the war, missing several series. During the war, he joined a Royal Artillery Unit and was attached for a period to the RAF. At his own request, he was taken on a bombing raid over Germany to experience that type of action from the other side.

At the age of 45, Allen took England on the 1947–48 West Indies tour, where they lost the four Test series 2–0. It was Allen's final appearance for England, and he took five wickets and averaged nearly 20 with the bat.

Allen stayed in touch with cricket after his playing career and was chairman of selectors in 1955 and served on various MCC committees and as treasurer of the MCC.

9. Clarrie Grimmett (AUS)

Test Record

Bat	M	Inn	NO	Runs	HS	Avg	100	50	Ct
	37	50	10	557	50	13.92	0	1	17
Bowl	M	Inn	Wkts	Avg	BBI	BBM	5i	10m	SR
	37	67	216	24.21	7/40	14/199	21	7	67.1

Until Shane Warne came along, Clarrie Grimmett was arguably Australia's greatest spinner of all time. Perhaps Bill O'Reilly fans might argue the point. It's always dangerous to compare players from different eras but Grimmett's and Warne's statistics are pretty close. Of course, Warne played over a hundred more Tests than Grimmett so he had to maintain his form more consistently, but there is nothing to say if Grimmett had been given the chance to play over a hundred Tests he wouldn't still be among the top couple of Australian wicket takers.

His great mate and leg-spin twin Bill O'Reilly scribed his obituary for *Wisden*, and noted that Grimmett's bowling, '... never insisted on spin as the chief means of destruction. To him it was no more important adjunct to unerring length and tantalising direction.' As a result of this approach Grimmett had a high proportion of bowled and LBW as dismissals with 56 and 38 respectively.

It took time for Grimmett's abilities to be recognised, but he was finally selected for Australia for the fifth Test of the 1924–25 Ashes series soon after he turned 33. His first Test wicket was bowling the great Frank Woolley, and he ended the match with outstanding figures of 5/45 and 6/37: the first of seven times he took ten or more wickets in a match, equal with Dennis Lillee.

The 1930 Ashes tour is often remembered as Bradman's, however without Grimmett the Australian success may not have been as complete. He took 29 wickets in the series including match figures of

10/201 in the first Test at Trent Bridge. Against Yorkshire he took all ten wickets in an innings.

In the ensuing home series against the West Indies and South Africa in the following years he improved again, nabbing 33 wickets against each team. However in the bodyline series he was out of form for the first time taking five wickets in the first three Tests then was dropped for the next two. 'Hopelessly wrong' was O'Reilly's take on the situation.

Grimmett was reinstated for the 1934 Ashes tour and added 23 wickets to his burgeoning tally. By this time, the partnership of Grimmett and O'Reilly was thought by many to be the greatest spin combination the world had seen.

The 1935–36 tour of South Africa was sensational for Grimmett. He took 44 wickets at 14.59 in the five Tests. This remains a record for most wickets in a series by an Australian. During the tour he became the first bowler to 200 Test wickets. Unbelievably, the fifth Test of this series where he took 7/100 and 6/73 was his last, and he was never again selected.

Grimmett was an inaugural inductee into the Australian Cricket Hall of Fame in 1996 and is also a member of the ICC Hall of Fame.

10. Bill Voce (ENG)

Test Record

Bat	M	Inn	NO	Runs	HS	Avg	100	50	Ct
	27	38	15	308	66	13.39	0	1	15

Bowl	M	Inn	Wkts	Avg	BBI	BBM	5i	10m	SR
	27	51	98	27.88	7/70	11/149	3	2	64.8

Bill Voce is perhaps best remembered for his back-up role to Harold Larwood on the 1932–33 bodyline tour of Australia. He was not as quick as Larwood but his left-arm deliveries, delivered from height, gave all batters he bowled to trouble and he gave them no relief.

When Voce first started out in cricket, he was a slow left-armer but had gradually changed to fast-medium by the time he debuted for Nottinghamshire in 1927.

He was selected to tour the West Indies in 1929–30 and played in all four Tests taking 17 wickets at 34.35 including 11/149 in the second Test. Voce's form continued on the 1930–31 tour of South Africa as he took the most wickets for either side with 23.

Voce played just a single Test against India in 1932, taking 3/23.

Then came the 1932–33 bodyline series in Australia. He played in four of the five Tests, missing the fourth due to an injury, and picked up 15 wickets at 27.13. Voce played his role in bowling at the bodies of the Australian batters but later in his career admitted to Gubby Allen that they had been wrong to pursue the leg theory tactic.

As a consequence of their bowling in 1932–33, both Voce and Larwood were left out of the 1934 series against Australia and Voce next played a Test in 1936 against India without much success.

Back in the touring party for the 1936–37 Ashes tour, Voce was forced to agree to forgo bodyline tactics and bowl over the wicket with an offside field. It worked as Voce took 10 wickets in the first Test and seven in the second as England took a 2–0 series lead before losing three to two. All up, Voce took a series leading 26 wickets at 21.53 despite a back injury that hampered him towards the end of the tour.

To round out his pre-war career, Voce took five wickets against New Zealand at Lord's in 1937.

After the war, he played a single Test versus India before again touring Australia. There, he played two wicketless Tests before age and injury brought an end to his career.

Voce became the coach for Nottinghamshire County for a period but the bowling attack was so weak Voce was called upon to bowl from time to time.

11. Bill O'Reilly (AUS)

Test Record

Bat	M	Inn	NO	Runs	HS	Avg	100	50	Ct
	27	39	7	410	56*	12.81	0	1	7

Bowl	M	Inn	Wkts	Avg	BBI	BBM	5i	10m	SR
	27	48	144	22.59	7/54	11/129	11	3	69.6

*not out

If Grimmett compared favourably to Warne, then his great mate and partner in leg-spin mastery, Bill 'Tiger' O'Reilly, does too. His average runs per over (1.94) and wickets per Test (5.3) are all just ahead of Warne. However, as for Grimmett, Warne has a much better strike rate of balls per wicket and again Warne played many more matches than O'Reilly wherein he had to maintain form.

O'Reilly was born in country New South Wales and on one occasion he played for Wingello against Bowral who happened to have a young Don Bradman on their side. Bradman knocked up 234 on day one but O'Reilly bowled him first ball on the second day. Much later Bradman would rate O'Reilly the finest bowler he had faced or watched (despite ongoing tension between them).

O'Reilly made his way into the New South Wales side in 1931–32 and by the end of the summer found himself making his Test debut against South Africa. He took two wickets in each innings and played in the fifth Test but was not required to bowl as South Africa made only 36 and 45.

O'Reilly played all five Tests in the bodyline series and was Australia's leading wicket-taker with 27 at 26.81 including a ten wicket haul in Australia's only win in the second Test.

He remained consistent on the 1934 England tour where he picked up 28 wickets at 24, which included his best match bowling figures of 11/129 in Australia's win in the first Test at Nottingham. By this time, he was proving troublesome for all batters, but in particular the great Wally Hammond, whom O'Reilly dismissed ten times in Test cricket. O'Reilly and Grimmett took 53 of the 72 wickets to fall.

Another 27-wicket haul in the 1935–36 series in South Africa followed, along with his highest score with the bat, 56 not out. Between him and Grimmett, they took 71 of the 98 wickets to fall to bowlers on tour. O'Reilly's remarkable consistency continued with 25 wickets in the 1936–37 Ashes series and another 22 in the 1938 series (where he only played four Tests).

As company secretary of a protected entity, O'Reilly was not allowed to serve in the war and at its end he played in one more Test, against New Zealand, where he helped decimate the Kiwis with 5/14 and 3/19.

O'Reilly had considered retirement back in the early 1930s, as his teaching career was also taking off, but fortunately he had pushed on. At the age of 40 it was time to stop. He came in from the Test against New Zealand and, knees aching, he tossed his boots out the window and declared that he was done.

After his cricket career, O'Reilly became a journalist and was known for speaking his mind and not worrying about whose toes he might have stepped on. By his own admission, O'Reilly was outspoken and gregarious, which could occasionally rub people the wrong way. But his views were always put honestly, from the heart if not from the head, and always with the best interests of cricket first.

O'Reilly was an inaugural inductee into the Australian Cricket Hall of Fame and ICC Hall of Fame.

1930s Second XI

1. Bill Woodfull (AUS) c
2. Bill Brown (AUS)
3. Stan McCabe (AUS)
4. Maurice Leyland (ENG) vc
5. Jack Fingleton (AUS)
6. Bert Oldfield (AUS) wk
7. Learie Constantine (WI)
8. Hedley Verity (ENG)
9. Ken Farnes (ENG)
10. Tim Wall (AUS)
11. Bert Ironmonger (AUS)

1940s and 1950s

It is hard to imagine that the 1950s were sometimes regarded as a somewhat boring decade of cricket, given the calibre of players included Neil Harvey, Keith Miller, Richie Benaud, Denis Compton, Everton Weekes and Clyde Walcott. However, the best runs per over was achieved by the West Indies and was only 2.76 (or 46 runs per 100 balls) with Australia the next best at 2.48 runs per over (or 41 runs per 100 balls). The batters were not exactly moving things along.

Australia was the most successful side of the period, winning 57% of matches played, with England the next best at 39% and the West Indies at 37%.

The 1948 Australian touring party to England got the era off to a winning start with an unbeaten tour of 34 matches. Known as 'The Invincibles' and skippered by Don Bradman on his final tour, the Australians won the five Test series 4–0 and in all won 25 matches and drew nine. Among their victories, they won the fourth Test at Leeds by seven wickets after chasing 404, Bradman and Morris adding 301 for the second wicket.

Jim Laker gave the outstanding individual performance when he took 19/90 at Old Trafford in the 1956 Ashes series. All up for the series he captured 46 wickets at an average of 9.60, which included four lots of five wickets in an innings.

The strength of this era's XI is shown by the players who missed out, both batting and bowling. To begin with, Miller and Benaud were chosen on their all-round ability with them batting at six and seven respectively. This left five spots for specialist batters and Hutton, Compton, Walcott and Weekes all demanded selection based on their records and their ability to move the game along. This left one opening spot, and Harvey was chosen out of position as his record was also too good to ignore. This left players the calibre of Arthur Morris and Lindsay Hassett from Australia, Peter May from England and Frank Worrell of the West Indies out of the XI.

With Miller providing express pace, Australian Ray Lindwall and Alec Bedser of England were chosen as his fellow seamers. This meant English greats Brian Statham and Frank Tyson and Australia's other great all-rounder of the 1950s, Alan Davidson, missed out. There was a toss of the coin between Bedser and Statham. Laker's performances during the era were also too hard to ignore and he shares the spinning duties with Benaud. Tony Locke makes a fine Second XI spinner.

England's Godfrey Evans and Australia's Don Tallon battled for the wicketkeeping spot in the side, with Evans' better batting ability counting in his favour.

Most Test Runs in Period

Player	Mat	Inns	NO	Runs	HS	Ave	100	50
L Hutton (ENG)	66	117	14	5626	206	54.62	14	30
DCS Compton (ENG)	70	119	12	5339	278	49.89	15	26
RN Harvey (AUS)	62	107	10	5107	205	52.64	18	19
ED Weekes (WI)	48	81	5	4455	207	58.61	15	19
PBH May (ENG)	59	93	8	4182	285*	49.20	13	20
CL Walcott (WI)	42	71	7	3714	220	58.03	15	13
AR Morris (AUS)	46	79	3	3533	206	46.48	12	12
KR Miller (AUS)	55	87	7	2958	147	36.97	7	13
AL Hassett (AUS)	39	61	3	2874	198*	49.55	10	10
FMM Worrell (WI)	32	57	5	2691	261	51.75	8	11

*not out

Most Test Wickets in Period

Player	Mat	Inns	Wkts	BBI	BBM	Ave	SR	5	10
AV Bedser (ENG)	51	92	236	7/44	14/99	24.89	67.4	15	5
RR Lindwall (AUS)	59	109	222	7/38	9/70	22.65	59.2	12	0
JC Laker (ENG)	46	86	193	10/53	19/90	21.24	62.3	9	3
KR Miller (AUS)	55	95	170	7/60	10/152	22.97	61.5	7	1
R Benaud (AUS)	42	74	165	7/72	11/105	23.95	67.8	11	1
MH Mankad (IND)	44	70	162	8/52	13/131	32.32	90.6	8	2
WA Johnston (AUS)	40	75	160	6/44	9/183	23.91	69.0	7	0
JB Statham (ENG)	47	87	159	7/39	9/88	23.50	62.8	5	0
HJ Tayfield (SA)	32	55	158	9/113	13/165	25.00	78.7	14	2
S Ramadhin (WI)	37	65	138	7/49	11/152	28.62	88.0	10	1

Results

Team	Mat	Won	Lost	Tied	Draw	W/L
England	115	45	31	0	39	1.451
Australia	75	43	12	0	20	3.583
West Indies	57	21	17	0	19	1.235
South Africa	47	12	22	0	13	0.545
Pakistan	29	8	9	0	12	0.888
India	57	6	23	0	28	0.260
New Zealand	38	1	22	0	15	0.045

1940s and 1950s XI

1. Len Hutton (ENG) vc
2. Neil Harvey (AUS)
3. Denis Compton (ENG)
4. Everton Weekes (WI)
5. Clyde Walcott (WI)
6. Keith Miller (AUS)
7. Richie Benaud (AUS) c
8. Godfrey Evans (ENG) wk
9. Ray Lindwall (AUS)
10. Alec Bedser (ENG)
11. Jim Laker (ENG)

1. Len Hutton (ENG) vc

Test Record

Bat	M	Inn	NO	Runs	HS	Avg	100	50	Ct
	79	138	15	6971	364	56.67	19	33	57

Bowl	M	Inn	Wkts	Avg	BBI	BBM	5i	10m	SR
	79	14	3	77.33	1-2	1-2	0	0	86.6

Another of the all-time great batters and certainly in the top handful of Test openers. Denis Compton described him as 'the greatest opening batsman I have ever seen'. In 1950 Bill O'Reilly wrote: 'His footwork is as light and sure and confident as Bradman's ever was. He is the finished player now ... one cannot fail to be impressed with the fluency and gracefulness of his strokemaking ... His control of the game is masterful.'

Hutton played county cricket for Yorkshire from a young age and debuted for England against New Zealand in 1937 when he had just turned 21. He began poorly with a duck and one but made an even 100 in the first innings of the second Test.

The next summer Hutton cut loose against the Australians with 473 runs at 118.25 in three Tests. His series was anchored by the then-Test high score of 364 at The Oval, batting for over 13 hours.

Hutton followed this up with a solid series against South Africa, where he scored 265 runs in the four Tests at 44.16 without reaching a century. Back in England in 1939, he faced the West Indies and excelled once again with 480 runs at 96 including centuries in the first and third Test (196 and 165 not out).

During the war, Hutton injured his left arm so badly in a gymnasium during commando training that three bone grafts were needed to repair the damage done by the compound fracture. He was in hospital for eight months before he was finally discharged, his left arm weakened and some two inches shorter than the other. He worked hard at rehabilitation and eventually returned to cricket and regained his old form.

Returning to Test cricket on the Australian tour of 1946–47, Hutton performed well with 417 runs in the five Tests at 52.12 with a hundred in the fifth Test at Sydney. A run of series followed against South Africa, the West Indies and Australia where Hutton averaged in the 40s.

Hutton then bounced back to his best with 577 runs in South Africa at 64.11 and then 469 in four Tests against New Zealand at an average of 78.16 with a double hundred. His form continued versus the West Indies in England averaging 66.60, and on the 1950–51 Ashes tour he scored heavily with 533 runs at 88.83 in five Tests and a top score of 156 not out.

In 1951 Hutton averaged 54 against South Africa, then 79.80 versus India the next summer including two centuries in a runs tally of 399 across four Tests. He captained England for the first time and was the first professional to do so. Australia then visited England and Hutton knocked up 443 runs at an average of 55.37 followed by a tour of the West Indies where he averaged 96.71.

Then Hutton's form fell away, and he ended his Test career three series later in New Zealand.

Hutton is an inductee into the ICC Cricket Hall of Fame and was knighted for his services to cricket.

2. Neil Harvey (AUS)

Test Record

Bat	M	Inn	NO	Runs	HS	Avg	100	50	Ct
	79	137	10	6149	205	48.41	21	24	64 |//
Bowl	M	Inn	Wkts	Avg	BBI	BBM	5i	10m	SR
	79	17	3	40.00	1/8	1/9	0	0	138.0

Due to the strength of the middle order batting in this XI, Harvey has been chosen out of position at the top of the order.

In 2012, Ashley Mallett wrote that the best batters the world had seen since Bradman were Garry Sobers, Viv Richards, Barry Richards, Sachin Tendulkar and Neil Harvey… exalted company indeed. In any conversation about the best Australian batter since Bradman, Harvey's name will always be in the argument. He was a brilliant and electrifying batter with shots all around the wicket who could bring misery on any bowling attack. On top of this, he is regarded as one of the greatest Australian fielders of all time, particularly in the covers. His arm and eye were so good he was twice chosen in the All Australian baseball team.

Harvey's unquestioned talent is recognised by his induction to the Australian Cricket Hall of Fame, an inaugural induction to the ICC Cricket Hall of Fame, and his naming in the Australian team of the century in 2000 by the Australian Cricket Board.

Such was his precocious ability that he was selected at age 19 for his Test debut against India in the fourth Test in the 1947–48 series. He began with only 13 in Australia's only innings. However, in the fifth Test Harvey carved his maiden century scoring 153, becoming the youngest Australian to score a hundred and beating Archie Jackson's effort in 1929. Harvey holds the record to this day.

Harvey was selected as the 'baby' of the 1948 England tour and got his chance in the fourth Test. He grabbed it with both hands making 112 and cementing his place in the Australian XI.

The Australian tour of South Africa in 1949–50 saw Harvey at his brilliant best as he hit four centuries and averaged 132 with a top score of 178. The Ashes series in 1950–51 saw a more subdued but still solid result of 362 runs at 40.22 but with no hundred. The 1952–53 series saw him flay the South Africans with a huge 834 runs at 92.67 with another four hundreds including his highest Test score of 205.

The captaincy opened up for the 1957–58 tour of South Africa and many thought Harvey deserved the position, but in a youth policy it went to 22-year-old Ian Craig with Harvey as vice-captain.

The famous series against the West Indies in 1960–61 saw Harvey make little impact, contributing only 143 runs across the five Tests. He regained form and proved himself in English conditions in 1961, averaging 42.25 with a hundred in the drawn first Test. The captain for the tour, Richie Benaud, was injured for the second Test and as his deputy Harvey finally got his chance at the captaincy, leading his country to a five-wicket win.

His final series was against England in the summer of 1962–63 where he made a more than useful contribution of 395 runs at 39.50 highlighted by 154 in the fourth Test at Adelaide Oval.

Post-international cricket, Harvey was a Test selector from 1967–79 which included the tumultuous years of World Series Cricket (WSC) when he was chairman of selectors.

3. Denis Compton (ENG)

Test Record

Bat	M	Inn	NO	Runs	HS	Avg	100	50	Ct
	78	131	15	5807	278	50.06	17	28	49
Bowl	M	Inn	Wkts	Avg	BBI	BBM	5i	10m	SR
	78	66	25	56.40	5/70	5/77	1	0	108.4

Another ICC Cricket Hall of Famer, his *Wisden* obituary described him thus: '[Compton] was not just a great cricketer but a character who transcended the game and became what would now be called a national icon. In the years after the war, when the British were still finding the joys of victory elusive, the exuberance of Compton's batting and personality became a symbol of national renewal. Almost single-handed (though his pal Bill Edrich helped), he ensured that cricket returned to its pre-war place in the nation's affections.'

As a batter, Compton was a risk taker who had all the shots. He would often stand outside his crease even to the quickest of bowlers.

Compton debuted for Middlesex as an 18-year-old and soon made his mark. He was chosen for England to play New Zealand in 1937 and made 65 before being flukily run out, backing up at the bowler's end.

He performed well against Australia in England in 1938, averaging 42.80 and bringing up his maiden Test ton. To round out the decade he averaged 63 against the West Indies with another century.

During the war (where Compton lost some of his best Test years) he served in the Royal Artillery and for a time in India as a sergeant-major in charge of getting troops fit for the war with Japan, a role he was overly lenient in.

On the resumption of Test cricket, Compton toured Australia with the English side and scored 459 runs at 51, which included a century in each innings at Adelaide.

South Africa toured England in 1947 and Compton had a summer to remember, scoring over 700 runs at 94.12 with four centuries including a high score of 208 in the second Test at Lord's.

Thereafter, struggling with a knee injury, Compton had a mixed bag of results, averaging 50 against South Africa away, New Zealand at home, South Africa at home and the West Indies away until he played Pakistan at home in 1954. Against Pakistan he scored 453 runs with his highest Test score of 278 and an average of 90.60.

A moderate Ashes series followed (average 38.20) before he carved up South Africa in England to the tune of 492 runs in five Tests in 1955 with a top score of 158. Compton then played just the one Test the following summer against Australia and just missed a century with 94.

His final Test matches came on the tour of South Africa in 1956–57, but he managed just 242 runs in 10 innings.

Post-cricket, Compton kept up his many cricketing friendships, notably with Keith Miller, and commentated for the BBC. He also wrote for newspapers, his articles often wildly optimistic about the prospects of up and coming young cricketers. On his death in 1997, aged 78, his memorial service was held in Westminster Abbey.

4. Everton Weekes (WI)

Test Record

Bat	M	Inn	NO	Runs	HS	Avg	100	50	Ct
	48	81	5	4455	207	58.61	15	19	49

Bowl	M	Inn	Wkts	Avg	BBI	BBM	5i	10m	SR
	48	10	1	77.00	1/8	1/8	0	0	122.0

One of the famed three Ws (Worrell, Walcott and Weekes), Everton Weekes was short and stocky but had the full array of attacking strokes at his disposal.

Weekes debuted against England in the West Indies in 1948 and scored 35 and 25. He was dropped to allow George Headley back in the side but was reinstated when Headley became unavailable. In the fifth Test the Kingston crowd wanted their own man and booed Weekes when he came out to bat but he won them over with a fine 141.

The 1948–49 tour of India was a standout for Weekes. He scored hundreds in his first four innings, thus giving him a record five centuries in a row; he would have made it six but for a controversial run out when he was on 90. All up he scored 779 runs in the five Tests at an average of 111.28.

In 1950, the West Indies toured England and Weekes batted well, scoring 338 runs in the four Tests at an average of 56.33 with a hundred in the third Test at Trent Bridge. All up, on tour he notched 2310 runs at 79.60 including a triple century against Cambridge.

Weekes did not perform up to his usual standard on the subsequent tour of Australia and New Zealand, but he returned to form against India at home in 1952–53. He scored a double century (207) in the first Test and another big hundred (161) in the third to end up with 716 runs in the five Tests at 102.28.

His form continued the next summer when England toured, as he notched another double century in scoring 487 runs in four

Tests while averaging 69.57. Australia were next to tour in 1955 and Weekes maintained his form with a further 469 runs at 58.62.

Weekes had a very good tour of New Zealand in 1955–56, as he notched up three centuries and averaged 83.60. His final series was a visit by Pakistan in 1957–58 and he went out on top with 455 runs at 65 with a high score of 197 in the first Test. Increasingly troubled by a thigh injury, Weekes decided to call it quits even though he was only in his early 30s.

He coached Barbados for a time and was also an ICC match referee. Weekes is also an ICC Hall of Famer and was knighted in 1995, the third of the three Ws to be so honoured.

5. Clyde Walcott (WI)

Test Record

Bat	M	Inn	NO	Runs	HS	Avg	100	50	Ct
	44	74	7	3798	220	56.68	15	14	53

Bowl	M	Inn	Wkts	Avg	BBI	BBM	5i	10m	SR
	44	22	11	37.09	3/50	3/50	0	0	108.5

Walcott was known for his powerful batting and David Frith wrote in *The Wisden Cricketer* that Walcott, 'At his peak, like Viv Richards later, he was one of those rare power-packed batsmen to whom bowlers preferred not to bowl on a long afternoon.'

Making his First Class debut on his 16th birthday, Walcott later scored a triple century in an unbroken fourth wicket stand of 574 with Worrell in an inter-island match at Port of Spain.

Chosen as wicketkeeper for his Test debut, Walcott also opened the batting against England at Bridgetown in 1948 but scored only eight and 16 and averaged 22.16 for the series.

The selectors kept faith with Walcott and he repaid them with 452 runs in India at 64.57, including two centuries (152 and 108).

The West Indies scored a joyful first win over England at Lord's in 1950, with Walcott contributing 168 not out. He did not add any other big scores during the tour and ended with an average of 45.80.

A poor tour of Australia followed, but he redeemed himself on the New Zealand portion of the tour with 115 in the second Test following a half-century in the first.

India toured the West Indies in 1953 with Walcott adding 457 runs at 76.16 with two centuries. He was in even better form the following summer against England, being the leading run scorer for either side with 698 at 87.25 including a double hundred (220) and two single hundreds (124 and 116).

A magnificent series followed versus Australia as Walcott racked up 827 runs in five Tests with five centuries at an average of 82.70. His efforts could not stop Australia winning the series 3–0.

Walcott had a mediocre tour of England in 1957 which was followed by another successful home series, this time against Pakistan as he averaged 96.25 across four Tests with a top score of 145.

His final series was two Tests against England at home in 1960 where he made nine, 53 and 22 and his Test career ended at Port of Spain.

Post-cricket, he was a West Indies tour manager, a selector and then board president before succeeding Colin Cowdrey as ICC's head. Knighted in 1993, Walcott is also an inductee in the ICC Cricket Hall of Fame.

6. Keith Miller (AUS)

Test Record

Bat	M	Inn	NO	Runs	HS	Avg	100	50	Ct
	55	87	7	2958	147	36.97	7	13	38
Bowl	**M**	**Inn**	**Wkts**	**Avg**	**BBI**	**BBM**	**5i**	**10m**	**SR**
	55	95	170	22.97	7/60	10/152	7	1	61.5

John Arlott, the respected cricket writer and commentator, wrote; 'If I had my choice of player to win a match off the last ball, whether it required a catch, a six or a wicket I would pick one player – Keith Ross Miller.' It is also said a true all-rounder's batting average is greater than their bowling average and in Miller's case the gap is significant. Miller's impact on Australian and world cricket is also emphasised by his admittance to the Australian Cricket Hall of Fame and as an inaugural inductee to the ICC Hall of Fame and selection in the Australian Cricket Board's team of the century for the twentieth century. He is also a 'Legend' in the Australian Sporting Hall of Fame. Neville Cardus dubbed Keith Miller 'the Australian in excelsis'. 'Swashbuckling' has also been used. You get the point.

Yet Miller didn't take cricket overly seriously. Sure, he was a fierce competitor. But when it came down to it, his experience as a flying officer with the RAAF in World War Two gave him the perspective that there were more important things to life than cricket. He also lived life to the fullest, some would say too full, outside of cricket. As he put it, 'I'll tell you what pressure is. Pressure is a Messerschmitt up your arse. Playing cricket is not.'

Miller made his Test debut against New Zealand after the war, scoring 30 and taking two wickets in the rout of the Kiwis. It was this Test that began his famed fast bowling partnership with Ray Lindwall, one of the greatest of all time.

The English felt the full wrath of Miller in the 1946–47 series as he was second to Bradman in the batting averages at 76.80, including his maiden Test century, 141 not out in Adelaide. He also chimed in with 16 wickets at 20.88 which included 7/60 in the first innings of the series.

Before long Miller was a favourite with the crowds, especially with the younger girls, although some older fans disapproved of his long hair that he would flick back before steaming in for another thunderbolt.

His career continued, regularly averaging in the 40s and picking up frequent wickets. Miller also had designs on the Australian captaincy but Ian Johnson was made captain and Miller was named vice-captain. Richie Benaud believed he was the best captain to have never captained Australia.

Of the many stories about Miller's love for life is the one where (as captain) he partied long and hard into the night during a Sheffield Shield match against South Australia. Bleary eyed, he turned up for play when his team was already on the field, so he threw on his whites and walked onto the field with his bootlaces still undone. Alan Davidson was ready to bowl, and Miller told him to get stuck in. However, Miller then noted the green state of the pitch and notified Davidson that he would not be bowling first but Miller himself would take the new ball. Miller took 7/12 and South Australia were out for 27.

7. Richie Benaud (AUS) c

Test Record

Bat	M	Inn	NO	Runs	HS	Avg	100	50	Ct
	63	97	7	2201	122	24.45	3	9	65
Bowl	M	Inn	Wkts	Avg	BBI	BBM	5i	10m	SR
	63	116	248	27.03	7/72	11/105	16	1	77.0

More a bowling all-rounder, having Benaud batting at seven in the order helps add a lot of depth to the 1950s side. And that's without what Benaud brings to the table, with his reputation as one of Australia's best captains. He did everything with a sense of purpose; there was planning behind it all, whether his next delivery, tactics in the field or managing his teammates. Behind this was an attacking approach and a desire for cricket to entertain, which gave rise to an intensity in his cricket.

Benaud debuted in 1952 without making an immediate impact. His potential began to blossom to results in the 1955 series in the West Indies where he notched 246 runs at 41 with his maiden Test century (121) at Sabina Park, Kingston. His century came in just 78 minutes – still the fourth fastest of all time, in terms of time. He dismissed 18 West Indians, ranking him just behind Lindwall and Miller who took 20 wickets each.

His Test career really took off on the 1957–58 tour of South Africa. He was second in the Australian batting averages with 54.83 with two centuries, and was the leading wicket-taker for either team with 30 wickets at 22. During the series he brought up his hundredth Test wicket with a ball that pitched on leg and took off stump. Thus, he was admitted to the exclusive club of those who had scored 1000 Test runs and taken 100 wickets.

With Ian Craig out ill, Benaud was elevated to captain for the 1958–59 Ashes series. While his batting was solid, he again topped the wicket-taking with 31. He also led Australia to a comprehensive 4–0 regaining of the Ashes.

Next came what was perhaps the highlight of Benaud's captaincy career: the famous series against the West Indies in 1960–61, including the tied Test. Both captains, Benaud and Frank Worrell, were credited with making the series such an enthralling one with attack being the name of the game, but the series was also played with great sportsmanship.

Benaud concluded his career with 15 wickets in England in 1961 and a further 17 back in Australia. Benaud's streak as captain of never losing a series was intact as Australia won the series 2–1.

By his retirement Benaud was the only player at that time to have taken 200 wickets and made over 2000 Test runs. His Australian record of 248 Test wickets was not overtaken until Dennis Lillee forged past nearly 20 years later.

His status as one of the most influential people in the game over his lifetime, both as a player and a commentator, is reflected in his membership of both the Australian Cricket and ICC Halls of Fame. Within the Australian Sporting Hall of Fame Benaud sits at the highest level: Legend.

8. Godfrey Evans (ENG) wk

Test Record

Bat	Mat	Inn	NO	Runs	HS	Avg	100	50	Ct	St
91	133	14	2439	104	20.49	2	8	173	46	

Wisden has described Godfrey Evans as arguably the best wicketkeeper the game has ever seen. Long before the Gilchrists and Dhonis came along, Evans made the role of wicketkeeper a spectator sport in itself. He was charismatic and ever ready to lend a hand where it was needed.

Evans may have had a career as a boxer, but the Kent cricket authorities told him to choose a sport and, fortunately for cricket, he chose the bat and ball. He was lightning fast behind the stumps and stood up to the likes of Alec Bedser with no diminution in his effectiveness.

Debuting in a single Test in the 1946 Indian series, Evans did not bat and made no dismissals. He was chosen on the tour of Australia and appeared in the second Test, where he did not concede a bye, as Australia racked up 659.

Evans had an excellent series with the bat against South Africa in 1947, averaging 41.80 with a top score of 74 in the first Test and making 14 dismissals.

The following summer, Evans scored 188 runs at 26.85 against the Australians and took 12 dismissals, eight catches and four stumpings. In 1950 Evans brought up his maiden Test ton (104) versus the West Indies, averaging 37.33 as he played three of the four Tests. He picked up three catches and six stumpings.

Evans's best batting series came in 1952 against India, with 242 runs at 60.50 with a second hundred (another 104 with 98 before lunch) and four catches and four stumpings.

Picking up dismissals at regular intervals, including 13 in the 1954–55 Ashes series, Evans's premier series as a keeper came in South Africa in 1956–57 where he took 18 catches and made two stumpings in the five Tests.

Evans then picked up another 15 dismissals at home to the West Indies in 1957. He also had an excellent series with the bat, scoring 201 runs at an average of 50.25 and a top score of 84.

He remained England's first choice of wicketkeeper until 1959 when 'team building' was given as the reason for dropping him despite averaging 36.50 in the two Tests he played against India. Evans promptly retired, perhaps prematurely.

Much later, Evans appeared in a seven a side competition and even at that stage the English bowler Mike Selvey noted that, 'Late out-swing just whispered into his gloves. I slipped in a full-length in-swinger on leg stump – the most difficult to take – and there he was, down the leg side as if by telepathy, flicking the bails away as the batsman changed feet.'

Post-cricket, he became known for his mutton chop whiskers and took up the role of adviser to bookmaker Ladbrokes, helping them analyse matches and set odds.

9. Ray Lindwall (AUS)

Test Record

Bat	M	Inn	NO	Runs	HS	Avg	100	50	Ct
	61	84	13	1502	118	21.15	2	5	26

Bowl	M	Inn	Wkts	Avg	BBI	BBM	5i	10m	SR
	61	113	228	23.03	7/38	9/70	12	0	59.8

Many cricket judges rate Lindwall as the greatest all-round fast bowler of all time. His variety of deliveries at extreme pace, combined with his accuracy and a fearsome bouncer, made him a nightmare for batters of his era. Whereas his partner in crime Keith Miller was all energy at the bowling crease, Lindwall was smooth and had a rhythmic approach with unerring accuracy. Ashes opponent John Warr said that, 'If one were granted one last wish in cricket, it would be the sight of Ray Lindwall opening the bowling in a Test match.' Testimony to his skill and accuracy was the fact 45% of his 228 wickets were bowled. Lindwall is in the argument for Australia's greatest fast bowler of all time.

Lindwall was an all-round athlete; he once ran the hundred yards in 10.6 seconds, and if he had chosen it he could probably have forged a career in rugby league. As a schoolboy he plundered 219 and 110 in one day, playing juniors in the morning and for a senior side in the afternoon. He joined the St George club where O'Reilly noticed him and took him under his wing.

He debuted in the first Test after the war against New Zealand. He made a duck and took two wickets but it mattered little as the more experienced players took charge. Lindwall's first series in Australia for the Ashes in 1946–47 was a success. Playing in four Tests, he averaged 32 with the bat and scored his maiden century in just 89 balls in the drawn third Test. He tied with McCool as the top wicket-taker for his country with 18, including 7/63 in the first innings of the fifth Test.

He stepped up even further on the 1948 tour and was a big part of the 'Invincibles' tag. Pulling a leg muscle in the first Test, he took a single wicket but added 42 with the bat. From there he took a series topping (tied with Bill Johnston) 27 wickets. His tour was highlighted by 6/20 in the fifth Test as he routed England for just 52. An average of 31 with the bat was also handy.

From thereon, Lindwall was the mainstay of the Australian attack and chipped in with runs when needed. He took 12 wickets against South Africa, 15 versus England in Australia, 21 against the West Indies in Australia, then 19 against South Africa again at home. This output continued until the Ashes tour of 1956 where the pace bowlers suffered on the dusty spinner's tracks.

By this time, Lindwall had lost some of his pace and was now a crafty medium-pace bowler, but still effective most of the time. After a few lean series Lindwall played his final Test in India in 1960. In the meantime, he joined the illustrious list of Australian captains when he stood in for Ian Johnson in the drawn second Test against India at Chennai (then known as Madras) in 1956.

Like several others in this 1950s team, Lindwall was an inaugural inductee into the Australian Cricket Hall of Fame and is also a member of the ICC Hall of Fame. Lindwall was also made a life member of the MCC and received an MBE in 1965.

10. Alec Bedser (ENG)

Test Record

Bat	M	Inn	NO	Runs	HS	Avg	100	50	Ct
	51	71	15	714	79	12.75	0	1	26
Bowl	M	Inn	Wkts	Avg	BBI	BBM	5i	10m	SR
	51	92	236	24.89	7/44	14/99	15	5	67.4

On ESPNcricinfo, Bedser has been described as, 'A powerfully built, naggingly accurate medium-fast bowler, with a classical action off a short run, Bedser used the inswinger as his stock ball; his most dangerous delivery was the leg-cutter, which fizzed off the pitch with noticeable deviation.'

The war likely delayed his Test debut, which he made on the resumption of Test cricket in 1946 against India at home. It was a debut series to remember as he took 24 wickets in the three Tests at just 12.41. From thereon, Bedser virtually carried the English attack until the mid-'50s and the emergence of bowlers such as Fred Trueman and Frank Tyson.

Bedser took 16 wickets in five Tests on the 1946–47 tour of Australia but was expensive, averaging over 50 per wicket. He picked up a further 18 when Australia toured England in 1948 and then 16 as England visited South Africa. Again, he was relatively expensive in both series with a bowling average in the mid- to high-30s.

His next big series was the Ashes of 1950–51 where he collected a series-leading 30 scalps at an impressive average of 16.06, including 10/105 in the final Test, bowling England to an eight-wicket win and avoiding a series whitewash.

Bedser added a further 30 wickets to his tally at an average of 17.23 when South Africa visited England in 1951. This included 12/112 as England won by nine wickets in the third Test.

The following summer, Bedser took 20 wickets against India at 13.95 with 5/27 in the second innings of the second Test as England won by an innings.

Bedser saved his best performance for late in his career, where he collected 39 wickets in five home Ashes Tests in 1953 at just 17.48. This included his career-best figure of 14/99 in the first Test at Trent Bridge. Despite his efforts the Test was drawn but England won the Ashes 1–0.

He played just four more Tests as he was dropped during the 1954–55 Ashes tour and recalled for a single Test against South Africa in 1955, taking four wickets.

Bedser was a long serving national selector, acting as chairman for a period and managing England on two overseas tours. He also ran successful businesses with his twin brother Eric. He was knighted in 1996 and is an inductee in the ICC Cricket Hall of Fame.

11. Jim Laker (ENG)

Test Record

Bat	M	Inn	NO	Runs	HS	Avg	100	50	Ct
	46	63	15	676	63	14.08	0	2	12

Bowl	M	Inn	Wkts	Avg	BBI	BBM	5i	10m	SR
	46	86	193	21.24	10/53	19/90	9	3	62.3

Off-spinner Jim Laker will always be remembered first for his record breaking 19/90 (9/37 and 10/53) at Old Trafford in the fourth Test of the 1956 Ashes series. Despite the dust bowl pitch, the effort was all the more remarkable because Tony Lock was bowling equally well from the other end and could easily have used up some of Laker's wickets. All up in the series he took 46 poles across the five Tests at an average of just 9.60.

Prior to 1956, Laker was not a fixture in the English side and was in and out of the team. He debuted on the 1947–48 tour of the West Indies and played in all four Tests, taking 18 wickets including 7/103 in his first outing.

Laker played just three Tests against Australia in 1948, taking nine wickets. But this Australian side was one of the strongest batting line-ups in the history of Test cricket and Laker was not spared as he averaged over 52.

Single Tests followed versus New Zealand and the West Indies. He was not chosen for the Ashes tour in 1950–51; a reflection of the lack of success off-spinners had in Australia as much as Laker's form.

In 1951 he was back in the English side, and nabbed 14 South African wickets at 14.85 in just two Tests.

Mediocre series followed with eight wickets against India, nine in the 1953 home Ashes, 14 versus the West Indies and two wickets in a single Test against Pakistan. Laker did take seven wickets including 5/56 in 1955 against South Africa.

Naturally after his 1956 Ashes series Laker saw a lot more game time for England. First up was a tour of South Africa where Laker picked up 11 dismissals at 29.45 and a best of 2/7.

In four Tests against the West Indies in 1957 he took 18 wickets at 24.88 and then 17 in four Tests against New Zealand at home including 5/17.

Laker's final series was in Australia in 1958–59 and he was solid with 15 wickets in four Tests at an average of 21.20, with his final five-for in the Sydney Test.

Post-cricket, Laker became a television commentator and was known for his forthright but fair views. In 2009 Laker was inducted into the ICC Cricket Hall of Fame.

1940s and 1950s Second XI

1. Arthur Morris (AUS)
2. Cyril Washbrook (ENG)
3. Lindsay Hassett (AUS) vc
4. Frank Worrell (WI) c
5. Peter May (ENG)
6. Polly Umrigar (IND)
7. Alan Davidson (AUS)
8. Don Tallon (AUS) wk
9. Tony Lock (ENG)
10. Brian Statham (ENG)
11. Frank Tyson (ENG)

1960s

The 1960s began with a bang with the West Indies touring Australia. Both captains, Richie Benaud and Frank Worrell, undertook to play attacking cricket and finally some of the dour play of the middle and end of the 1950s was left behind.

The series started in Brisbane with the first-ever tied Test in the history of Test cricket. Led by a typically attacking Sobers innings of 132 the West Indies rattled up 453. When Australia replied with 505, anchored by Norm O'Neill's 181, it appeared the Test was headed for a draw. Alan Davidson added to his five wickets in the first innings with 6/87 in the second, bowling the West Indies out for 284 and leaving Australia a very gettable 233. But Wes Hall, at his fiery best, reduced the home team to 6/92.

When Bradman asked Benaud at the tea interval whether they were playing for a win or draw, Benaud assured him they were going for a win. They went for it and Davidson and Benaud brought up half-centuries leaving Australia needing just seven runs to win in the last two (eight ball) overs with four wickets in hand. Davidson was then run out for 80 by Joe Solomon and, with an over left, six were still needed. Scores were tied as five runs were added in the first six balls for the loss of two wickets. Next ball Ian Meckiff took off for the winning run but was beaten by another of Joe Solomon's brilliant direct hits from side on and the Test was tied.

The outstanding individual performer of the decade was undoubtedly Garry Sobers who was in the top-four for runs made and wickets taken, and sat second in the batting averages behind Doug Walters (who did not qualify for the 1960s XI).

While some very talented players missed out on a spot in the batting line-up, the batters essentially chose themselves, with Australia's Bob Simpson and Bill Lawry the standout openers in front of Pakistan's Hanif Mohammad. England's Ken Barrington, South Africa's Graeme Pollock and the West Indies' pair Sobers and Rohan Kanhai make up the middle order – their records and performances superior even to England's Colin Cowdrey and Ted Dexter, and West India's Seymour Nurse.

The standout pace bowlers of the decade were England's Fred Trueman, West Indian Wes Hall and Australian Grahame McKenzie, with Sobers to also bowl some medium pace as required. The spinner's spot came down to Lance Gibbs of the West Indies or Fred Titmus of England. As Gibbs took more wickets at a slightly better average and strike rate than Titmus, he was preferred.

Wally Grout picked up the keeper's position in this XI based on anecdotal evidence from the decade describing his superior ability as a wicketkeeper.

For the decade overall, the West Indies had the best win rate at 37% of matches won, closely followed by Australia and England at 34% and 32% respectively.

Most Runs in Period

Player	Mat	Inns	NO	Runs	HS	Ave	100	50
KF Barrington (ENG)	75	122	15	6397	256	59.78	20	31
MC Cowdrey (ENG)	65	110	12	4788	182	48.85	16	21
WM Lawry (AUS)	58	105	10	4717	210	49.65	13	23
GS Sobers (WI)	49	86	10	4563	226	60.03	15	19
ER Dexter (ENG)	55	92	8	4232	205	50.38	8	26
RB Simpson (AUS)	46	84	6	3995	311	51.21	8	23
RB Kanhai (WI)	43	76	1	3739	153	49.85	10	18
JH Edrich (ENG)	40	63	4	2711	310*	45.94	8	10
G Boycott (ENG)	41	70	9	2609	246*	42.77	6	13
CG Borde (IND)	45	79	10	2562	177*	37.13	4	15

*not out

Most Wickets in Period

Player	Mat	Inns	Wkts	BBI	BBM	Ave	SR	5	10
GD McKenzie (AUS)	54	102	238	8/71	10/91	27.91	67.7	16	3
LR Gibbs (WI)	42	77	184	8/38	11/157	27.84	84.1	12	2
FS Trueman (ENG)	36	67	179	7/44	12/119	22.01	50.1	12	3
GS Sobers (WI)	49	89	162	6/73	8/80	32.29	82.7	6	0
WW Hall (WI)	40	76	146	7/69	9/105	29.10	58.1	6	0
FJ Titmus (ENG)	47	81	145	7/79	9/162	30.82	96.1	7	0
DA Allen (ENG)	39	65	122	5/30	9/162	30.97	92.5	4	0
EAS Prasanna (IND)	22	40	113	6/74	10/174	27.05	66.8	8	1
PM Pollock (SA)	24	44	101	6/38	10/87	25.22	57.7	8	1
RC Motz (NZ)	32	55	100	6/63	8/113	31.48	70.3	5	0

Results

Team	Mat	Won	Lost	Tied	Draw	W/L
England	100	32	15	0	53	2.133
Australia	67	23	14	1	29	1.642
West Indies	49	18	13	1	17	1.384
India	52	9	21	0	22	0.428
South Africa	31	7	8	0	16	0.875
New Zealand	43	6	18	0	19	0.333
Pakistan	30	2	8	0	20	0.250

1960s XI

1. Bill Lawry (AUS)
2. Bob Simpson (AUS) vc
3. Ken Barrington (ENG)
4. Graeme Pollock (SA)
5. Garry Sobers (WI) c
6. Rohan Kanhai (WI)
7. Wally Grout (AUS) wk
8. Wes Hall (WI)
9. Fred Trueman (ENG)
10. Graham McKenzie (AUS)
11. Lance Gibbs (WI)

1. Bill Lawry (AUS)

Test Record

Bat	M	Inn	NO	Runs	HS	Avg	100	50	Ct
	67	123	12	5234	210	47.15	13	27	30

Bowl	M	Inn	Wkts	Avg	BBI	BBM	5i	10m	SR
	67	2	0	-	-	-	0	0	-

'It's all happening at the MCG,' Bill Lawry would often cry from the commentators' box as his excitement and passion for the game of cricket overflowed into his commentary. Yet his approach to the game as an opening batter was quite the opposite. Lawry was a left-handed accumulator of runs, eschewing attacking play for the relative safety of defending his wicket first and foremost. His methods even brought the English cricket writer Ian Wooldridge to unkindly refer to him as, 'The corpse with pads on.'

Selected to make his Test debut in the first Test of the 1961 England tour, he began well with 57 and followed it up with 130 in the first innings of the second Test at Lord's. Again unkindly, the English press responded with 'Plumber's ton at Lord's'. He added another hundred in the fourth Test and ended the series with 420 runs at 52.50.

During the 1962–63 Ashes series, he opened the batting with Bob Simpson for the first time, beginning one of Australia's greatest opening pairs (3590 runs in partnership, still the third best for Australian opening partners). Against the West Indies in 1965, he hit his highest Test score of 210 in his 382 partnership with Simpson (still an Australian opening partnership record). It wasn't easy either, as Wes Hall and Charlie Griffith hurled thunderbolts at them. Eventually Griffith was warned for intimidatory bowling but not before Lawry had his cheek grazed by a bouncer.

A passionate Victorian, Lawry was elevated to captain when Bob Simpson retired in the middle of the 1967–68 series. Lawry captained Australia 25 times for nine wins and eight losses.

Things started to go awry for Lawry on the 1969–70 tour of South Africa where Australia were belted 4–0. By the end of the tour Lawry was being criticised as being aloof and lacking diplomacy.

The pressure was on for the six Test 1970–71 Ashes tour, and after England led 1–0 Lawry was not just dumped as captain for Ian Chappell but was removed from the team altogether. Australia had not won a Test in the last eight, but it was the first time a regular captain had been removed mid-series.

Lawry was inducted into the Australian Cricket Hall of Fame in 2010.

2. Bob Simpson (AUS) vc

Test Record

Bat	M	Inn	NO	Runs	HS	Avg	100	50	Ct
	62	111	7	4869	311	46.81	10	27	110

Bowl	M	Inn	Wkts	Avg	BBI	BBM	5i	10m	SR
	62	84	71	42.26	5/57	8/97	2	0	96.9

Bob Simpson had a long association with Australian cricket broken into three distinct episodes. First, there was his initial, 'traditional' career in the 1960s. This was followed by his second career as a player as the Australian Cricket Board brought him out of retirement at 41 to captain the national team when the bulk of the Australian side defected to World Series Cricket. Finally, he was again called on to rescue Australian cricket, this time as coach to join with captain Allan Border in helping drag Australia out of its mid-1980s hole.

As well as his batting prowess, Simpson was a brilliant slip-fielder and occasional leg-spin bower where he was good enough to capture 71 Test wickets. His all-round contribution is recognised by his membership in the Australian Cricket Hall of Fame.

Simpson debuted in the 1958–59 series versus England and made a duck in his only bat. Inconsistent form followed and, despite not having scored a century and arguably not cemented his place in the national side, Simpson was made captain for the last four Tests against South Africa in 1963–64.

By the fourth Test of the 1964 Ashes series Simpson had gone 30 Tests without a century. He broke through in a big way scoring 311 in 12 hours 42 minutes, averaging 76 in the series and leading Australia to a 1–0 victory.

Against India in 1967–68 Simpson scored 55, 103 and 109, and then promptly resigned from the captaincy. He was dropped as well, despite being Australia's best batter.

Fast forward to the Indian tour in 1977–78 when the Australian side had been decimated by World Series Cricket: Simpson was cajoled out of retirement, aged 41, and captained the young, very inexperienced side in an exciting series that ended up Australia's way 3–2. Simpson also added two centuries and averaged just under 54. The following series in the West Indies was a different story and Simpson called stumps. All up Simpson led Australia 39 times for 12 wins, 12 losses and 15 draws.

Fast forward again, and Simpson was made the first coach of the struggling Australian side and brought a hard edged, disciplined approach to his role with fitness a key focus. Gradually the team was rebuilt until it won the World Cup in 1987 and then regained the Ashes in emphatic fashion in England in 1989. Simpson spent ten years in the role. This set the scene for eventual domination by the Australians by the mid-'90s.

3. Ken Barrington (ENG)

Test Record

Bat	M	Inn	NO	Runs	HS	Avg	100	50	Ct
	82	131	15	6806	256	58.67	20	35	58

Bowl	M	Inn	Wkts	Avg	BBI	BBM	5i	10m	SR
	82	29	29	44.82	3–4	5/111	0	0	93.6

When Barrington debuted for England in 1955, he was a naturally attacking batter but made a duck in his first outing, and 34 and 18 in his second Test, and was dropped.

It was not until 1959 that he returned to the English side by which time he had become the ultimate stonewaller. It worked in his favour as he carved out a storied career which ended as the second leading run-maker for England. Against India he played all five Tests in the summer and scored 357 runs at 59.50 with three scores in the 80s without going on to a century.

Barrington's maiden Test hundred came up on the tour of the West Indies in 1959–60 where he notched 128 in the first Test. He followed it up with a second century in the next Test and ended the series with an average of 46.66.

Playing all five Tests on Australia's tour of England in 1961, Barrington averaged a respectable 45.50 and was consistent but did not reach three figures.

Barrington then had an outstanding tour of the sub-continent in 1961–62 as he scored a hundred in Pakistan and averaged 76.33 in the two Test series. His form went to another level in the five Tests in India as he knocked up three centuries in scoring 594 runs at 99.

His away form continued on the tour Down Under in 1962–63 and he scored 582 runs in Australia at 72.75 with two hundreds to help England draw the series. Barrington then averaged in the 70s in three Tests in New Zealand.

Barrington's good form against Australia continued in the 1964 Ashes with 531 runs at 75.85 including his highest Test score of 256. He maintained his form in South Africa scoring a further 508 runs at over 100.

The Ashes of 1965–66 saw him lead the way again for England with 464 runs at 66.28, including twin centuries.

In 1967 he averaged in the 60s in three Tests at home versus India and followed it up against Pakistan with 426 runs in just three Tests at 142, including three centuries.

Barrington's final series was the 1968 Ashes in England where he played in three Tests and again averaged over 50 against the old foe. A heart attack brought about an abrupt end to his career.

He was assistant manager on the England tour of the West Indies in 1980 when a second heart attack claimed his life at just 50.

Barrington is an inductee in the ICC Cricket Hall of Fame.

4. Graeme Pollock (SA)

Test Record

Bat	M	Inn	NO	Runs	HS	Avg	100	50	Ct
	23	41	4	2256	274	60.97	7	11	17

Bowl	M	Inn	Wkts	Avg	BBI	BBM	5i	10m	SR
	23	13	4	51.00	2/50	2/50	0	0	103.5

Graeme Pollock's Test career was cut short in its prime by South Africa's exclusion from Test cricket in the 1970s. Short as it was, his Test career was prolific and his average is second-highest of all time for batters with at least 40 innings.

A left-handed batter with exquisite timing and immense power, Pollock could carve up any attack. Bradman once described him as the greatest left-hand bat he had seen along with Sobers.

At the age of 16, Pollock scored his maiden First Class century, the youngest centurion in the history of South Africa's domestic competition the Currie Cup.

Pollock was selected to tour Australia at the age of 19 in 1963–64, and he made his Test debut in the first Test scoring 25 at his only bat. He made his maiden Test hundred (122) in the third Test and brought up a second century (175) in the next Test scoring 399 runs at 57 for the series.

England toured South Africa in 1964–65 and Pollock knocked up 459 runs at 57.37 with a highest score of 137 in the drawn fifth Test.

South Africa then toured England for a three Test series where Pollock averaged 48.50 with one century at Trent Bridge in the second Test won by South Africa.

Pollock then decimated the Australians in two Test home series. In 1966–67 he scored 537 runs at 76.71 with a top score of 209 in the second Test and another century in the fourth Test.

In 1970 against Australia, Pollock led the runs aggregate and averages for both sides with 517 runs in the four Tests at 73.85. His series was highlighted by 274 in the second Test at Durban. This series was his final one before South Africa's exclusion.

All up in his First Class career, Pollock scored over 20,000 runs at an average of 54.67. He also claimed 43 wickets with his leg-spin.

Pollock played in unofficial 'Tests' against touring sides and his final match at the age of 42 saw him score a hundred against the rebel touring Australians in 1987.

Along with other players such as Barry Richards and Mike Proctor, Pollock took part in protests against apartheid and supported the selection of the national side based on merit alone.

Pollock is one of two South African batters inducted in the ICC Cricket Hall of Fame.

5. Garry Sobers (WI) c

Test Record

Bat	M	Inn	NO	Runs	HS	Avg	100	50	Ct
	93	160	21	8032	365*	57.78	26	30	109

Bowl	M	Inn	Wkts	Avg	BBI	BBM	5i	10m	SR
	93	159	235	34.03	6/73	8/80	6	0	91.9

*not out

Sir Garfield Sobers was the complete all-rounder and could have held his spot in the West Indian sides of the 1960s and '70s for his batting or bowling alone. As a batter he had all the shots, playing with a powerful elegance. His bowling was a mix between left-arm fast-medium and spin, both orthodox and wrist spin. As a fielder he was superb in any position.

If the mark of an all-rounder is that their batting average is greater than their bowling average, then this measure suggests Sobers is the greatest of all-rounders as his difference of 23.74 is greater than any other cricketer who played a meaningful number of Tests.

Sobers was actually born with six fingers on each hand but had the extras removed at birth. He excelled at many sports including playing soccer and basketball for Barbados.

He made his First Class debut at 16 and his Test debut a year later, chosen more as a bowler and scoring 40 runs and taking four wickets against England.

Sobers contributed over the next few series before his breakthrough came when Pakistan visited the West Indies in 1958. He brought up his first Test century in the third Test and made it worthwhile going on to a world record score of 365 not out. Sobers scored two centuries in the next Test to bring up 864 runs at 137.33 for the series.

Maintaining his form versus India away, Sobers scored 557 runs at 92.83 to go with ten wickets. Sobers brought up 709 runs against England at home in 1959–60 at 101.28.

Probably his best all-round series came versus India in 1961–62, with 424 runs at 70.66 and 23 wickets at an average of 20.56. Competing with this series was the West Indies visit to England in 1966 when Sobers scored 722 runs at 103.14 and took 20 wickets at 27.25.

Sobers then averaged 114 in a series in India and 90.83 against England in the West Indies.

A couple of moderate series followed before he sprung back to form against India with over 500 runs at 74.62, including three centuries. Sobers also scored a magnificent 254 for the Rest of the World versus Australia.

His career was ended with an away and home series against England where he brought up a century at Lord's and averaged 76.50 in three Tests in England. Sobers' final Test came at Port of Spain where he managed just 20 and took three wickets.

Sobers captained the West Indies 39 times for nine wins and ten losses.

He was knighted for his services to cricket in 1975 and was an inaugural inductee into the ICC Cricket Hall of Fame. Sobers was made a National Hero of Barbados by the Cabinet of Barbados in 1998 and is thus accorded the honorary prefix 'The Right Excellent'.

6. Rohan Kanhai (WI)

Test Record

Bat	M	Inn	NO	Runs	HS	Avg	100	50	Ct
	79	137	6	6227	256	47.53	15	28	50

Bowl	M	Inn	Wkts	Avg	BBI	BBM	5i	10m	SR
	79	9	0	-	-	-	0	0	-

A pugnacious, attacking right-handed batter, Kanhai's career began in 1954–55 and extended to 1973–74. He was also a cornerstone of the West Indies batting line-up in the 1960s. He is an inductee into the ICC Cricket Hall of Fame.

Kanhai debuted against England at Birmingham and kept wicket and opened the batting for his first three Tests before Gerry Alexander took the gloves.

It took him until his 13th Test in 1958 to bring up his first hundred but it was a mighty one – 256 against India at Kolkata and then he scored 99 in his next Test. He was second leading run scorer for the series (behind Sobers) with 538 runs at 67.25. Kanhai added a further 274 runs in Pakistan at 54.80.

In 1960–61 Kanhai had a good tour of Australia, knocking up 503 runs with two centuries at 50.30. He then followed it up at home against India, leading the runs aggregate at 495 with an average of 70.71 and two more hundreds.

Kanhai again led the runs aggregate away to England with 497 at 55.22, but failed to pass three figures although he had two scores in the 90s. It helped the West Indies to a 2–0 series win.

He had a solid series in Australia in 1964–65, with two hundreds and an average of 46.20, and followed it up in 1966 with an average of 40.50 back in England.

Visiting India in 1966–67, Kanhai powered 227 runs at 56.57 and then had an outstanding series when England toured the West

Indies, with over 500 runs at 59.44 including 153 at Port of Spain and then 150 at Georgetown.

As Kanhai's career entered the '70s, his form continued against India at home and he again averaged over 50 in scoring 433 runs with a top score of 158 not out.

Kanhai replaced Sobers as captain for the 1972–73 series against Australia in the West Indies but couldn't conjure a series win as Australia won 2–0. Captaincy didn't affect Kanhai's batting as he scored 385 runs at 51.14.

A better result awaited Kanhai in England as the West Indies won 2–0 and Kanhai averaged 44.60 with a top score of 157.

Kanhai's final series was a one all draw with England at home, but he was disappointed with his personal form with just 157 runs in the five Tests and he promptly retired from Test cricket.

Indian great Sunil Gavaskar described Kanhai as, 'Off the field, he was one of the nicest guys I ever met. Naming my son after him was a no-brainer.' Gavaskar also commented that, 'In my debut series, if I played a bad shot, when crossing over me to go to the slips for the next over, if he was not within earshot of the wicketkeeper, he would whisper in my ear: "Concentrate! Don't you want a 100? What's the matter with you?"'

7. Wally Grout (AUS) wk

Test Record

Bat	Mat	Inn	NO	Runs	HS	Avg	100	50	Ct	St
	51	67	8	890	74	15.08	0	3	163	24

A lucky charm to the Australian team, as they did not lose a series during Grout's time behind the stumps. He was a genial man with a sense of humour that hid the serious heart condition he carried that resulted in him passing away at 41 after finishing his Test career, aged 39. Over the last four years of his tenure, he was warned that his heart could cause him to drop dead at any time, and he went on the West Indies tour in 1964 after hiding a heart attack from officialdom.

Wally 'Griz' Grout was widely regarded as a fine keeper; Bob Simpson rated him as the greatest wicketkeeper he ever saw, Bradman rated him very highly, and even opponents were complimentary including Wes Hall who said, 'He was the finest wicketkeeper I either played with or against in my ten years of big cricket.' Ultimately he was elevated to the Australian Cricket Hall of Fame.

His batting at Test level was not up to the standard of modern keeping greats, but he chipped in from time to time and was even a stand in opener, scoring 50 in a Test against India.

Grout's first tour was to South Africa in 1957 and, despite a hairline fracture to his thumb, he was selected over Barry Jarman for the first Test. Here he set a then-world record of six catches in an innings and contributed 21 down the order in Australia's only innings. Despite his Test opportunities being limited by Grout, Jarman would go on to admit, 'I could not speak too highly of Wally as a wicketkeeper. He was one of the game's greatest characters. I never begrudged playing second fiddle to him.' Grout ended the series with 16 catches and three stumpings and a top score of 35 not out. An aside from the tour diary was Neil Harvey and Grout having a narrow escape when they were chased by lions and elephants on safari trying to get the perfect photo.

Grout collected dismissals consistently over the ensuing series, and as for any great keeper he was also essential in keeping an eye on batter's faults and the rhythm of the match. Richie Benaud spoke of this when he commented, 'He was able to read a match as well as any captain, and was always of tremendous value to me in captaining the Australian side.'

Against the West Indies in the tied Test series, Grout equalled the record for dismissals by a keeper in a series with 23. In the last Test, which was the decider, Australia needed four runs with three wickets in hand. Grout late-cut Valentine but despite the ball knocking the bails off Grout was ruled not out. Demonstrating his sportsmanship, Grout 'committed suicide' and hit the next ball up in the air.

In England in 1961, Grout claimed 21 dismissals – a new Ashes record for wicketkeepers. It was noted that his speed, consistency, agility, and uncanny capacity to read play were the hallmarks of wicketkeeping greatness.

Grout continued to the home series against England in 1965–66 and showed he still had the skills to keep at the highest level, with 15 catches and one stumping. This was his last series and he retired just shy of his 39th birthday.

8. Wes Hall (WI)

Test Record

Bat	M	Inn	NO	Runs	HS	Avg	100	50	Ct
	48	66	14	818	50*	15.73	0	2	11

Bowl	M	Inn	Wkts	Avg	BBI	BBM	5i	10m	SR
	48	92	192	26.38	7/69	11/126	9	1	54.2

*not out

Wes Hall's Test career began in 1958 and for a decade he terrorised opposition batters. At a muscular 188 centimetres tall (6 foot 2 inches) and with a lithe approach and a classical action, Hall struck fear into the hearts of many a batter.

He started his cricket career as a wicketkeeper-batter, but took the new ball one day when an opening bowler failed to show and never looked back.

Hall was chosen for the 1957 England tour but played only one First Class match. He was then picked to tour India and Pakistan in 1958–59 and excelled on pitches that are a graveyard for fast bowlers. In five Tests in India, he took 30 wickets including 11/126 in the second Test. He then added a further 16 in Pakistan in three Tests, averaging just 17 in both series.

England toured the West Indies in 1959–60 and Hall picked up a further 22 wickets at the more expensive 30.86 runs per wicket, including 7/69 in the first innings of the Kingston Test.

Hall performed well in Australia in 1960–61, dismissing 21 batters which included 9/203 in the famous tied Test which involved bowling the last over when Australia needed six to win with three wickets left (Hall took one wicket, dropped a caught and bowled, and there were two run outs).

With India in the West Indies in 1961–62, Hall collected 27 wickets at 15.74 and averaged 40 with the bat.

Hall's form never quite reached those levels again as he picked up 16 wickets in England, 16 at home to Australia (instrumental in gaining the West Indies first series win over Australia) and then 18 back in England again – all in five Test series and with an average in the high 20s to low 30s.

His output dropped further in his last few series and he took eight, nine and eight wickets against India, England and Australia.

Hall's final Test came in New Zealand where he took one wicket in the match. *Wisden* noted that, 'Old age, as cricketers go, had finally had its say.'

Post-cricket, Hall became an ordained minister as well as serving as Minister for Tourism and Sport in the Barbados government. He also managed several West Indian tours and was President of the West Indies Cricket Board, helping bring the World Cup to the Caribbean in 2007.

Hall is an inductee in the ICC Cricket Hall of Fame.

9. Fred Trueman (ENG)

Test Record

Bat	M	Inn	NO	Runs	HS	Avg	100	50	Ct
	67	85	14	981	39*	13.81	0	0	64

Bowl	M	Inn	Wkts	Avg	BBI	BBM	5i	10m	SR
	67	127	307	21.57	8/31	12/119	17	3	49.4

*not out

A genuinely fast bowler, Trueman would have played many more Tests and taken many more wickets had it not been for various disciplinary infractions.

Trueman burst out of the blocks in his first series at home to India in 1952 with 29 wickets in four Tests at 13.31, including 8/31 in India's first innings at Old Trafford where he helped have the tourists 4/0.

Playing only a minor role in the next few series, Trueman returned to near his best when the West Indies toured in 1957, capturing 22 wickets with a best of 5/63.

A few mediocre series followed before Trueman picked up 24 wickets at home to India in 1959 at an average of 16.70, and then 21 in the West Indies in 1959–60 including 5/35 in the second Test at Port of Spain.

It was during the second half of the '50s that Trueman formed one of the great all-time fast bowling partnerships with Brian Statham, who raced Trueman to the 250 wicket mark.

Trueman followed this up in 1960 as South Africa visited, collecting 25 dismissals at 20.32 with a best of 5/27 at Trent Bridge.

He took 20 wickets, including an innings five-wicket haul, in each of his next three series; home and away to Australia and at home to Pakistan.

Trueman then collected 14 wickets in the two Tests against the Kiwis in New Zealand, with a best of 7/75 in the first innings of the Christchurch Test.

He had his best series with the ball in 1963 at home to the West Indies, and picked up 34 wickets at 17.47 including 7/44 at Birmingham.

In Trueman's penultimate series he became the first bowler to take 300 Test wickets as he took 17 in the home Ashes summer of 1964.

Trueman's final series came in 1964 when he took just six wickets in two Tests versus New Zealand in England.

Part of Yorkshire's dominance in the 1960s, Trueman then turned his hand to commentating (which ex-player doesn't?) and was a natural raconteur who had a penchant for tall stories.

Trueman was an inaugural inductee into the ICC Cricket Hall of Fame in 2009.

10. Graham McKenzie (AUS)

Test Record

Bat	M	Inn	NO	Runs	HS	Avg	100	50	Ct
	60	89	12	945	76	12.27	0	2	34

Bowl	M	Inn	Wkts	Avg	BBI	BBM	5i	10m	SR
	60	113	246	29.78	8/71	10/91	16	3	71.8

McKenzie carried the Australian attack in the 1960s and thoroughly deserves his place in this XI. With 238 wickets, he captured more than twice the next-best Australian, Alan Davidson (who claimed 94 in the second half of his career).

He was big and broad shouldered, a super-hero come to life. He had a well-oiled action, perfect for a fast bowler and if it were not for the heavy workload he carried he may well have had an even better record. An example was the fourth Test of the 1964 Ashes series when he bowled a mammoth 60 overs for 7/153. As it was, he had 100 Test wickets by age 23 and 200 by 27. When he retired soon after, he was just shy of Richie Benaud's all-time Australian wicket tally.

McKenzie toured with the 1961 Ashes party and made his Test debut in the second Test, taking 5/37 in the second innings. Thereafter McKenzie was at or near the top of wicket tallies and bowling averages for virtually every series he appeared in.

In India in 1964, McKenzie ignored the presumption the wickets were a fast bowler's graveyard and topped the wicket aggregate for Australia with 13 wickets at 16 in the three Tests. He had his best ever Test match figures of 10/91 in the first Test.

However by this time McKenzie was being seriously overbowled. He bowled 101.4 overs in the two Pakistan Tests and 108.3 overs in the Indian Tests. Even this super-fit super-hero was suffering from exhaustion. Nonetheless, he stepped up for the West Indies tour in

1965 to contribute 17 wickets but this time his average had blown out to nearly 40.

He burst back to form with 30 wickets against the West Indies at home in 1968, including his best bowling in an innings of 8/71 in the second Test. However, McKenzie took a single wicket for 333 runs in the 4–0 drubbing in South Africa. But he wasn't finished, and soldiered on into the 1970s, playing four Tests in the 1970–71 Ashes summer with just seven wickets. His last Test was the fourth of the series as the changing of the guard took place as the Chappells, Lillee, Marsh et al era began.

McKenzie also has the most Test dismissals by hit wicket for any bowler with four.

One of Australia's all-time greatest fast bowlers, McKenzie was admitted to the Australian Cricket Hall of Fame in 2010.

11. Lance Gibbs (WI)

Test Record

Bat	M	Inn	NO	Runs	HS	Avg	100	50	Ct
	79	109	39	488	25	6.97	0	0	52

Bowl	M	Inn	Wkts	Avg	BBI	BBM	5i	10m	SR
	79	148	309	29.09	8/38	11/157	18	2	87.7

With an unusual chest-on action, Gibbs generated turn and bounce with his right-arm off-spin, generally with a high degree of accuracy as his career economy rate of just 1.98 runs per over demonstrates.

When Gibbs finished his Test career in 1976, he was the leading wicket-taker in the history of the game and just the second Test bowler to go past 300 wickets.

Gibbs debuted against Pakistan at Port of Spain in 1958 and picked up 4/70 for the match. In the third Test of the series he collected his first five-for (5/80) and ended the series with 17 wickets at a respectable 23.05.

Playing only three Tests (he wasn't picked for the first two) on the West Indies tour of Australia in 1960–61, Gibbs nabbed 19 wickets with two five-fors and a best of 5/66.

Gibbs captured 24 wickets when India toured the West Indies in 1961–62, including bowling his country to victory in the second innings of the third Test with 8/38 (his figures were 53.3–37–38–8).

In 1963 the West Indies toured England, and Gibbs had his best series with 26 wickets at 21.30 with a couple of five-fors and a best of 6/98, helping the West Indies to a ten-wicket win in the first Test.

Australia toured the West Indies in 1965 and Gibbs took 6/29, again bowling the West Indies to victory in the final innings of the third Test. All up, he picked up 18 wickets in the series.

Four years later the West Indies toured Australia and Gibbs led the way for the West Indies with 24 wickets in the five Tests including

5/88 in a winning effort in the first Test. Gibbs's efforts were to no avail, however, as Australia won the series 3–1.

Gibbs's success against Australia continued in 1972–73 when he took 26 wickets at 26.76 equalling Max Walker for leading wicket-taker in the series.

His final series was again versus Australia away in 1975–76, and he dismissed 16 batters at 40.75 with 5/102 being his best.

Post-cricket, Gibbs emigrated to the United States. He is an inductee in the ICC Cricket Hall of Fame.

1960s Second XI

1. Conrad Hunte (WI)
2. Hanif Mohammed (PAK)
3. Basil Butcher (WI)
4. Colin Cowdrey (ENG) c
5. Seymour Nurse (WI)
6. Ted Dexter (ENG) vc
7. Peter Pollock (SA)
8. James Parks (ENG) wk
9. Fred Titmus (ENG)
10. Charlie Griffith (WI)
11. Dick Motz (NZ)

1970s

The 1970s began with a South African side full of rising stars smashing Australia 4–0 in a four-Test series in South Africa. The future was looking bright for the South Africans but the international sporting community, cricket included, pulled the rug out from under them and excluded them from international competition in response to the South African Government's apartheid policy. With more Test cricket it is possible there would be more than a solitary South African in this XI.

The Australians rejuvenated after the South African debacle and ended up with the best winning record for the decade at 36% of matches won, just edging England who won 35% of the Tests they played. Australia dominated at home in the middle of the decade with Dennis Lillee and Jeff Thomson arriving as one of the most damaging opening bowling duos in Test history. However, by the end of the decade the West Indies had emerged as the force in world cricket with their quartet of fast bowlers causing havoc, and a dynamic batting line-up including Viv Richards, Clive Lloyd and Gordon Greenidge.

While the focus of this book is on Test cricket, it would be remiss not to mention the first One Day World Cup in 1975 in England. Australia and the West Indies made it through to the final. Clive Lloyd led with a century as the West Indies made 8/291 off 60 overs. However, the deadly arm of Viv Richards combined with some less than competent running saw Australia slump to 9/233 with seven overs to go. Lillee and Thomson added 41 as they swung and hit and swung and missed until Thomson was run out, 17 short of victory. The West Indies won again in 1979.

World cricket was also disrupted towards the end of the 1970s by World Series Cricket. Whole books have been written about the planning, execution and the outcome in relation to World Series Cricket but we don't have space to go into that detail here. Suffice to say Australian media mogul Kerry Packer wanted the television rights to Tests and the ever expanding One Day International Cricket. The Australian Cricket Board said no, so Packer set up his own competition and poached the best Australian players and most of the others from around the world. Global superstars such as the Chappells, Lillee, Barry and Viv Richards, Lloyd, Imran Khan and Tony Greig among many others signed on to the cause.

Choosing the 1970s XI started with the difficult task of opening batters. Gavaskar and Boycott both averaged mid-50s for the decade, although Boycott's overall record is somewhat less. Then there was South African Barry Richards who averaged in the 70s in his one Test series against Australia and then carved out a storied First Class career in county cricket and Australia's Sheffield Shield, as well as performing well in World Series Cricket against the best in the world. The decision was made to go with all three and bat Richards at number three.

Greg Chappell was the standout middle order batter and an automatic selection at number four, while Gundappa Viswanath, Alvin Kallicharan and Doug Walters were in competition for the number five spot with Viswanath being preferred for scoring runs for India when it really counted. Tony Greig was chosen at number six as the all-rounder in the XI.

The pace bowling positions went firstly to Lillee as the leading fast man of the decade. Thomson was chosen because at his destructive best there was no-one better. This left the third spot between West Indian Andy Roberts and Englishmen Bob Willis and John Snow, with Roberts just getting the nod as his best was also probably the best of the three. The spinner's role was a genuine coin toss between India's Bishen Bedi and England's Derek Underwood. Bedi was preferred based on his ability to deceive batters with flight, whereas Underwood was a slightly quicker bowler, but either deserves the spot.

Finally, the wicketkeeping spot came down to a decision between Alan Knott of England and Australia's Rod Marsh. Both were fine keepers, and the position went to Knott only for his slightly superior batting record.

Most Runs in Period

Player	Mat	Inns	NO	Runs	HS	Ave	100	50
SM Gavaskar (IND)	60	108	7	5647	221	55.91	22	25
GR Viswanath (IND)	62	108	8	4611	179	46.11	10	28
GS Chappell (AUS)	54	96	13	4398	247*	52.98	15	21
AI Kallicharran (WI)	53	89	9	3956	187	49.45	11	20
RC Fredericks (WI)	49	90	7	3809	169	45.89	8	22
G Boycott (ENG)	44	77	9	3806	191	55.97	12	21
AW Greig (ENG)	58	93	4	3599	148	40.43	8	20
IM Chappell (AUS)	45	84	5	3512	196	44.45	10	17
APE Knott (ENG)	71	112	10	3509	135	34.40	5	23
DL Amiss (ENG)	45	80	9	3487	262*	49.11	11	11

*not out

Most Wickets in Period

Player	Mat	Inns	Wkts	BBI	BBM	Ave	SR	5	10
DL Underwood (ENG)	59	106	202	8/51	13/71	27.65	76.1	10	4
BS Bedi (IND)	48	84	196	6/71	10/194	29.79	80.7	10	1
DK Lillee (AUS)	35	68	184	6/26	11/123	23.78	51.6	12	4
RGD Willis (ENG)	51	95	182	7/78	9/118	24.78	54.4	11	0
BS Chandrasekhar (IND)	42	70	180	8/79	12/104	29.20	62.2	14	1
JR Thomson (AUS)	34	61	152	6/46	9/105	25.60	49.4	6	0
AW Greig (ENG)	58	93	141	8/86	13/156	32.20	69.5	6	2
AME Roberts (WI)	29	57	140	7/54	12/121	25.15	52.4	9	2
MHN Walker (AUS)	34	63	138	8/143	8/143	27.47	73.1	6	0
CM Old (ENG)	41	73	129	7/50	9/88	27.86	60.1	4	0

Results

Team	Mat	Won	Lost	Tied	Draw	W/L
England	95	33	21	0	41	1.571
Australia	83	30	29	0	24	1.034
West Indies	63	18	15	0	30	1.200
India	64	17	19	0	28	0.894
Pakistan	46	9	11	0	26	0.818
South Africa	4	4	0	0	0	-
New Zealand	41	3	19	0	19	0.157

1970s XI

1. Sunil Gavaskar (IND)
2. Geoff Boycott (ENG)
3. Barry Richards (SA)
4. Greg Chappell (AUS) c
5. Gundappa Viswanath (IND)
6. Tony Grieg (ENG) vc
7. Alan Knott (ENG) wk
8. Dennis Lillee (AUS)
9. Andy Roberts (WI)
10. Bishan Bedi (IND)
11. Jeff Thomson (AUS)

1. Sunil Gavaskar (IND)

Test Record

Bat	M	Inn	NO	Runs	HS	Avg	100	50	Ct
	125	214	16	10,122	236*	51.12	34	45	108

Bowl	M	Inn	Wkts	Avg	BBI	BBM	5i	10m	SR
	125	29	1	206	1/34	1/34	0	0	380

*not out

Sunil Gavaskar is one of the greatest opening batters of all time and when he finished his Test career he was the leading run scorer in Test history, as well as centuries made. His records have since been broken, of course, but generally by players playing significantly more Tests. He was the first to pass 10,000 Test runs.

His game was built on solid defence, but he could play all the shots. His position in the Indian team demanded solidity rather than flair and he helped lay the foundations for the success India eventually enjoyed.

Gavaskar burst onto the Test scene playing four of the five Tests on the 1970–71 tour of the West Indies. He scored 65 and 67 not out in his first Test, 116 in his second, 117 not out in the third, and topped it off with a century and double century in the fourth. All up he scored 774 runs at an incredible 154.80.

A few lean series followed before India toured New Zealand in 1975–76, and Gavaskar knocked up 266 runs in the three Tests at 66.50. He followed this up, averaging over 50 on the tour of the West Indies.

Gavaskar hit another purple patch in 1978–79 as he rattled up 447 runs in a three Test series versus Pakistan at 89.40. He then scored 732 runs in six Tests against the West Indies at home with an average of 91.50, including a double century. 542 runs followed in England at 77.42, including yet another double ton.

More than respectable series at home to Australia and Pakistan saw Gavaskar again average over 50.

In 1981–81, Gavaskar scored 500 runs in six Tests versus England and averaged 62.50, including a top score of 172 in the second Test at Bengalaru.

Gavaskar added 352 runs in Australia in three Tests in 1985–86 and averaged over a hundred, including 166 not out at Adelaide and 172 in Sydney.

His penultimate series resulted in an average of 85 in three Tests against Sri Lanka before his final series versus Pakistan in 1986–87, where he scored 295 runs at a tick under a 50 average.

Post-cricket, Gavaskar has worked as a commentator and columnist as well as in various roles with the BCCI and as chair of the ICC cricket committee.

Naturally, Gavaskar is an inductee in the ICC Cricket Hall of Fame.

2. Geoff Boycott (ENG)

Test Record

Bat	M	Inn	NO	Runs	HS	Avg	100	50	Ct
	108	193	23	8114	246*	47.72	22	42	33

Bowl	M	Inn	Wkts	Avg	BBI	BBM	5i	10m	SR
	108	20	7	54.57	3/47	3/47	0	0	134.8

*not out

Geoff Boycott was a polarising figure in his playing days. John Woodcock wrote in *One Hundred Greatest Cricketers,* 'Even in his native Yorkshire he attracted either fanatical support or uncompromising opposition.'

The source of any opposition came from his obdurate approach to batting that some argued bordered on selfishness. Once in he was one of the most difficult batters to remove, but at the same time he hardly moved the game along. Bazball would have been a nightmare for Boycott.

Boycott debuted in the 1964 Ashes series and made 48 at his only bat and brought up his first Test ton (113) in his fourth Test. He managed 291 runs in the four Tests he played at an average of 48.50.

He followed up his successful debut series with a solid outing against South Africa away, averaging just under 50 in the five Tests with another hundred (117).

In 1967 at Headingly versus India, Boycott made his highest Test score of 246 not out at a strike rate of 44.3. He hit 30 fours and even managed a six.

A successful tour of the West Indies followed against the might of Hall, Griffith, Sobers and Gibbs with 463 runs at 66.14 including a top score of 116.

Perhaps Boycott's best series was in Australia in 1970–71 when he compiled 657 runs in five Tests at 93.85 leading both the aggregate and averages in the series. He included two hundreds – at Sydney (142 not out) and Adelaide (119 not out).

Boycott then scored twin centuries against Pakistan including one at Lord's, ensuring his name on the honour board.

He missed 30 Tests in the mid-'70s as it was thought he felt he should have been made captain (rather than Mike Denness) after Ray Illingworth had retired.

Boycott returned triumphantly in 1977, playing three Tests in the Ashes series and scoring 442 runs at 147.33 with two centuries and a top score of 191. He followed it up by averaging 82.25 against Pakistan.

In 1979 he averaged 75.60 versus India at home, scoring 378 runs in the four Tests with two more hundreds and leading the way for England.

Boycott's final series came in India in 1981–82 and he performed solidly with an average of 44.57 – not far below his career effort.

Post-cricket, Boycott turned to commentating, was knighted (some say controversially) for his service to cricket and inducted into the ICC Cricket Hall of Fame.

3. Barry Richards (SA)

Test Record

Bat	M	Inn	NO	Runs	HS	Avg	100	50	Ct
	4	7	0	508	140	72.57	2	2	3

Bowl	M	Inn	Wkts	Avg	BBI	BBM	5i	10m	SR
	4	3	1	26.00	1/12	1/12	0	0	72.0

Barry Richards played in only one Test series, against Australia, before South Africa were excluded from international cricket for their government's apartheid policy. Were it not for South Africa's isolation, it is likely Richards would have been an integral part of what had the makings of a great South African side.

However, the one series he played – plus a stellar First Class record – sees Barry Richards as an inductee in the ICC Hall of Fame. In addition, the great Don Bradman chose Richards as an opener in his best team of the twentieth century.

An attacking opening batter, Richards has been selected at three in the 1970s XI even though he was likely a better batter than the openers and certainly a more entertaining one.

On top of his brief Test record, Richards scored over 28,000 First Class runs at an average of 54.74 playing for Natal, Hampshire and South Australia. His highest score of 356 came for South Australia, which included 325 in a day against an attack including Dennis Lillee and Graham McKenzie. Richards scored nine hundreds before lunch and reached 1000 runs in a season on 15 occasions.

Richards also turned out for Kerry Packer's World Series Cricket, playing for the World side and scoring 554 runs in five 'Super Tests' against the best bowlers in the world.

The one Test series Richards did play was against Australia in 1970 at home, which saw South Africa skittle the Australian 4–0.

He began slowly with 29 and 32 on debut, but in the second Test brought up his first Test century of 140 at his only bat as South Africa won by an innings.

In the third Test at Johannesburg, Richards made 65 and 35. Richards brought up his second century (126) in second innings of the fourth Test after making 81 in the first innings.

Post-cricket, Richards did the obligatory commentating for a period.

4. Greg Chappell (AUS) c

Test Record

Bat	M	Inn	NO	Runs	HS	Avg	100	50	Ct
	87	151	19	7110	247*	53.86	24	31	122

Bowl	M	Inn	Wkts	Avg	BBI	BBM	5i	10m	SR
	87	88	47	40.70	5/61	5/61	1	0	113.3

*not out

If you were to have a discussion about who the best Australian batter of the 1970s was it wouldn't last long, because the answer would be Greg Chappell. If you also wanted a discussion about, say, the best batter in the world in the 1970s, or maybe who is the best Australian batter ever is apart from Bradman, then Greg Chappell is well in the conversation.

Tall and upright, Chappell had a gracefulness about his batting. Always unruffled, it seemed he had all the time in the world to unravel what the bowler had tossed his way. Along with his undoubted batting prowess, Chappell was an outstanding slip-fielder and held the record for most catches by a non-wicketkeeper by the end of his career. He also changed his bowling from leg-spin to medium pace which was a very useful addition to the teams he played in.

Chappell debuted in the second Test at Perth in 1970 and came in at 5/107. He took his time to get settled in and crafted a century on debut (108) and added 219 with Ian Redpath. Playing against the rest of the World in 1972, Chappell knocked up 425 runs at 106.25. In New Zealand in 1974 he also notched his highest Test score of 247 not out in the first Test, putting on 264 with brother Ian.

Chappell continued to contribute heavily to Australia's success in the mid-1970s but then lost some of his more productive years to World Series Cricket. In the first series of WSC, he scored 661 runs at 60 – including a century – and 85 in the Antigua 'Super Test' against the hostility of Roberts, Holding, Croft and Garner.

Once the players were brought back together, Chappell resumed the captaincy and his Test run-making. But the 1980–81 season was also the undoubted low point of Chappell's career as, with New Zealand needing six to win in the One Day Internationals finals series, he ordered his brother Trevor to bowl underarm. As you would expect this was roundly condemned, especially by Richie Benaud from the commentary box. Chappell was contrite afterwards, apologising and blaming the decision on the pressure and demand of the amount of cricket being played.

Chappell's final series was in 1983–84 against the Pakistanis. He announced his decision to retire after the fourth Test and went in to the fifth and final Test of the series, needing 84 runs to break Bradman's Australian Test run scoring record and two catches to pass Colin Cowdrey's world record for most catches by a non-wicketkeeper. He managed both, with an epic 182 in his only bat (Australia won by ten wickets) and snaring a catch in Pakistan's first innings and two in their second.

Post-cricket, Chappell pursued various business interests.

5. Gundappa Viswanath (IND)

Test Record

Bat	M	Inn	NO	Runs	HS	Avg	100	50	Ct
	91	155	10	6080	222	41.93	14	35	63

Bowl	M	Inn	Wkts	Avg	BBI	BBM	5i	10m	SR
	91	7	1	46.00	1/11	1/11	0	0	70.0

Gundappa Viswanath's statistics don't tell the full story of his worth to the Indian team in the 1970s. He often made his runs when the chips were down and was every bit as important to his national side as Gavaskar.

Viswanath was an artist with the willow, whether using dazzling footwork to the spinners or waiting with all the time in the world against the pace bowlers. Having said that, he was a lot more successful at home averaging 47.32 in India versus 36.30 away from home.

He debuted for India aged 20 in 1969 against Australia at Kanpur, and made a duck in his first innings but a hundred (137) in the second innings, helping India draw. Viswanath played in all four Tests and scored 334 runs at 47.71.

Viswanath then had to wait until 1971 for his second century (113) which he brought up against New Zealand at home as he scored 365 runs in the series at around a 40 average.

The West Indies toured India in 1974–75, and Viswanath led the way for India with 568 runs at 63.11 – including a best score of 139 – but couldn't stop the West Indies winning the series 3–2. Viswanath also scored 97 not out against a fiery Andy Roberts at Chennai, helping India to a win. He also notched a 95 in the series.

When New Zealand toured a couple of years later, Viswanath led the runs aggregate for either side with 324 runs in the three Tests at 64.80, and a century at Kanpur in the second Test.

With the West Indies back in India in 1978–79, Viswanath carved out 497 runs at 71 including 124 out of 255 on a bouncy Chennai wicket, leading India to a win.

Viswanath's best series was probably against Australia at home in 1979–80 when he scored 518 runs at 74, leading the runs aggregate and averages for India. This included his then-highest Test score of 161 not out in the drawn second Test.

Viswanath's last series of note was versus England in 1981–82 as he brought up his maiden double ton (222) in scoring 466 runs in six Tests at 58.25.

He played a few more series in the 1980s, but his best was behind him and he faded into retirement.

6. Tony Greig (ENG) vc

Test Record

Bat	M	Inn	NO	Runs	HS	Avg	100	50	Ct
	58	93	4	3599	148	40.43	8	20	87
Bowl	M	Inn	Wkts	Avg	BBI	BBM	5i	10m	SR
	58	93	141	32.20	8/86	13/156	6	2	69.5

Tony Greig's career was cut short by his defection to World Series Cricket in the late '70s but his Test record as an all-rounder is impressive, with his batting average over eight runs in front of his bowling average. His ability with the bat saw him make hundreds against the likes of Lillee and Thompson, Roberts and Holding, and Bedi and Chandra. His bowling alternated between extracting bounce from his height with medium pace, and subtle variations bowling off-spin.

Greig was born in South Africa but moved to Sussex in 1965 with the aim of eventually qualifying to play for England. He was first chosen for the Rest of the World side that toured Australia in 1971–72 before he debuted for England against Australia in mid-1972, where he made a pair of fifties and took five wickets.

He followed this up with a successful tour of India where he scored 383 runs at 63.66 – including his maiden Test century of 148, which would remain his highest Test score. Greig also picked up his first five-for in the second innings of the second Test at Eden Gardens, collecting nine wickets for the series.

England toured the West Indies in 1974 and Greig picked up match figures of 13/156, bowling England to victory in the fifth Test at Port of Spain. He took 24 wickets for the series and was the leading wicket-taker for either side. He also added 430 runs at 47.77 with two hundreds.

Back in England, Greig scored 159 runs in three Tests against India at an average of 79.50 and took six wickets.

Greig had a solid tour of Australia in 1974–75 as his teammates fell apart around him – England were thumped 4–1. He led the English runs aggregate with 446 runs at 40.54 and was equal leading wicket-taker with 17.

The subsequent tour of New Zealand saw Greig take his second ten-wicket match haul with 10/149, along with a half-century in the first Test at Auckland.

Greig was again solid on the 1976–77 tour of India, as he picked up 342 runs at 42.75 along with ten wickets.

As well as his contribution with bat and ball, Greig captained England 14 times for three wins and five losses.

After World Series Cricket, Greig became a television commentator in Australia. He became known for his morning pitch reports and running battle in the commentary box with Bill Lawry.

7. Alan Knott (ENG) wk

Test Record

Bat	Mat	Inn	NO	Runs	HS	Avg	100	50	Ct	St
	95	149	15	4389	135	32.75	5	30	250	19

It was a tight call between Knott and Australia's Rod Marsh for the keeping spot in this XI, but Knott's slightly superior batting average saw him get the nod.

In the ten years before Knott joined World Series Cricket in 1977, he played in 89 of England's 93 Tests – 20 more than England's next best. Rarely did Knott miss a chance in that period.

Knott debuted against Pakistan in 1967 and made a duck but took seven catches. He followed this up with five catches and a stumping in the next Test.

In two Tests versus the West Indies in 1967–68, he made 149 runs and was dismissed just once.

On tour to Australia in 1970–71, Knott took 21 catches and made three stumpings as well as scoring 222 runs at 31.71. Against New Zealand on the same tour, Knott brought up his maiden Test century (101).

A second century (116) followed against Pakistan as Knott claimed a further ten catches and a stumping in three Tests in 1971. The next summer he took 17 catches versus the touring Australians.

Despite England's lack of success on the 1974–75 tour of Australia, Knott had a solid series contributing down the order with 364 runs at 36.40 including a century in the fifth Test at Adelaide. He also added 22 catches along with a stumping.

In India in 1976–77, Knott scored 268 runs at 38.28 and took 13 catches with two stumpings to help England win the five Test series 3–1.

Knott's final Test series before joining World Series Cricket – and being omitted from the English side as a result – was against Australia in 1977. He averaged 36.42 with the bat, including a top score of 135, and made a dozen keeping dismissals.

Post-World Series Cricket, Knott played a handful of Tests before retirement beckoned.

Knott was awarded an MBE for his services to cricket and, on the occasion of the thousandth Test, was named in England's greatest XI by the England Cricket Board.

8. Dennis Lillee (AUS)

Test Record

Bat	M	Inn	NO	Runs	HS	Avg	100	50	Ct
	70	90	24	905	73*	13.71	0	1	23

Bowl	M	Inn	Wkts	Avg	BBI	BBM	5i	10m	SR
	70	132	355	23.92	7/83	11/123	23	7	52.0

*not out

The crowd's chant would begin 'Lilleeee, Lilleeee' and he would turn and steam in, chain bobbing around his neck and top shirt buttons undone, before launching into a perfect action. He terrorised the batter with electrifying pace in the first part of his career, and then with guile, cut and swing in the second part after a back injury threatened his career.

Lillee was one of the world's greatest ever Test fast bowlers and arguably Australia's greatest of all time. It may also surprise some who view him as mainly a '70s player to learn that Lillee played 35 Tests in the '70s and 35 in the '80s. However, as he took more wickets in the '70s (184) than the '80s (171), he narrowly qualifies for this era.

Lillee debuted for Australia after the side was cleared out in the 1970–71 season. For his first game – the sixth Test of the Ashes series – he picked up 5/84 in the first innings.

Following the cancellation of the South African tour, a Rest of the World side toured Australia the next summer. The tourists included greats such as Sobers, Kanhai, Gavaskar, Graeme Pollock, Greig, Zaheer Abbas and others. Lillee announced himself on the world stage in the second unofficial Test at Perth where he took 8/29, including six for none in 15 balls.

An Ashes tour followed in 1972, and Lillee topped the wicket-taking for either side with 31 wickets at just 17.68. This included his first of seven ten-wicket match hauls in Australia's win in the final Test to draw the series.

Unfortunately, Lillee broke down in the West Indies in 1973 with stress fractures in his lower back in the first Test and played no further part in the series. His career was in jeopardy, but he worked assiduously on his rehabilitation and returned to cricket over a year later.

He returned just in time to forge another famous partnership, this one an opening bowling one with the newly arrived Jeff Thomson. They blew England away in 1974–75 and then the West Indies the next summer. England again felt his wrath in the Centenary Test in 1977 as Lillee took 6/26 and 5/139 to bowl Australia to victory. This was his last Test before joining World Series Cricket as one of its marquee signings.

On return from the World Series Cricket, Lillee continued his stranglehold over England in 1981 with 39 wickets at 22. Lillee continued to collect wickets and, by his retirement in 1984 was the leading-wicket taker in Test history with 355.

Lillee was an inaugural inductee into the Australian Cricket Hall of Fame in 1996 and the International Cricket Hall of Fame in 2009. He was also selected in the Australian Cricket Board's Team of the Century for the twentieth century and is a Legend of Australian sport, the very pinnacle of the Australian Sporting Hall of Fame.

9. Andy Roberts (WI)

Test Record

Bat	M	Inn	NO	Runs	HS	Avg	100	50	Ct
	47	62	11	762	68	14.94	0	3	9

Bowl	M	Inn	Wkts	Avg	BBI	BBM	5i	10m	SR
	47	90	202	25.61	7/54	12/121	11	2	55.1

Andy Roberts marked the start of the West Indies obsession with the four-pronged pace attack. ESPNcricinfo noted that, 'Here was a bowler whose pace came from timing, with power from a huge pair of shoulders. His bouncer was regarded as one of the most dangerous. He varied its pace, often setting batters up with a slower one and then poleaxing them when they were late on the quickie.'

Roberts debuted against England at Bridgetown in 1974 and took three wickets, including Dennis Amiss.

His second series was in India where fast bowlers often do it tough. Roberts had no issues with the slow pitches and was the leading wicket-taker for either side, with 32 at an average of 18 including 7/64 and 5/57 at Chennai.

Despite the West Indies being belted 5–1 in Australia in 1975–76, Roberts was the leading wicket-taker for the West Indies with 22, including 7/54 in the second innings of the second Test in Perth as he bowled the West Indies to their sole victory in the series.

Roberts again led the wickets tally (tied with Michael Holding) with 28 as the West Indies toured England in 1976. At Lord's, Roberts took 10/123 in a drawn match and 6/37, bowling the West Indies to victory in the second innings at Old Trafford and securing a 3–0 series win.

He then picked up 19 wickets against Pakistan as they toured the West Indies, and then 12 in two Tests versus the Australians.

Roberts played for the West Indies in World Series Cricket, where his variation and skill made up for the loss of outright pace. This was in evidence when India toured the West Indies in 1982–83 and Roberts took 24 wickets at 22.70 to once again head the wickets tally for either side.

His final two Tests came in India in 1983, and he picked up five wickets and made his top score of 68.

Post-cricket, Roberts worked as an administrator and coach and was a West Indies selector for a period. He was knighted for his services to cricket and is an inductee in the ICC Cricket Hall of Fame.

10. Bishan Bedi (IND)

Test Record

Bat	M	Inn	NO	Runs	HS	Avg	100	50	Ct
	67	101	28	656	50*	8.98	0	1	26

Bowl	M	Inn	Wkts	Avg	BBI	BBM	5i	10m	SR
	67	118	266	28.71	7/98	10/194	14	1	80.3

*not out

The spinner's position for the 1970s XI came down to a coin toss between Bishan Bedi and England's Derek Underwood. Underwood has an undoubted claim to the spot, but in the end the coin came down on the side of Bedi. Bedi is also rated higher by respected cricket journalist John Woodcock in his *One Hundred Greatest Cricketers*.

Left-armer Bedi was a master of deception, who used subtle variations in flight, bounce, length and turn to his advantage and wasn't afraid to be hit for six by giving the ball plenty of air. He finished with 1560 First Class wickets, many for Northamptonshire, which is the most for any Indian bowler.

Bedi wasn't just effective on Indian pitches, but took wickets worldwide including 35 in England and Australia and 33 in the West Indies.

He debuted against the West Indies at Eden Gardens in 1967, taking the wickets of Basil Butcher and Clive Lloyd in the only innings he bowled in (West Indies won by an innings).

In New Zealand in 1967–68, Bedi took 16 wickets at 23 across the four Tests, including his first five-for with 6/127 at Christchurch.

Australia toured India in 1969–70, and Bedi picked up 21 wickets which included his best bowling figures of 7/98 in the fourth Test at Eden Gardens.

In 1972–73, England toured India and Bedi collected 25 wickets at an average of 25.28 with best bowling figures of 5/63. He helped bowl India to victory by 28 runs in the second Test, and to a 2–1 series win.

England were back in 1976–77, and Bedi again collected 25 wickets, once more bowling India to victory in the fourth Test with 6/71.

Bedi's most successful series came in 1977–78 in Australia when he was captain. He led the wicket tally for either side with 31, including three five-fors and match figures of 10/194 at Perth. This didn't stop India going down 3–2 in an enthralling series, with Australia weakened by the absence of their World Series Cricket stars.

Bedi captained India 22 times for six wins and 11 losses.

Bedi had occasional run ins with officialdom and was a strident critic of modern ways from time to time. In 2008, *Wisden* named Bedi one of the five best players to never have been named as a cricketer of the year. Bedi is also an inductee in the ICC Cricket Hall of Fame.

11. Jeff Thomson (AUS)

Test Record

Bat	M	Inn	NO	Runs	HS	Avg	100	50	Ct
	51	73	20	679	49	12.81	0	0	20
Bowl	M	Inn	Wkts	Avg	BBI	BBM	5i	10m	SR
	51	90	200	28.00	6/46	9/105	8	0	52.6

Thommo terrorised batters probably more than any bowler in the history of cricket. His slingshot action made him frighteningly quick (he was clocked over 160 kilometres an hour, or 100 miles per hour) but it was his unpredictability that made him so difficult to combat. Even he admitted he didn't always know where the ball was going, one smashing into the batter's toes and the next clattering full bore into the sight screen without bouncing again. Adding to this he was one of the nastiest, even by fast bowling standards – Thomson once admitted he loved to see blood on the pitch, a statement he recanted later in life.

The great Viv Richards was quoted as saying, 'For that special delivery, no-one could match Jeff Thomson for raw, lethal pace. He was very special, you know.' Another great, Greg Chappell, on Thomson: 'He was so quick – and so frightening – that blokes just didn't want to bat against him. There were guys literally running away.'

Of course, there is also the partnership with Dennis Lillee which was virtually unbeatable in the mid-'70s. From 1974 to 1983, sharing the new ball they took 214 wickets between them (Lillee 116, Thomson 98). Australia won 14 Tests with the dynamic duo in action and lost only three. As the saying went, 'If Lillee don't get you then Thommo must.'

Given some time to mature after an early debut, Thomson was recalled for the 1974–75 Ashes series and this time he overwhelmed England, pummelling them into submission with 33 wickets in five

Tests at 17.94. In 1975–76 it was the West Indies turn to feel the wrath of Thomson, and he nailed 29 batters at 28 – again leading the wicket table.

Disaster struck for Thomson the next summer as he collided with teammate Alan Turner in the field and was hospitalised with his bowling shoulder injured.

Initially, Thomson refused to sign on to World Series Cricket and played in the 1977–78 Indian series, experimenting with a host of fast-bowlers to give the attack some much-needed experience. He was then allowed to tour the West Indies as part of WSC, and missed the disastrous 1978–79 Ashes.

On the return of the WSC players to Test cricket, Thomson was not as influential and he played a handful of Tests until the 1982–83 Ashes summer as he again tormented the old enemy with 22 wickets. He also found form with the bat in the fourth Test, as he batted with Border to add 70 for the last wicket but falling just three runs short of an unlikely victory.

Missing several series, he returned for a last hurrah in England in 1985 but played only two Tests for three wickets.

1970s Second XI

1. Roy Fredericks (WI)
2. Majid Khan (PAK)
3. Ian Chappell (AUS) vc
4. Alvin Kallicharan (WI)
5. Clive Lloyd (WI) c
6. Doug Walters (AUS)
7. Mike Proctor (SA)
8. Rod Marsh (AUS) wk
9. Derek Underwood (ENG)
10. John Snow (ENG)
11. Bob Willis (ENG)

1980s

The 1980s were dominated by the mighty West Indian sides, who won 52% of the Tests they played and lost only 10% of the time. As a result, five of this decade's XI come from the West Indies. Pakistan were next best, as they won 29% of the matches they played.

One of the West Indies' outstanding performances was the 5–0 drubbing of England in England in 1984 at the height of their powers. They won two of the five Tests by an innings and comfortably won the other three.

At home the West Indies were especially dominant, winning 18 of 30 Tests (60%) and losing only once – against Pakistan in 1988.

There were also two One Day International World Cups played in the 1980s and they were won by India in 1983, upsetting the West Indies in the final and by Australia in 1987 – a surprise result as Australia were in a rebuilding phase following some dire results in the middle of the decade.

Allan Border was the leading batter of the decade, often called upon to shore up a shaky Australian batting line-up. Border was more than a thousand runs in front of the next best run-maker in David

Gower. On the bowling side of things, the West Indian pacemen dominated with Malcolm Marshall leading the wickets tally for the decade followed by New Zealand great Richard Hadlee.

The openers for the XI chose themselves, with the most prolific opening pair in the history of Test cricket in West Indians Gordon Greenidge and Desmond Haynes being a natural choice. There were some fine batters in the 1980s but the standout trio was Viv Richards, Javed Miandad and Border. On the next level were batters such as Gower, Richie Richardson, Martin Crowe and Zaheer Abbas.

There is one thing the 1980s is not short of, and that's all-rounders. Imran Khan, Ian Botham and Kapil Dev are among the greatest all-rounders the game has seen and Richard Hadlee could also be considered a bowling all-rounder. It was decided to include all of them, so this is a very deep batting line-up with Hadlee at ten. Marshall was also an automatic selection, meaning pace bowlers of the calibre of Joel Garner and Michael Holding missed out.

Choosing the all-rounders also means there is no room for a specialist spinner, with Pakistan's Abdul Qadir the unlucky omission. Spin would have to be provided by part-timers Richards, Border and Miandad.

The leading wicketkeeper of the decade by some margin was not surprisingly from the West Indies – Jeff Dujon. Dujon also had the best batting record of the leading keepers, and it was an easy job to choose him as custodian for the 1980s XI.

Most Runs in Period

Player	Mat	Inns	NO	Runs	HS	Ave	100	50
AR Border (AUS)	97	164	30	7386	205	55.11	20	40
DI Gower (ENG)	89	157	11	6196	215	42.43	12	32
J Miandad (PAK)	76	110	7	5642	280*	54.77	16	26
IVA Richards (WI)	78	112	8	5113	208	49.16	15	28
CG Greenidge (WI)	75	123	12	5094	223	45.89	12	25
DL Haynes (WI)	81	139	16	5074	184	41.25	12	28
DB Vengsarkar (IND)	71	112	16	4501	166	46.88	12	22
SM Gavaskar (IND)	65	106	9	4475	236*	46.13	12	20
IT Botham (ENG)	75	124	4	4051	208	33.75	10	19
GA Gooch (ENG)	56	105	2	3970	196	38.54	8	23

*not out

Most Wickets in Period

Player	Mat	Inns	Wkts	BBI	BBM	Ave	SR	5	10
MD Marshall (WI)	63	120	323	7/22	11/89	19.91	44.5	22	4
Sir RJ Hadlee (NZ)	53	91	289	9/52	15/123	19.28	47.9	28	7
NK Dev (IND)	80	134	272	9/83	11/146	29.54	62.1	16	2
IT Botham (ENG)	75	120	258	8/103	13/106	32.39	61.6	15	2
I Khan (PAK)	54	90	256	8/58	14/116	19.12	47.0	18	5
A Qadir (PAK)	57	94	216	9/56	13/101	32.31	70.2	14	5
J Garner (WI)	49	93	210	6/56	9/108	20.62	51.8	7	0
MA Holding (WI)	45	84	184	6/21	11/107	23.38	50.3	9	1
GF Lawson (AUS)	46	78	180	8/112	11/134	30.56	61.7	11	2
DK Lillee (AUS)	35	64	171	7/83	11/138	24.07	52.3	11	3

Results

Team	Mat	Won	Lost	Tied	Draw	W/L
West Indies	82	43	8	0	31	5.375
Australia	97	27	31	1	38	0.870
Pakistan	80	23	13	0	44	1.769
England	104	20	39	0	45	0.512
New Zealand	59	17	15	0	27	1.133
India	81	11	21	1	48	0.523
Sri Lanka	29	2	16	0	11	0.125

1980s XI

1. Gordon Greenidge (WI)
2. Desmond Haynes (WI)
3. Viv Richards (WI) c
4. Javed Miandad (PAK)
5. Allan Border (AUS) vc
6. Ian Botham (ENG)
7. Imran Khan (PAK)
8. Jeff Dujon (WI) wk
9. Kapil Dev (IND)
10. Richard Hadlee (NZ)
11. Malcolm Marshall (WI)

1. Gordon Greenidge (WI)

Test Record

Bat	M	Inn	NO	Runs	HS	Avg	100	50	Ct
	108	185	16	7558	226	44.72	19	34	96

Bowl	M	Inn	Wkts	Avg	BBI	BBM	5i	10m	SR
	108	2	0	-	-	-	0	0	-

Together with Desmond Haynes, Greenidge formed the most prolific opening partnership in Test cricket history. They were the platform on which the West Indies' 1980s success was built. In total, they added 6482 runs at an average of 47.31 with 16 stands of a hundred or more (four over 200) and a highest partnership of 298.

Greenidge was a massively destructive opening batter who cut savagely, pulled and hooked at will and drove both sides of the wicket. While attack was his general approach, he also had a solid defensive game cultivated on the soft English pitches of his childhood.

Debuting in 1974 against India at Bengaluru, he announced himself with 93 and 107 to help the West Indies to a Test win. The rest of the series wasn't as successful, but he still ended with an average of 41.22.

In 1976 in England, Greenidge helped himself to 592 runs at 65.77 which included a century in each innings at Old Trafford and another hundred at Headingly.

Pakistan then toured the West Indies, and Greenidge maintained his form with 536 runs at 53.60 with an even hundred in the fifth Test at Kingston.

Greenidge's form was solid but not spectacular until India's visit in 1983, where he averaged 78.60 – followed by a series in India where he averaged 51.37 with a top score of 194.

Australia toured in 1984 and Greenidge was on top of his game with 393 runs at 78.60 including two centuries. England then felt the full force of Greenidge's bat as he topped the runs aggregate and averages with 572 runs at 81.71, with two double centuries including a masterful 214 at Lord's.

In New Zealand in 1987, Greenidge added 344 runs in three Tests at 68.80 including a top score of 213 at Auckland in the second Test.

Greenidge's last series before retirement was at home to Australia in 1991, and he showed he could still bat with an average of 45.75 and his highest Test score of 226 in the fourth Test at Bridgetown.

After his playing days, Greenidge turned to coaching and was head coach of the Bangladesh side for a period and was also a West Indian selector.

Greenidge is a member of the ICC Cricket Hall of Fame and was knighted for his services to cricket and the development of sport.

2. Desmond Haynes (WI)

Test Record

Bat	M	Inn	NO	Runs	HS	Avg	100	50	Ct
	116	202	25	7487	184	42.29	18	39	65

Bowl	M	Inn	Wkts	Avg	BBI	BBM	5i	10m	SR
	116	3	1	8.00	1–2	1–2	0	0	18.0

One half of the famed Haynes-Greenidge opening partnership, Haynes could be an attacking batter but was generally happy to sit back and let Greenidge do the majority of the blasting.

Haynes debuted against Australia at Port of Spain in 1978 and made 61 in his only bat. He followed this up with scores of 66 and 55 in the next Test at Bridgetown.

It was not until 1980 in New Zealand that Haynes scored his maiden Test century – 105 out of a total of 212 at Dunedin. He followed this up with another century in the next Test at Christchurch. Haynes led the runs aggregate for the series with 339 at 56.50.

Haynes followed this up with a 50-plus average on the West Indies' tour of England in 1980, which included his highest Test score of 184 made at Lord's, putting on a double hundred stand with Viv Richards.

In 1984, Haynes had an outstanding series at home versus Australia where he led the runs aggregate for the West Indies and the overall averages with 468 runs at 93.60 including two centuries of 103 not out and 145.

England toured the West Indies in 1986 and it was Haynes again leading the batting aggregate and averages in scoring 469 runs at 78.16 with a top score of 131 in the fifth Test at St John's.

In 1988–89 on the Australian tour Haynes mustered 537 runs at 59.66, once again leading the total runs scored for either side. His tour included two centuries, including 143 out of a total of 256 on a turning dustbowl in Sydney.

Haynes again showed his liking for Australian bowling when they toured in 1991 with 412 runs at 51.50.

Yet again, Haynes led the runs aggregate against Pakistan in 1993 with 402 runs in three Tests at the very impressive average of 134 including two centuries.

Haynes exited Test cricket after the series at home to England in 1994, where he averaged a below-par 36.16.

Captaining the West Indies four times, Haynes collected a win, a loss and two draws.

After Test cricket, Haynes served on various cricket boards and was a selector for Barbados. Haynes is also an inductee in the ICC Cricket Hall of Fame.

3. Viv Richards (WI) c

Test Record

Bat	M	Inn	NO	Runs	HS	Avg	100	50	Ct
	121	182	12	8540	291	50.23	24	45	122
Bowl	**M**	**Inn**	**Wkts**	**Avg**	**BBI**	**BBM**	**5i**	**10m**	**SR**
	121	103	32	61.37	2/17	3/51	0	0	161.5

John Woodcock wrote, 'Others have made more runs at a higher average but the most daunting figure to have walked through a pavilion gate must be Vivian Richards. In the right mood he was a magnificent, irresistible player. It is unimaginable that anyone has ever hit the ball harder or with more thrilling strokes.'

Wisden, the cricketer's bible, rated Richards one of the top-five players of the twentieth century (alongside Bradman, Hobbs, Warne and Sobers).

He was also brilliant in the field: three run outs in the 1975 World Cup final against Australia is evidence of this, and he bowled some useful off-spin.

Richards debuted against India in India in 1974, and brought up his maiden Test century in just his second Test with 192 not out in Delhi. All up in his debut series, he scored 353 runs at 50.42.

India toured the West Indies in 1976 and Richards hit his straps, leading the runs total and averages for either side with 556 runs at 92.66 including three hundreds.

More was to follow in England as Richards thrashed the Poms to the tune of 829 runs in four Tests at 118.42 with two double hundreds (including his highest Test score of 291 at The Oval) and a single hundred.

In Australia in 1979–80, Richards plundered 386 runs in just three Tests at an average of 96.50 to lead the runs aggregate and averages yet again.

Richards scored a further 340 runs at 85 when England toured in 1981 including two centuries with a top score of 182 not out.

Never wearing a helmet, Richards continued to score heavily through the 1980s and was an integral part of the West Indies domination during that period (they lost only 8 Tests out of 82 in the decade). His final series came away against England and while he averaged over 50, he failed to pass three figures.

Eagerly awaiting the West Indian captaincy following the eventual retirement of Clive Lloyd, Richards skippered the West Indies 50 times for 27 wins and just eight losses.

After his playing days, he turned his hand to some commentating and also mentored various T20 sides in India and Pakistan. Knighted for his services to cricket, Richards is of course inducted in the ICC Cricket Hall of Fame.

4. Javed Miandad (PAK)

Test Record

Bat	M	Inn	NO	Runs	HS	Avg	100	50	Ct
	124	189	21	8832	280*	52.57	23	43	93

Bowl	M	Inn	Wkts	Avg	BBI	BBM	5i	10m	SR
	124	36	17	40.11	3/74	5/94	0	0	86.4

*not out

Javed Miandad is arguably Pakistan's best ever batter. He has the best average of any Pakistani batter with more than 20 innings, just shading Mohammad Yousuf.

Miandad was a tenacious batter with a homespun technique that relied heavily on the bottom hand. He was also an improviser which added to his genius as a batter. Niggling the opposition was part of his make-up, but he had the game to back it up: just ask Dennis Lillee after he and Miandad faced off in Perth in 1981.

Debuting against New Zealand at home in 1976, Miandad started with a century (163) on debut then followed it up with a double ton in his third Test alongside an 85. He scored 504 runs in three Tests at 126 and well and truly announced his arrival on the international scene.

In 1977/78, England toured Pakistan and Miandad knocked up 262 runs in three Tests at an average of 131. He did even better in the three Test series against India in 1978 with 357 runs at an incredible 178.50.

Miandad's form continued in New Zealand, averaging just shy of a hundred in scoring 297 runs in three more Tests.

Miandad had a memorable series versus India at home in 1982–83 where he scored 594 runs at 118.80 including his highest Test score of 280 as he and Mudassar Nazar added a 451 run partnership for the third wicket – the equal fourth-highest partnership in Test history.

Sri Lanka toured in 1985 and Miandad carved them up with 306 runs in three Tests at 153 including a top score of 203 not out at Faisalabad.

In 1988 it was Australia's turn to face Miandad's brilliance, and they conceded 412 runs in three Tests at an average of 82.40 including a double hundred (211) at Karachi.

New Zealand again suffered in two Tests in 1989 to the tune of 389 runs in just two Tests, with scores of 118 and 271.

Miandad's final series came in 1993–94 versus Zimbabwe, where he made little impact and moved into retirement.

Miandad captained Pakistan 34 times for 14 wins and six losses.

Following his retirement, Miandad coached Pakistan across a number of stints and also did some commentating. He is also an inductee in the ICC Cricket Hall of Fame.

5. Allan Border (AUS) vc

Test Record

Bat	M	Inn	NO	Runs	HS	Avg	100	50	Ct
	156	265	44	11,174	205	50.56	27	63	156

Bowl	M	Inn	Wkts	Avg	BBI	BBM	5i	10m	SR
	156	98	39	39.10	7/46	11/96	2	1	102.7

Allan Border was Australian cricket in the '80s. Without him, the national team would have been a complete shambles (rather than simply very poor). By the time he had finished his Test career, he held the all-time records for most runs (11,174), most Tests played (156), most successive Tests played (153), most Tests as captain (93) and most catches by a fielder (156). On top of that, he averaged over 50 over a lengthy career. He is also the only player to score over 150 in each innings of a Test. Of course, records are made to be broken – and they have been – but Border's record still leaves him amongst the all-time greats.

His left-arm trundlers were very useful, no more so when he took 11 wickets and bowled Australia to victory at the SCG against the West Indies. He was also very effective as a cover, short mid-wicket or slips fielder.

As captain he was initially reluctant, but with Bob Simpson brought a hard-edged approach to the Australian side which culminated in the 4–0 Ashes win in 1989 and eventual return to the top of the cricketing tree. Border led Australia in 93 Tests for 32 wins, 22 losses, 38 draws and a tie as well as a One Day International World Cup in 1987.

In addition to the above records, Border was selected as twelfth man in Australia's Team of the Century in 2000. Border is also an inductee in the Australian Cricket Hall of Fame, an inaugural inductee in the ICC Hall of Fame and received an Order of Australia (AO).

Border's character was never on show as much in his battles with the might of the West Indies. As his fellow teammates crumbled around him Border would stand firm, absorbing blows where necessary and blunting Holding, Marshall, Garner and co. There was no better example of this than in the 1984 series in the West Indies where he averaged 74.43 (when the next best Aussie, Graeme Wood, averaged 44) with a century and two 98s.

His other tour by tour achievements are too numerous to mention, but the trophy played for between Australia and India is named the Border-Gavaskar Trophy, and the honour awarded to the men's international player of the year for Australia is the Allan Border Medal.

6. Ian Botham (ENG)

Test Record

Bat	M	Inn	NO	Runs	HS	Avg	100	50	Ct
	102	161	6	5200	208	33.54	14	22	120

Bowl	M	Inn	Wkts	Avg	BBI	BBM	5i	10m	SR
	102	168	383	28.40	8/34	13/106	27	4	56.9

Ian Botham took 27 fewer Test matches to get to 100 wickets and 1000 runs than the great Sobers did. He could swing a match in a matter of hours with the bat, and be equally destructive with the ball in hand when he was on. If there was one criticism it would be he was not always on, particularly against the great West Indian sides of the 1980s.

The series that best demonstrates Botham's brilliance is the 1981 Ashes series. Botham began the series as England's captain but was relieved of that duty after two Tests. It seemed to provoke him to life, as in the third Test with England following on 227 runs behind and 7/135, Botham conjured an innings of 149 not out off 148 balls to give England a lead of 129 which they defended. In the next Test he took 5/1 off 28 balls to bowl Australia out for 121, chasing 151 to win. In the fifth Test he scored another hundred and picked up five wickets to claim his third man of the match in as many Tests.

Botham had debuted in 1977 against Australia and began slowly, but in his next series against New Zealand managed 212 runs at 53 including his maiden Test century and took 17 wickets in three Tests – the most for either side.

England toured India for six Tests in 1981–82, and Botham racked up 440 runs at 55 as well as taking 17 wickets (the most for England) with a best of 5/61.

When India then toured England in 1982, Botham continued his form with 403 runs in three Tests at an average of 134.33

including his highest Test score of 208 at The Oval. He also picked up nine wickets.

Botham was again in form for the 1985 Ashes and picked up 31 wickets in the series as well as 250 runs at 31.25. It was rare for both his batting and bowling to be out of form at the same time.

He only scored one more hundred which was on the 1986–87 Ashes tour where he scored 138 at the Gabba in Brisbane.

Botham's appearances became sporadic thereafter and he played his final Test at Lord's against Pakistan in 1992.

Botham did captain England on a dozen occasions but had no wins and four losses.

He was always one to attract attention from the media, especially the tabloids, and he stayed active in the game as a commentator after he finished playing. Botham was also involved in several charitable causes and has become a member of the House of Lords. He was inducted into the ICC Cricket Hall of Fame in 2009.

7. Imran Khan (PAK)

Test Record

Bat	M	Inn	NO	Runs	HS	Avg	100	50	Ct
	88	126	25	3807	136	37.69	6	18	28
Bowl	M	Inn	Wkts	Avg	BBI	BBM	5i	10m	SR
	88	142	362	22.81	8/58	14/116	23	6	53.7

Imran Khan began as a fast bowler, excelling on the mud-baked pitches of Pakistan and paving the way for the likes of Wasim Akram and Waqar Younis. His batting steadily improved to the point where he could hold his place in his national team for batting or bowling. In fact, it improved to the point where he averaged over 50 in the last ten years of his Test career. His bowling average was 19 in the same period, giving a difference between bat and ball of 31 – better than even the great Sobers whose difference was 23.

The other thing about Imran was his good looks and charisma, being equally at home in the salons of London as he was striving for pace on the dead wickets of Pakistan.

Imran played a solitary Test against England in 1971 but then did not appear for Pakistan again until 1974 when he started to cement his place in the national setup.

On the 1976–77 tour of Australia, Imran led the way for Pakistan with the ball taking 18 wickets in three Tests with a best of 6/63. He followed this up with 25 wickets in the West Indies, again leading the Pakistani wickets tally.

In 1982 in England, Imran began to show his potential as an all-rounder and made 212 runs in three Tests at 53 as well as picking up 21 wickets at 18.57.

In the six Test series versus India in 1982–83, Imran knocked up 241 runs at 61.75 including his maiden Test ton and bagged 40 wickets at just 13.95.

Pakistan toured India in 1986–87, and Imran scored 324 runs at 64.80 including a hundred (135 not out) at Chennai but managed just eight wickets.

When India toured Pakistan in 1989–90, Imran ran up 262 runs in the four Tests at an average of 87.33 with another century and captured 13 wickets.

In his final series which was versus Sri Lanka in 1991–92 Imran averaged 57.50 with the bat but did not take a wicket.

Imran captained Pakistan 48 times for 14 wins and eight losses, as well as to World Cup victory in 1992.

Following his cricket career, Imran entered the fraught world of Pakistan politics and served as Prime Minister for a time but now finds himself in legal difficulties as he lost his position.

8. Jeff Dujon (WI) wk

Test Record

Bat	Mat	Inn	NO	Runs	HS	Avg	100	50	Ct	St
	81	115	11	3322	139	31.94	5	16	267	5

Jeff Dujon sits in sixth place on the all-time wicketkeeping dismissals table and at the top of the West Indian tally. Never playing in a losing series, Dujon was the hub of the great West Indies sides of the 1980s. He was athletic and spent most of his career keeping to a quartet of outright pace bowlers, as reflected in his relatively low stumping dismissals. He was often required to fly high to pull in a one-handed screamer as the ball flew off the batter's edge.

Dujon was also very handy with the bat and his best efforts often came when there was rare failure at the top of the West Indian batting order. Five centuries and an average over 30 is testament to his ability.

He debuted as a batter against Australia in Melbourne in 1981 and made a pair of 40s in a low scoring affair the Windies lost. Another pair of 40s followed in Sydney, again as a batter only, before he took the gloves in Adelaide, made a fifty and never looked back.

Dujon's second series was even more successful – against India in 1983, he made 259 runs at 51.80 including his maiden Test hundred (110), took 18 catches and made a stumping.

In Australia in 1984–85, Dujon scored 341 runs at an average of 48.71 including 139 in the first Test at Perth, rescuing the West Indies from 6/186. He also collected 19 catches behind the stumps.

Pakistan toured the West Indies in 1987–88 and Dujon averaged 46.25 with the bat with a top score of 110 not out. In the three Tests he bagged five catches and a stumping.

The next tour was to England and Dujon had one of his best series with bat and gloves, scoring 305 runs at an average of 50 and taking 20 dismissals, all caught.

Dujon's best series with the gloves was at home to Australia in 1991 when he grabbed 23 catches – including five in the first innings at St John's – and averaged just under 30 with the bat.

His final series was in England in 1991 and he collected another 17 victims but was not as successful with the bat, averaging just 12.

Dujon was one of *Wisden's* five Cricketers of the Year in 1989. After cricket, he acted as assistant coach to the national side as well as helping develop youth in Jamaica.

9. Kapil Dev (IND)

Test Record

Bat	M	Inn	NO	Runs	HS	Avg	100	50	Ct
	131	184	15	5248	163	31.05	8	27	64
Bowl	M	Inn	Wkts	Avg	BBI	BBM	5i	10m	SR
	131	227	434	29.64	9/83	11/146	23	2	63.9

This XI would be better balanced if Abdul Qadir of Pakistan had been selected as a specialist spinner, but Kapil's all-round record demanded he be selected and spin be left up to the part-timers Richards, Border and Miandad. In any event, the theme of the 1980s – set by the West Indies – was pace, so this XI is also dominated by pace.

Kapil would probably be considered a bowling all-rounder, although his batting average does just exceed his bowling average. He relied on swing to pick up wickets, and when he finished his career he was the leading wicket-taker in Test history. His batting was attacking and conducted with uncomplicated flair. *Wisden* named him India's cricketer of the twentieth century, ahead of Gavaskar and Tendulkar.

He debuted against Pakistan away in 1978 in a team dominated by the great Indian spinners, and he took seven wickets in the series and averaged 31.80 with the bat.

Kapil's next series, at home to the West Indies, was more successful as he scored 329 runs at 65.80 including his first Test ton (129 not out) and he collected 17 wickets.

In 1979–80 versus Pakistan, Kapil bagged a series-leading 32 scalps with a best of 7/56 as well as adding 278 runs at 30.88 and a top score of 84.

In England in 1982, Kapil batted well for 318 runs at 53 including a century and bagged 22 dismissals. He immediately followed this up with 292 runs at 73 in three Tests against Pakistan, just missing a century and taking ten wickets.

Touring the West Indies in 1982–83, Kapil averaged 42.16 including an even hundred with the bat, and claimed 17 dismissals.

Kapil's best bowling in an innings came against the West Indies, with 9/83 in the third Test at Ahmedabad in 1983, taking 29 wickets in the series – the most for India.

Kapil made a hundred and was joint man of the match with Dean Jones in the celebrated tied Test at Chennai in 1986.

In a three Test series with Sri Lanka in 1986–87, Kapil had his best time with the bat making 234 runs at 117 with his highest Test score of 163 at Kanpur. He picked up just nine wickets in the series.

Kapil again led the way for India in Australia in 1991–92, with 25 victims at around an average of 25. He was less successful with the bat, however, averaging just 18.33.

His last match was versus New Zealand in 1994 in Hamilton.

Kapil captained India 34 times for just four wins, seven losses, a tie and 22 draws.

He had an ill-fated stint as coach of the Indian side when he had finished playing and also worked as a bowling consultant and chair of the National Cricket Academy.

Kapil is an inductee in the ICC Cricket Hall of Fame.

10. Richard Hadlee (NZ)

Test Record

Bat	M	Inn	NO	Runs	HS	Avg	100	50	Ct
	86	134	19	3124	151*	27.16	2	15	39
Bowl	M	Inn	Wkts	Avg	BBI	BBM	5i	10m	SR
	86	150	431	22.29	9/52	15/123	36	9	50.8

*not out

One of the greatest fast bowlers in the history of Test cricket, Hadlee was the first bowler to 400 wickets (in just 79 Tests) and finished his career as the leading Test wicket-taker.

He had a whippy, side on action that produced bounce and movement that troubled all the batters of his day. Hadlee also carried the New Zealand attack in the 1980s and much of their success was down to him. In particular, he saved some of his best for the trans-Tasman rivalry with the Australians.

Hadlee's batting was also good enough for him to score two Test hundreds and be considered an all-rounder.

Debuting at home to Pakistan as far back as 1973, it took Hadlee a little while to find his feet in Test cricket. He picked up useful wickets, but it wasn't until 1978 that he made a big impact. Hadlee took ten wickets against England including 6/26 in the second innings to bowl New Zealand to their first win over England.

Hadlee picked up 19 wickets in three Tests when the West Indies toured in 1980 (and scored his maiden Test century) and another 19 in Australia in three Tests in 1980–81. Both efforts led the wickets tally for either side.

The Kiwis toured England in 1983, and Hadlee bagged 21 wickets in four Tests with a best of 6/53. He added 301 runs at 50.16 for an outstanding all-round series.

Hadlee saved his very best for Australia in 1985–86, as he dismissed 33 batters in just three Tests at 12.15. This included 9/52 and 6/71 in the first Test at the Gabba. He led New Zealand to a 2–1 series victory.

Against Sri Lanka in 1987 at Colombo, Hadlee recorded his highest Test score of 151 not out and picked up four wickets in his only bowling innings.

Hadlee's final series was in England in 1990, and he was still good enough to take 16 wickets in three Tests including 5/53 in the second innings of his final Test. He took a wicket with his last delivery in Test cricket – Devon Malcolm trapped LBW.

Post-cricket, Hadlee became an outspoken media personality and chair of New Zealand's selectors. Hadlee was knighted for his services to cricket and inducted into the ICC Cricket Hall of Fame – the only Kiwi included thus far.

11. Malcolm Marshall (WI)

Test Record

Bat	M	Inn	NO	Runs	HS	Avg	100	50	Ct
	81	107	11	1810	92	18.85	0	10	25

Bowl	M	Inn	Wkts	Avg	BBI	BBM	5i	10m	SR
	81	151	376	20.94	7/22	11/89	22	4	46.7

Another of the all-time greats in this XI, Marshall was deadly effective as his strike rate of 46.7 reveals. In another side his wickets tally would probably be higher, as he shared the spoils around with his fellow fast bowlers.

Standing at under 6 foot, Marshall was not as physically imposing as some of his contemporaries but was just as quick and skidded the ball onto the batter, making his bouncer particularly troublesome. His batting was also useful down the order, and he is the best number 11 in all the XIs in this book.

Marshall was just 20 when he debuted against India in 1978–79 without making an immediate impact. However, by 1980 he had a permanent place in the national setup and took 15 wickets in four Tests in England.

On the spin-friendly pitches of India in 1983–84, Marshall led the wickets table with 33 at 18.81 with a best of 6/37 in the second innings at Eden Gardens, helping the West Indies to an innings win.

The Australian tour of 1984–85 saw Marshall once again lead the wickets table for either side with 28 at 19.78 with four five-fors and a best of 5/38.

In successive tours by New Zealand and England, Marshall collected 27 dismissals at an average of around 18.

Marshall often saved his best for England, and the West Indies tour in 1988 saw him pick up 35 wickets in five Tests at just 12.65 including 7/22 at Old Trafford as the West Indies thumped England 4–0.

In 1989, Marshall destroyed India with 19 wickets in three Tests at 15.26 including bowling the West Indies to victory in the second Test with 5/34 and 6/55 at Port of Spain.

Marshall maintained his form to the end and took 20 wickets in his last series in England in 1991.

He coached the West Indies for a period before illness brought an end to that pursuit. Marshall died from cancer aged just 41.

Along with most of the others in this XI, he is a member of the ICC Cricket Hall of Fame.

1980s Second XI

1. Mudassar Nazar (PAK)
2. Zaheer Abbas (PAK)
3. Richie Richardson (WI)
4. Martin Crowe (NZ) c
5. Dilip Vengsarkar (IND)
6. David Gower (ENG)
7. Ravi Shastri (IND) vc
8. Ian Smith (NZ) wk
9. Michael Holding (WI)
10. Joel Garner (WI)
11. Abdul Qadir (PAK)

1990s

The West Indies started the decade as the undisputed kings of world cricket, but by the mid-'90s Australia had taken the crown from them. Australia had the best winning record in Tests in the 1990s, with a win rate of 50% of matches played, followed by South Africa – who returned to world cricket in 1991 – at 44%. To look at it from another angle, South Africa had the lowest loss rate at 20% followed by Australia who lost 23% of the Tests they played.

The series where the crown was handed over was Australia in the West Indies for four Tests in 1995. The West Indies had not lost a home series in over 20 years, but Australia comfortably won the first Test at Bridgetown by ten wickets and the second was drawn at St John's. The West Indies struck back to win the third Test at Port of Spain by nine wickets, sending the series to a decider in Kingston. The West Indies were bowled out for 265 and Australia replied with 531, led by a double century from Steve Waugh. The West Indies could only manage 213 in their second innings and Australia won the Test by an innings and 53 runs to claim the series and the unofficial title of world's best.

In addition to Test cricket, there were three One Day International World Cups played during the decade. The first was won by an Imran Khan-led Pakistan, who beat England in the final at the Melbourne Cricket Ground. The next edition was on the sub-continent, and an inspired Sri Lanka defeated Australia in the final at Lahore. Finally, in 1999, Australia knocked off Pakistan in the final at Lord's.

Alec Stewart from England was the leading run scorer for the decade, but a spot could not be found for him in the decade's XI as others had stronger claims with better averages. Leg-spinner Shane Warne led the wicket-taking for the 1990s, with Curtly Ambrose the leading fast man in terms of wickets taken.

Saeed Anwar of Pakistan had the best record of the 1990s openers and nailed down one opening spot. The second was given to Mark Taylor – even though fellow Australian Michael Slater may have had a slightly better average – as Taylor adds a lot to the side as captain and first slipper. Gary Kirsten of South Africa also had a claim to the position. Andy Flower of Zimbabwe averaged over 50 in Test cricket and deserves to be one of the first picked in the middle order. Likewise for Steve Waugh. The other two batting spots went to Mohammad Azharuddin of India and Aravinda de Silva of Sri Lanka, although arguments could also be made for Australia's David Boon and Mark Waugh, Salim Malik of Pakistan and Alec Stewart.

The pace bowling line-up is lethal and was easy to choose with Wasim Akram, Allan Donald and Ambrose the standout performers, although the second XI attack of Waqar Younis, Craig McDermott and Courtney Walsh is not too shabby. Warne was far and away the best spinner qualified for selection for the decade, with Mushtaq Ahmed of Pakistan a distant second best.

It was tempting to choose Stewart as the wicketkeeper for the XI based on his batting performances, but it was decided that Australia's Ian Healy was the better keeper and deserved to be picked in the XI. In any event, Healy still had a solid batting record with four centuries. It would also be possible to choose an extra batter and give the gloves to Andy Flower, who kept for Zimbabwe for part of his career.

Most Runs in Period

Player	Mat	Inns	NO	Runs	HS	Ave	100	50
AJ Stewart (ENG)	93	169	12	6407	190	40.80	12	34
ME Waugh (AUS)	99	164	11	6371	153*	41.64	17	37
MA Taylor (AUS)	93	166	12	6306	334*	40.94	15	35
MA Atherton (ENG)	91	168	6	6217	185*	38.37	13	38
SR Waugh (AUS)	89	143	26	6213	200	53.10	18	28
SR Tendulkar** (IND)	69	109	12	5626	217	58.00	22	21
BC Lara** (WI)	65	112	4	5573	375	51.60	13	29
PA de Silva (SL)	62	104	9	4448	267	46.82	14	18
MJ Slater (AUS)	58	103	5	4425	219	45.15	13	16
DC Boon (AUS)	62	108	13	4303	164*	45.29	13	18

**qualify for the 2000s era *not out

Most Wickets in Period

Player	Mat	Inns	Wkts	BBI	BBM	Ave	SR	5	10
SK Warne (AUS)	80	146	351	8/71	12/128	25.66	64.3	16	4
CEL Ambrose (WI)	71	128	309	8/45	11/84	20.14	52.2	21	3
CA Walsh (WI)	78	143	304	7/37	13/55	25.97	59.4	13	1
W Akram (PAK)	62	111	289	7/119	11/160	21.45	48.9	17	3
AA Donald (SA)	59	105	284	8/71	12/139	21.83	45.7	19	3
W Younis (PAK)	56	101	273	7/76	13/135	21.71	40.9	21	5
GD McGrath* (AUS)	58	112	266	8/38	10/78	22.87	52.4	15	1
A Kumble* (IND)	58	103	264	10/74	14/149	27.80	68.9	15	3
M Muralidaran* (SL)	48	74	227	9/65	16/220	27.04	65.5	17	2
CJ McDermott (AUS)	47	85	211	8/97	11/157	26.52	54.7	11	2

*qualify for the 2000s era

Results

Team	Mat	Won	Lost	Tied	Draw	W/L
Australia	108	54	25	0	29	2.160
Pakistan	76	32	21	0	23	1.523
West Indies	81	30	28	0	23	1.071
South Africa	66	29	13	0	24	2.230
England	107	26	43	0	38	0.604
India	69	18	20	0	31	0.900
New Zealand	81	17	32	0	32	0.531
Sri Lanka	67	14	22	0	31	0.636
Zimbabwe	39	3	19	0	17	0.157

1990s XI

1. Mark Taylor (AUS) c
2. Saeed Anwar (PAK)
3. Mohammad Azharuddin (IND)
4. Andy Flower (ZIM)
5. Aravinda de Silva (SL)
6. Steve Waugh (AUS) vc
7. Ian Healy (AUS) wk
8. Wasim Akram (PAK)
9. Shane Warne (AUS)
10. Curtly Ambrose (WI)
11. Allan Donald (SA)

1. Mark Taylor (AUS) c

Test Record

Bat	M	Inn	NO	Runs	HS	Avg	100	50	Ct
	104	186	13	7525	334*	43.49	19	40	157

Bowl	M	Inn	Wkts	Avg	BBI	BBM	5i	10m	SR
	104	2	1	26.00	1/11	1/11	0	0	42.0

*not out

Given Taylor's masterful opening batting, brilliant slip-fielding and astute captaincy – one of Australia's best ever – he is sometimes referred to as an all-rounder. While his batting could never be considered attacking, his captaincy was adventurous and he was prepared to lose a match to win it.

Taylor formed a very successful opening partnership with Michael Slater, and they opened together in 78 innings for a total of 3887 runs (the sixth most prolific opening partnership of all time) at an average of 51.14.

He debuted in 1989 against the West Indies at home in Sydney and scored 25 and three. Taylor was then run out twice in his second Test.

However, the selectors kept faith with him and were repaid on the 1989 Ashes tour where Taylor scored 839 runs at 83.90, with a highest score of 219 at Trent Bridge as Australia regained the Ashes 4–0.

Taylor maintained his form in twin Tests against Sri Lanka, averaging 76, then scored 390 runs in three Tests versus Pakistan at 97.50.

He assumed the captaincy from Allan Border in 1994, and began with a pair of ducks in the first Test of Australia's tour of Pakistan.

However, he had a solid Ashes series in 1994–95 knocking up 471 runs at 47.10 including 113 in the second innings at Sydney to help Australia to a draw.

Taylor then scored a series-leading 338 runs against Pakistan at home with an average of 67.60. This was followed by a lean spell where his captaincy probably kept him in the side.

His funk was broken by a century at Edgbaston on the 1997 Ashes tour, and his run-making was turned back on.

Taylor's greatest innings came against Pakistan at Peshawar in 1998, where he ran up 334 not out equalling the then-Australian record held by Bradman for highest Test score. He would likely have surpassed it, but he declared overnight to chase the win (the match ended in a draw).

Taylor finished his Test career in Australia in the 1998–99 Ashes where he managed only 228 runs at 22.80 and retired at the relatively young age of 34.

All up, Taylor captained Australia 50 times for 26 wins and 13 losses.

Once he had finished playing cricket, Taylor turned to television commentary and was inducted into the Australian Cricket Hall of Fame in 2011.

2. Saeed Anwar (PAK)

Test Record

Bat	M	Inn	NO	Runs	HS	Avg	100	50	Ct
	55	91	2	4052	188*	45.52	11	25	18

Bowl	M	Inn	Wkts	Avg	BBI	BBM	5i	10m	SR
	55	4	0	-	-	-	0	0	-

*not out

Saeed Anwar first rose to prominence as a One Day player, but he seamlessly transitioned his game to Test cricket. Anwar relied on precision timing rather than brute force to get the innings off to a flying start. He has been described as 'gracefully compelling' and as having 'majestic timing and placement'.

He would have played many more Tests if he had played for another country, but Pakistan's Test series seemed to be limited to just two or three Tests per series in the 1990s.

Anwar debuted with a duck against the West Indies in 1990 and then had to wait a couple of years before scoring 261 runs in three Tests in New Zealand at 52.20, including his maiden Test century of 169.

Two Tests versus Sri Lanka followed, and Anwar chalked up another 261 runs at an average of 87 including 136 at Colombo.

Pakistan toured England in 1996 for three Tests, and Anwar was Pakistan's leading batter with 362 runs at 60.33, with 74 and 88 at Lord's and 176 at The Oval. Pakistan won the series 2–0.

Anwar followed this up by averaging 91 against Zimbabwe and 52.33 versus New Zealand, both two Test series and played in Pakistan.

In another two Test series in 1998, this time against Australia, Anwar scored 145 at Rawalpindi then 126 at Peshawar but couldn't stop the Australians from winning the series 1–0.

The Asian Test Championship in 1999 saw Anwar play three Tests and score 290 runs at 72.50 including his highest Test score of 188 not out versus India at Eden Gardens.

Following the tragic death of his daughter in August 2001, Anwar took a break from the game and while he returned to One Day cricket (he scored a hundred in the 2003 World Cup) he did not play another Test match.

For a time, Anwar held the record for the highest score in a One Day International with 194, but the great Tendulkar and others have since surpassed it.

He also captained Pakistan seven times for one win and four losses.

3. Mohammad Azharuddin (IND)

Test Record

Bat	M	Inn	NO	Runs	HS	Avg	100	50	Ct
	99	147	9	6215	199	45.03	22	21	105

Bowl	M	Inn	Wkts	Avg	BBI	BBM	5i	10m	SR
	99	3	0	-	-	-	0	0	-

Azharuddin wielded the bat like a magician's wand, majestically caressing the ball away through the onside. If he had a weakness, it was against the short stuff from the express bowlers, but then who doesn't have a problem with this?

He was a far better batter at home, averaging 55.93 in India while he averaged 36.40 away.

Unfortunately, Azharuddin's career came to an abrupt halt following allegations of match fixing and a life ban from cricket which was later overturned in 2012 by the Andhra Pradesh High Court.

Azharuddin began Test cricket like no other, with three centuries in his first three Tests against England in 1984: 110 at Eden Gardens on debut, 105 at Chennai and 122 at Kanpur. His only 'failure' in the series was 48 in the second Test at Chennai.

He had to wait until 1986 for his next Test century, and it was his highest Test score of 199 versus Sri Lanka at Kanpur given out LBW.

In early 1987, Pakistan toured India and Azharuddin scored 315 runs at over 50 with two hundreds, his best being 141 in the drawn second Test at Eden Gardens.

In three Tests away to New Zealand in 1990, he scored over 300 runs at 75.75 and led the runs aggregate and averages for India. He again fell just short of a double century with 192 at Auckland.

Azharuddin again led the way for India versus England away, scoring 426 runs at 85.20 including a magnificent 121 at Lord's.

Topping the runs aggregate and averages against Sri Lanka in a three Test series in 1994, he scored 307 runs at an average of 102.33 with two more tons.

South Africa toured India in 1996–97 for three Tests, and Azharuddin once more topped the runs aggregate and averages for either side with 388 runs at 77.60 including two centuries.

In 1998, the Australians toured India for three Tests and Azharuddin added a further 311 runs at 77.75 including 163 not out at Eden Gardens.

Azharuddin's final innings before his ban came in 2000 versus South Africa at Bengalaru, and he went out of Test cricket the way he came in – with a century.

Azharuddin also captained India 47 times for 14 wins and 14 losses, with 13 of the wins coming at home.

4. Andy Flower (ZIM)

Test Record

Bat	Ma	Inn	NO	Runs	HS	Avg	100	50	Ct	St
	63	112	19	4794	232*	51.54	12	27	151	9

*not out

Andy Flower is the elder of two brothers to have played for Zimbabwe (Grant Flower played 67 Tests). He is undoubtedly Zimbabwe's greatest international cricketer and is their leading run scorer: more than 1300 runs in front of his brother Grant, he is their only player to average over 50 (minimum ten innings). Flower is also Zimbabwe's only inductee in the ICC Cricket Hall of Fame.

As well as being an attractive left-handed batter, Flower also kept wicket for Zimbabwe. However, he has been chosen as a batter only in this XI. Flower's number of Tests and thus runs scored were restricted by the number of one and two Test series that Zimbabwe played in over the course of his career, as well as his generally limited Test opportunities.

Flower debuted against India at Harare in 1992 and made 59 and one not out while claiming a solitary catch. He followed this up with 81 versus New Zealand at Bulawayo.

Touring India for a single Test at Delhi in 1993, Flower brought up his maiden Test century and backed it up with 62 not out in the second dig. Despite his efforts Zimbabwe still lost by an innings, which unfortunately was a theme throughout Flower's career – individual success but he did not have the team to back him up.

It was not long before Flower was elevated to captain of Zimbabwe and he led them to their first Test victory, an innings win against Pakistan at Harare in 1995 with Flower contributing a fine 156. Unfortunately for Zimbabwe, Pakistan hit back to claim the next two Tests and thus the series. The win against Pakistan was Flower's single success as captain in 20 matches.

Flower had to wait until the end of 1996 to score his next hundred (112) which came against England at Bulawayo in a drawn match. Zimbabwe then played only two Tests in 1997 before Flower racked up another ton (105 not out) versus Sri Lanka at Colombo in early 1998. Back home, he added another undefeated century against Pakistan at Bulawayo.

In 1999, Flower was given the opportunity to play in a three Test series at home to Sri Lanka. He topped the batting aggregate and averages for both sides with 388 runs at 97 including 74 and 129 in the second Test at Harare, again in vain as Sri Lanka won by six wickets. Flower followed this up with 194 runs in two Tests in the West Indies in early 2000 with a high score of 113 not out.

Zimbabwe toured India at the end of 2000 and Flower was in rare form, scoring 540 runs in just two Tests and being dismissed just twice for an average of 270. This included his highest Test score of 232 not out at Nagpur as he batted Zimbabwe to the safety of a draw. This is also the highest Test score by a wicketkeeper.

When South Africa toured in 2001, Flower again led the runs chart with 422 runs at an average of 211 including 142 and 199 not out at Harare, once more in a losing effort. He followed this up in a match away against Bangladesh, collecting 142 runs for once out – yet another hundred. In 2003, Flower and Henry Olonga wore black armbands in the One Day International World Cup to protest the Zimbabwe Government's human rights record. This led to pressure being brought to bear against the duo and resulted in Flower's retirement from international cricket.

After his playing days Flower has had a successful coaching career, most notably as England's coach.

5. Aravinda de Silva (SL)

Test Record

Bat	M	Inn	NO	Runs	HS	Avg	100	50	Ct
	93	159	11	6361	267	42.97	20	22	43

Bowl	M	Inn	Wkts	Avg	BBI	BBM	5i	10m	SR
	93	58	29	41.65	3/30	3/34	0	0	89.4

Aravinda de Silva was one the game's entertainers: he had an unrufflable technique and was strong with the cross bat shots even though he stood at only 5 foot 3 inches. Like many of the sub-continent players, most of the series he played in were only two or three Tests so he could have played many more Tests if he were, say, Australian.

Arguably his greatest innings was not in Test cricket but the 1996 World Cup final, when he scored a match-winning century against the all-conquering Australians.

Aravinda debuted at Lord's in 1984 but could manage just 16 and three. It was a year later that he got another chance, against India, and was solid but not spectacular with an average of 33.60.

Versus Pakistan in 1985–86, Aravinda found his feet in Test cricket and scored two hundreds in the three Tests and averaged an even 50.

He had an excellent pair of Tests in Australia in 1989–90, making 314 runs at 104.66 and a top score of 167 on the bouncy Gabba wicket in Brisbane.

Aravinda led the way for Sri Lanka against New Zealand in 1990–91, scoring 493 runs in three Tests with an average of 98.60 and two hundreds including his highest Test score of 267 at Wellington.

India toured Sr Lanka in 1993, and Aravinda topped the runs aggregate for either side with 266 runs at an average of 53.20 with one century – 148 at Colombo.

A few lean series by his standards ensued, although he picked up hundreds here and there.

His best series was the two Test series against Pakistan at home in 1997 when he scored three hundreds (168, 138 not out and 103 not out) and averaged 216.

Aravinda also averaged over 100 in Test series against India in 1997 and Zimbabwe in 1998. Later in 1998, he knocked up 152 in a single Test versus England at The Oval.

He picked a good Test to finish on, as he carved 206 in just 234 balls in his only bat against Bangladesh in 2002 (Sri Lanka won by an innings).

Aravinda's worth to Sri Lankan cricket goes beyond his mere stats: he set the platform for the great Sri Lankan batters to come, including Kumar Sangakkara, Mahela Jayawardene and Sanath Jayasuriya.

Aravinda acted as a national selector on his exit from Test cricket.

6. Steve Waugh (AUS) vc

Test Record

Bat	M	Inn	NO	Runs	HS	Avg	100	50	Ct
	168	260	46	10,927	200	51.06	32	50	112
Bowl	M	Inn	Wkts	Avg	BBI	BBM	5i	10m	SR
	168	150	92	37.44	5/28	8/169	3	0	84.8

Steve Waugh began life in Test cricket at age 20 as an attacking batter who flailed at everything, and a medium-pace bowler who was prepared to bounce Viv Richards. Over time, he reigned in his tempestuous nature to become a tough-as-nails competitor who would not give his wicket away cheaply. Back issues also meant his bowling became less and less a part of his game.

Waugh was also a hard edged captain, always looking for a way to win no matter the situation. It helped he had a great Australian side at his disposal, but he won 41 of 57 Tests he skippered in – a win rate of 71.93% which is the best for anyone who has captained a meaningful amount of Tests.

He came into the national side at a time when Australian cricket was at its lowest ebb and looking towards the future. Waugh was an integral part in dragging Australia from the bottom to the top rung of world cricket.

It was the Boxing Day Test of 1985 against India that Waugh made his debut. He made just 13 and five but over the following Tests showed glimpses of his potential without delivering on the promise. This included the integral part he played in Australia's World Cup victory in 1987.

The Ashes tour of 1989 was Waugh's breakthrough series, coinciding with Australia's rise from the canvas. He made 393 runs in the Tests before he was dismissed, and ended the series with 506 runs at 126.50 and a top score of 175 not out at Headingly.

Losing form, Waugh lost his place (to his brother Mark) for a period but was back for the 1993 Ashes and again put England to the sword with 416 runs at 83.20

Waugh's highest Test score of 200 is also probably his greatest innings, as it was made against the West Indies at Kingston in the series-deciding Test won by Australia, thus handing the Windies their first home series loss in 20 years. He averaged 107.25 for the series.

The 2001 Ashes was another series to remember for Waugh, who scored 321 runs in four Tests with an average of 107 and a top score of 157 not out.

Waugh had many other successful series, home and away, against all opposition – he scored a hundred against every opposition he played against. At 36 he won the Allan Border medal for Australia's best male player of the year.

He finished his Test career at home in Sydney scoring 40 and 80 against the Indians.

After his career, Waugh did not pursue a life with cricket either as a commentator or administrator, but instead helped set up a charity for the daughters of lepers in Calcutta.

Waugh is an inductee of both the Australian and ICC Cricket Halls of Fame, and was named Australian of the Year in 2004.

7. Ian Healy (AUS) wk

Test Record

Bat	Ma	Inn	NO	Runs	HS	Avg	100	50	Ct	St
	119	182	23	4356	161*	27.39	4	22	366	29

*not out

Ian Healy had played only a handful of First Class games when he was a shock call up to the Australian side, part of the youth policy from Australian selectors desperate to pull Australian cricket out of the doldrums. For ten years thereafter, Healy was the heart and soul of the Australian side. His keeping to the fast men improved from good to great, but it was his work standing up to Shane Warne that really shone. By the time he retired he held the record for most dismissals by a keeper in Test history and still sits in third place.

Healy's batting was good enough for four Test centuries and he was a dependable lower order batter with slashing cuts and pulls.

The Australian Cricket Board considered him good enough to be named as wicketkeeper in the Australian XI of the twentieth century, in front of other greats such as Rod Marsh, Wally Grout and Don Tallon.

It was a torrid introduction to Test cricket for Healy: thrown in at the deep end on a three Test tour of Pakistan in 1988, he took six catches and made two stumpings. The selectors saw enough to stick with him.

In the 1990–91 Ashes series in Australia, Healy held 24 catches in the five Tests along with 175 runs at an average of 25.

Healy held a further 19 catches and made four stumpings when the West Indies toured Australia in 1992–93, but disappointed with the bat.

His breakthrough series with the bat came on the 1993 Ashes tour when he made much-needed runs – 296 in total at 59.20 including his maiden Test hundred of 102 not out at Old Trafford. He also took 21 catches and made five stumpings in the six Tests.

Healy followed this up with another century in Australia versus New Zealand in the first Test at Perth.

The 1994–95 Ashes was another successful series for Healy, with 25 dismissals, 23 caught and two stumped, along with 249 runs at 35.57 and a top score of 74.

Sri Lanka toured Australia in 1995–96, and in three Tests Healy claimed 19 dismissals and averaged over 50 with the bat.

Healy's highest Test of 161 not out score came at Brisbane in 1996 against the West Indies. He added 45 not out in the second innings and took four catches to claim man of the match.

His final Test was at Harare versus Zimbabwe in 1999 where he was not required to bat and took a single catch.

As well as his role as a keeper-batter, Healy also served time as vice-captain and even captained Australia in a handful of ODIs.

Healy is an inductee in the Australian Cricket Hall of Fame.

8. Wasim Akram (PAK)

Test Record

Bat	M	Inn	NO	Runs	HS	Avg	100	50	Ct
	104	147	19	2898	257*	22.64	3	7	44
Bowl	M	Inn	Wkts	Avg	BBI	BBM	5i	10m	SR
	104	181	414	23.62	7/119	11/110	25	5	54.6

*not out

Many argue that Wasim Akram is the greatest left-arm fast bowler of all time, and his record backs this up. Akram bowled at pace and could swing or seam the ball both ways, and had a lethal bouncer and a well-disguised slower ball: all of this on home pitches that were not conducive to pace bowling. He is also Pakistan's leading wicket-taker in both Test and ODI cricket.

His batting was better than his statistics reveal although he did have a monumental innings of 257 against Zimbabwe along with two other centuries.

Akram debuted in New Zealand in 1985 and took 12 wickets in two Tests including 5/56 and 5/72 at Dunedin in his second Test.

Akram picked up regular wickets over the next few years without a really big series until 1990–91, when he picked up 21 wickets in just three Tests against the West Indies at home – the most for either side.

A further 21 wickets came his way in England in 1992 at an average of 22 and a best of 6/67 at The Oval.

In just three Tests in New Zealand in 1994, Akram dismissed 25 Kiwi batters at 17.24 with his best bowling in an innings of 7/119.

The West Indies toured Pakistan in 1997–98 and Akram collected 17 wickets in the three Tests at an average of 17.29.

He took a further 15 wickets in three Tests in the Asian Test Championship in 1999 at the cost of 18.40 runs per wicket.

On the 2000 tour of the West Indies, Akram took another 15 scalps in the three Tests including 6/61 and 5/49 at St John's for match figures of 10/110, but couldn't stop the West Indies winning by one wicket.

Akram's last five-wicket haul came against Sri Lanka at Colombo where he picked up 5/45.

His final Test was at Dhaka in Bangladesh where he got through just 2.4 overs before having to stop.

A natural successor to Imran Khan as Pakistan's captain, Akram led his country 25 times for 12 wins and eight losses.

After his Test career ended, Akram has coached and taken up a position in the commentary box.

Akram is an inductee in the ICC Cricket Hall of Fame.

9. Shane Warne (AUS)

Test Record

Bat	M	Inn	NO	Runs	HS	Avg	100	50	Ct
	145	199	17	3154	99	17.32	0	12	125

Bowl	M	Inn	Wkts	Avg	BBI	BBM	5i	10m	SR
	145	273	708	25.41	8/71	12/128	37	10	57.4

Shane Warne is not only one of the greatest spin bowlers of all time but one of the greatest bowlers full stop. He was nominated by *Wisden* as one of the five best cricketers of the twentieth century when his career was only a little over half way done. Warne is also a member of the Australian and ICC Cricket Halls of Fame.

For a leg-spinner, he had great control and variety and could bowl long spells with no drop off in his potency. He was a great competitor and probably willed a large number of his victims out.

An occasional contributor with the bat, Warne missed out on a Test century trying to slog when a nudge for single would have got him there. Then again, that was Warne's approach to cricket and life as a whole.

Warne was plucked from relative obscurity to play his first Test against India in 1992. It's fair to say he began slowly, as he took 1/150 as the Indians got stuck in. His sole wicket was Ravi Shastri, who was 206 when Warne had him caught in the deep.

Yet he persevered, and in the Boxing Day Test in 1992 bowled Australia to victory over the West Indies taking 7/52 in 22.2 overs.

That put him on the 1993 Ashes tour, and his first ball of the series to Mike Gatting has gone down in history as 'the ball of the century'. It dipped and swerved and pitched outside leg before spinning back past Gatting's bat to clip off. Warne had arrived. In all he took 34 wickets in the series, the most for either side.

From there it was a procession of wicket-taking for Warne, including 18 in three Tests against South Africa at 17.05 in 1993–94 and another 18 in three Tests against Pakistan the following summer.

Warne claimed 27 wickets in the 1994–95 Ashes at home which included his best bowling figures in an innings of 8/71 and a hat-trick.

He grabbed another 20 dismissals in just three Tests versus South Africa in 1997–98 and again bowled Australia to victory with 6/31 in the second innings of the Sydney Test.

In 2002, Warne dismissed 27 Pakistani batters in just three Tests at an average of 12.66 and a best of 7/94.

Warne tested positive to a banned substance on the eve of the 2003 World Cup and spent a year out of the game. He was always adamant that what he took was for weight reduction and the pill was given to him by his mother.

A mighty Ashes tour ensued in 2005, where Warne took 40 wickets in five Tests at 19.92 including three five-fors. It couldn't stop Australia losing the Ashes, however.

Warne bowed out of Test cricket after the 2006–07 Ashes in Australia. During the series, he became the first bowler to take 700 Test wickets (only Muraliduran has taken more wickets) and ended up with 23 wickets for the series.

He did a number of things post-cricket, including commentary. Warne died of a heart attack in Thailand in 2022, aged 52.

10. Curtly Ambrose (WI)

Test Record

Bat	M	Inn	NO	Runs	HS	Avg	100	50	Ct
	98	145	29	1439	53	12.40	0	1	18

Bowl	M	Inn	Wkts	Avg	BBI	BBM	5i	10m	SR
	98	179	405	20.99	8/45	11/84	22	3	54.5

A tall and menacingly fast bowler, Ambrose was the most threatening bowler of his generation. At 6 foot 7 inches, Ambrose was releasing the ball from over 10 foot, which created steepling bounce. Yet when his pace started to desert him, Ambrose – like other great fast bowlers – found seam movement from a well-grooved action.

Ambrose debuted versus Pakistan at Georgetown in 1988, picking up two wickets – his first being Mudassar Nazar. He ended up with seven wickets for the series.

He retained his place for the tour of England later in 1988 and bagged 22 scalps at 21.46 in a consistent series. Ambrose then backed this up with 26 wickets in Australia – the most for either side.

Back in England in 1991, Ambrose took another series-leading wicket tally with 28 in five Tests with a best effort of 6/52 in a losing effort at Headingly.

The 1992–93 tour of Australia was one of Ambrose's finest, as he snared 33 victims – the most for either side – at an average of 16.42. This included a withering spell of 7/1 in Perth, bowling Australia out for 119, in the deciding Test match of the summer which the West Indies won by an innings.

England toured the West Indies in 1994 and Ambrose picked up another series-leading tally of 26 at 19.96 including helping bowl England out for 46 in the third Test at Port of Spain with 6/24.

When the English came back in 1998, Ambrose was again waiting for them and collected 30 wickets with 5/25 his best at Port of Spain in the third Test.

Towards the end of his career, he was still good enough to take 19 wickets in four Tests against Australia in 1999 with 5/94 at St John's – his best figures.

Ambrose's final series was versus England in 2000 and he nabbed 17 wickets at 18.64 with a best of 4/30 at Lord's.

Ambrose was admitted into the ICC Cricket Hall of Fame, was named in the West Indies greatest ever XI by a panel of journalists, and has been knighted for his services to cricket.

11. Allan Donald (SA)

Test Record

Bat	M	Inn	NO	Runs	HS	Avg	100	50	Ct
	72	94	33	652	37	10.68	0	0	18

Bowl	M	Inn	Wkts	Avg	BBI	BBM	5i	10m	SR
	72	129	330	22.25	8/71	12/139	20	3	47.0

The final position in this XI came down to Allan Donald and Courtney Walsh. Walsh had far more wickets (519) but played far more Tests than Donald (132). In the end it was decided that Donald on his day was slightly ahead of Walsh, but it was a close call.

Donald was another genuine fast bowler who could swing the ball both ways with unerring accuracy, never giving the batter a moment's peace. As the South Africans' one strike bowler, he was often overbowled and injuries complicated his career in later years. ESPNcricinfo claims that, 'If the credit for South Africa's success in the modern era could be given to one player, that cricketer would be Allan Donald.'

Debuting against the West Indies in Bridgetown in 1992, Donald took 2/67 and 4/77. Then, in his first full series versus India at home, he took a series-leading 20 wickets at 19.70 including 7/84 at Gqeberha, helping South Africa to an eventual easy win.

A couple of 12 and 13 wicket hauls in three Test series followed, until a one off Test against Zimbabwe at Harare where Donald collected 3/42 and 8/71 for match figures of 11/113.

India toured South Africa in 1996–97 for three Tests and Donald again led the wickets tally with 20 at an average of 15.95 including 5/40 at Durban.

Donald's best series came in England in 1998 where he bagged 33 victims at 19.78, including 5/32 at Lord's, 6/88 at Old Trafford and 5/109 at Trent Bridge.

When England toured South Africa in 1999/2000, Donald took 22 wickets in four Tests including 6/53 and 5/74 at Johannesburg to bowl his side to an innings victory.

Donald called it quits after South Africa were thrashed at home by Australia, losing by an innings and 360 runs in the first Test at Johannesburg in 2002.

Post-cricket, Donald did some commentating and has worked as a coach, particularly as a bowling coach.

Donald is an inductee in the ICC Cricket Hall of Fame.

1990s Second XI

1. Michael Atherton (ENG)
2. Michael Slater (AUS)
3. Gary Kirsten (SA)
4. David Boon (AUS) vc
5. Mark Waugh (AUS)
6. Salim Malik (PAK)
7. Alec Stewart (ENG) wk
8. Mushtaq Ahmed (PAK)
9. Waqar Younis (PAK)
10. Craig McDermott (AUS)
11. Courtney Walsh (WI) c

2000s

Australia ended the 1990s and began the 2000s with a record-breaking 16 consecutive Test wins. The streak was only brought to an end in a defeat by India after they had followed on. It took a partnership of 376 between Rahul Dravid and VVS Laxman to help halt the Australian juggernaut.

However, to prove their run was no fluke, the Australians again won 16 in a row from the end of 2005 to the beginning of 2008, India once more bringing their run to an end.

Not surprisingly, Australia ended with the best win rate for the decade, winning a huge 69% of Tests played. South Africa were next best at 49% and Sri Lanka 45%.

One series that did get away from the all-conquering Australians was the 2005 Ashes in England. Australia had an easy win at Lord's in the first Test, but England hit back to claim the second by just two runs. The third Test was an exciting draw before England went ahead 2–1 by winning the fourth Test by three wickets. The fifth Test was drawn and the Ashes were England's. Australia did take revenge 18 months later in Australia, destroying England 5–0.

Bangladesh also played their first Test – against India at Dhaka – which they lost by nine wickets.

Australia won both One Day International World Cups while India and Pakistan won one T20 World Cup each.

The ICC voted Australian Ricky Ponting as the player of the decade, and he also topped the runs aggregate for the decade in front of South Africa's Jacques Kallis. Sri Lanka's Muttiah Muralidaran was the leading bowler for the 2000s, well in front of Makhaya Ntini of South Africa.

Choosing the XI for this decade was actually pretty easy until you realise which players have been left out. The openers came down to a choice of three between Australian Matthew Hayden, India's Virender Sehwag and South African Graeme Smith. Hayden and Sehwag were ultimately chosen for their ability to get the innings off to a rapid-fire start and have the opposition on the back foot from the get-go.

Kallis was chosen as an all-rounder, although his batting alone would have seen him selected. Three all-time greats in Ponting, Sachin Tendulkar and Brian Lara fill the specialist batting spots. This means batters who averaged in the 50s have missed out including Kumar Sangakkara, Rahul Dravid, Mahela Jayawardene, Mohammad Yousuf and Shivnarine Chanderpaul. In fact, if you add up the batting averages of the second XI members it totals 425 (the first XI total of averages is 431 so it's close) – good enough to be ranked third in the averages table in the Sundry Lists section at the end of this book.

Glenn McGrath's career was split nearly evenly between the 1990s and 2000s, so you need to look at his overall record not just his 2000s numbers. From there it's clear that he is the standout fast bowler of the era. Sean Pollock of South Africa was chosen over his countryman Ntini as the second paceman due to his ability as an all-rounder. Having Kallis as the third seamer allows two specialist spinners to be chosen. Muralidaran was a walk up starter and the second spot came down to a choice between Indians Anil Kumble and Harbhajan Singh, with Kumble's marginally better record getting him the nod.

Mark Boucher of South Africa made the most dismissals as a wicketkeeper in the decade, but Australia's Adam Gilchrist was far superior with the bat. A case could also be made for Sangakkara as he kept from time to time for Sri Lanka. However, Gilchrist was a better full-time keeper than Sangakkara and also had a better batting average as keeper (Sangakkara's average as keeper was 40.48 and Gilchrist's 47.60) so he was selected.

Most Runs in Period

Player	Mat	Inns	NO	Runs	HS	Ave	SR	100	50
RT Ponting (AUS)	107	184	22	9458	257	58.38	62.51	32	40
JH Kallis (ICC/SA)	101	174	27	8630	189*	58.70	46.50	27	42
R Dravid (ICC/IND)	103	179	23	8558	270	54.85	43.49	22	42
ML Hayden (AUS)	96	172	14	8364	380	52.93	60.85	29	29
DPMD Jayawardene (SL)	95	160	12	8187	374	55.31	53.46	25	30
KC Sangakkara (SL)	88	147	10	7549	287	55.10	55.53	21	32
SR Tendulkar (IND)	89	150	16	7129	248*	53.20	54.35	21	31
GC Smith (ICC/SA)	79	139	9	6451	277	49.62	60.58	18	26
M Yousuf (PAK)	71	121	11	6439	223	58.53	53.02	23	23
S Chanderpaul (WI)	86	148	25	6435	203*	52.31	43.63	19	35

*not out

Most Wickets in Period

Player	Mat	Inns	Wkts	BBI	BBM	Ave	SR	5	10
M Muralidaran (ICC/SL)	84	154	565	9/51	13/115	20.97	50.9	49	20
M Ntini (SA)	97	182	380	7/37	13/132	28.64	52.8	18	4
SK Warne* (AUS)	65	127	357	7/94	12/246	25.17	50.7	21	6
A Kumble (IND)	74	133	355	8/141	13/181	31.02	63.7	20	5
H Singh (IND)	72	132	322	8/84	15/217	30.31	64.3	23	5
B Lee (AUS)	75	148	303	5/30	9/171	31.27	53.8	9	0
GD McGrath (AUS)	66	131	297	8/24	10/27	20.53	51.4	14	2
SM Pollock (SA)	70	135	260	6/30	10/147	24.76	61.0	6	1
MJ Hoggard (ENG)	67	122	248	7/61	12/205	30.50	56.0	7	1
WPUJC Vaas (SL)	77	141	247	7/71	14/191	29.69	65.1	8	1

*does not qualify for this period

Results

Team	Mat	Won	Lost	Tied	Draw	W/L
Australia	115	79	18	0	18	4.388
England	129	55	37	0	37	1.486
South Africa	108	53	32	0	23	1.656
Sri Lanka	96	44	31	0	21	1.419
India	103	40	27	0	36	1.481
Pakistan	83	30	31	0	22	0.967
New Zealand	80	23	32	0	25	0.718
West Indies	108	18	59	0	31	0.305
Zimbabwe	44	5	30	0	9	0.166
Bangladesh	61	3	52	0	6	0.057
ICC World XI	1	0	1	0	0	0.000

2000s XI

1. Matthew Hayden (AUS)
2. Virender Sehwag (IND)
3. Ricky Ponting (AUS) c
4. Jacques Kallis (SA)
5. Sachin Tendulkar (IND) vc
6. Brian Lara (WI)
7. Adam Gilchrist (AUS) wk
8. Shaun Pollock (SA)
9. Anil Kumble (IND)
10. Muthiah Muralidaran (SL)
11. Glenn McGrath (AUS)

1. Matthew Hayden (AUS)

Test Record

Bat	M	Inn	NO	Runs	HS	Avg	100	50	Ct
	103	184	14	8625	380	50.73	30	29	128
Bowl	M	Inn	Wkts	Avg	BBI	BBM	5i	10m	SR
	72	3	0	-	-	-	0	0	-

Matthew Hayden was strong, both physically and mentally, and is one of Australia's greatest opening batters. He had to endure a torrid start in Test cricket against the West Indies and South Africa, tough for any opening batter, and he took his time in finding his place. Once settled, he dominated attacks worldwide. He was also a fine fielder at slip or gully.

Hayden formed a prolific opening partnership with Justin Langer and together they added 5655 runs, setting the platform for the Australian success the side enjoyed in the early to mid-2000s. They sit behind only Greenidge and Haynes on the all-time openers list.

He debuted against South Africa at Johannesburg in 1994 but played just one Test. Hayden didn't play again until the 1996–97 series versus the West Indies, and he scored his maiden Test ton of 125 at Adelaide.

Hayden didn't lock down his spot at the top of the order until the 2001 tour of India, where he scored an Australian record for a three Test series of 549 runs at over a hundred with a top score of 203 at Chennai.

In 2001–02, Hayden scored three hundreds in three Tests against South Africa at home at an average of 107.25, and followed it up back in South Africa with 309 runs in three Tests at 61.80.

Hayden scored another three centuries in the 2002–03 Ashes in Australia, notching 496 runs at 62.00 with a top score of 197 at the Gabba.

Against Zimbabwe at Perth in 2003, Hayden overtook Brian Lara's record for the highest Test innings as he racked up 380 off 437 balls (Lara has of course taken the record back). He also brought up another hundred in the next Test in Sydney.

When the West Indies toured in 2005–06, Hayden scored a series-leading 445 runs in three Tests at 89 with two centuries and a best of 118.

Hayden added a further 410 runs at 82 (leading the averages for either side) in 2007–08 against the touring Indians with three more hundreds.

A few leaner series followed, prompting Hayden to call stumps after the South Africa Test in Sydney in 2009.

Hayden turned to commentating after cricket and is an inductee in the Australian Cricket Hall of Fame.

2. Virender Sehwag (IND)

Test Record

Bat	M	Inn	NO	Runs	HS	Avg	100	50	Ct
	104	180	6	8586	319	49.34	23	32	91

Bowl	M	Inn	Wkts	Avg	BBI	BBM	5i	10m	SR
	104	91	40	47.35	5/104	5/118	1	0	93.2

Perhaps Rahul Dravid or Kumar Sangakkara deserve a spot in this XI at the expense of Sehwag, but that would have meant batting them out of their usual position. Sehwag makes it, but only just.

Virender Sehwag made a career out of blasting boundary after boundary, often with minimal footwork but always with maximum intent. The most remarkable aspect of Sehwag's career is his ability to build massive scores at breakneck speed. He holds the Indian record for highest number of Test double hundreds, and came within seven runs of becoming the first batsman to score three triple hundreds.

Sehwag debuted batting at number six with a century (105) versus South Africa at Bloemfontein in 2001, going stroke for stroke with Sachin Tendulkar in adding 220 for the fifth wicket.

2003–04 was a big period for Sehwag as he made 177 runs in two Tests against New Zealand at 44.25 and 464 in four Tests in Australia at 58. He then scored 438 in three Tests in Pakistan at an average of 109.50 including his first triple century, 309 made at Multan.

In 2004–05, Sehwag scored 299 runs at 42.71 versus Australia at home followed by 262 in two Tests against South Africa with an average of 87.33 and a high score of 164.

Sehwag scored a series-leading 544 runs against Pakistan at home in 2005 at 90.66, including a top score of 201 made at Benglauru and another century (173) at Mohali.

In Australia in 2007–08, Sehwag played in two Tests – running up 286 runs at 71.50 – then followed it up with 372 runs in three

Tests versus South Africa – again averaging over 70 – but most of his runs came in one innings of 319 (off 304 balls).

Sehwag belted Sri Lanka in 2009–10 at home with 491 runs in the three Tests at 122.75 with a top score of 293 off just 254 balls.

Two series later, Sehwag faced South Africa and played in two Tests scoring 290 runs at 96.66 with a hundred in each Test.

He also put the Kiwis to the sword in 2010–11, knocking up a series-leading 398 runs at a tick under a hundred average and a top score of 173 off 199 balls.

Sehwag played on for a couple of more years but never reached these heights again, and retired after Australia toured in 2013 scoring just 27 in two Tests.

Captaining India four times, Sehwag had two wins and a loss.

3. Ricky Ponting (AUS) c

Test Record

Bat	M	Inn	NO	Runs	HS	Avg	100	50	Ct
	168	287	29	13,378	257	51.85	41	62	196

Bowl	M	Inn	Wkts	Avg	BBI	BBM	5i	10m	SR
	168	36	5	55.20	1/0	1/0	0	0	117.4

Ricky Ponting is arguably the greatest batter Australia has produced after Bradman (do I hear any Greg Chappell or Steve Smith fans?). Ponting was a fluent, attacking player who played all the shots but was particularly savage with the pull and cover drive. His fielding was also second to none, whether catching or conjuring a run out with a direct hit.

Ponting was named player of the decade by the ICC and is an inductee in the Australian and ICC Cricket Halls of Fame.

He first played for Tasmania at just 17 and debuted for Australia aged 20, scoring 96 against Sri Lanka in 1995 before being unluckily given out LBW in the days before DRS.

Ponting had some issues as a youngster and didn't score his first hundred (127) until 1997 which came at Headingly. Gradually, as he matured, he cemented his place in the Australian XI and dominated world cricket.

He had his first big series against Sri Lanka in 1999 when he managed 253 runs at 84.33 in the three Tests with a hundred at Colombo.

Ponting scored a series-leading 375 runs against India at 125 in 1999–2000 including his highest Test score to date of 141 not out.

On the 2003 tour of the West Indies, Ponting racked up 523 runs in three Tests at an average of 130.75 with three centuries including his first double century (206) at Port of Spain.

Another hundred-plus average series came in two Tests versus Zimbabwe and in four Tests at home to India, where he scored double hundreds in successive Tests including his highest score of 257.

Pakistan toured Australia in 2004–05 and Ponting again averaged a hundred in scoring 515 runs in three Tests with three centuries.

Ponting's last series where he averaged over a hundred was at home to India in 2011–12, where he ran up 544 runs in four Tests.

His last series was versus South Africa in 2012–13 but, finding himself out of form, he retired from Test cricket.

Ponting captained Australia 77 times for 48 wins, a win rate of 62%, and lost just 16. He stood aside from the captaincy near the end of his career to allow Michael Clarke to take over.

After Test cricket Ponting has coached, with success in the IPL, and is a wise voice in the commentary box.

4. Jacques Kallis (SA)

Test Record

Bat	M	Inn	NO	Runs	HS	Avg	100	50	Ct
	166	280	40	13,289	224	55.37	45	58	200
Bowl	M	Inn	Wkts	Avg	BBI	BBM	5i	10m	SR
	166	272	292	32.65	6/54	9/92	5	0	69.2

Jacques Kallis is the odd man out in this XI of dashers, with his Test strike rate just 45.97. He eschewed the attacking role to become the foundation on which many South African innings, and victories, were built. It wasn't that he couldn't attack – his strike rate in ODIs and T20s was substantially higher – he just chose to prize his wicket for the sake of his side.

Kallis's statistics also place him near the top of the pile of all-rounders in Test cricket history, with his fast-medium bowling taking nearly 300 wickets. The difference between his batting and bowling averages is 22.72 which sits just behind Sobers, whose difference is 23.75. His bowling also allows two spinners to be chosen in this XI.

Debuting in 1995 at Durban against England, Kallis made just one at his only bat and didn't bowl.

In his seventh Test against Australia in 1997, Kallis scored his maiden Test ton in the second innings of the Melbourne Test and in so doing helped South Africa hang on for a draw on a wearing pitch.

In 1998–99, Kallis had his first substantial all-round series at home to the West Indies as he scored 485 runs at 68.28 with one century and picked up 17 wickets with his first five-for of 5/90.

Kallis led the runs aggregate when New Zealand toured for three Tests in 2000–01 with 287 at 71.75 including 160 at Bloemfontein.

In 2001, Kallis had his best series with the ball taking 20 wickets at 19.75 in the West Indies with best figures of 6/67.

Kallis's best series with the bat was also against the West Indies in 2004 at home, where he scored 712 runs in four Tests at a huge average of 178 with a century in each Test and a high of 177 at Durban.

In 2004–05 England toured, and Kallis led the way for South Africa scoring 625 runs in the five Tests at an average of 69.44 with three more hundreds.

Kallis led the runs tally and averages against India in three Tests in 2010–11, with 498 runs at 166 including his first double ton.

Kallis's career came to an end after the 2013–14 series versus India at home, where he managed a credible average of 49.66.

He has coached in various roles since finishing his playing career.

5. Sachin Tendulkar (IND) vc

Test Record

Bat	M	Inn	NO	Runs	HS	Avg	100	50	Ct
	200	329	33	15,921	248*	53.78	51	68	115
Bowl	M	Inn	Wkts	Avg	BBI	BBM	5i	10m	SR
	200	145	46	54.17	3/10	3/14	0	0	92.1

*not out

Sachin Tendulkar is in the discussion for the greatest batter ever after Sir Donald Bradman. ESPNcricinfo wrote of him: 'Tendulkar's considerable achievements seem greater still when looked at in the light of the burden of expectation he had to bear from his adoring but somewhat unreasonable followers, who were prone to regarding anything less than a hundred in every innings as a failure. He still remains, by a distance, the most worshipped cricketer in the world.'

He had all the shots and no single one stood out because they were all so good, with perfect balance at the crease and an attacking mindset that could be tempered if the need arose.

Tendulkar debuted as a 16-year-old in 1989 against Pakistan and managed 215 runs in four Tests at 35.83. His debut also involved getting hit in the face by Waqar Younis.

He brought up his first Test century as a 17-year-old at Old Trafford, undefeated on 119, averaging 61.25 for the series. Two years later he took apart the Australian attack in Sydney to the tune of 148 not out. Tendulkar's career was up and running.

Tendulkar averaged over 100 versus England at home and then against Sri Lanka away in 1993.

Further series with hundred-plus averages followed against Australia in 1998 and New Zealand in 1999, against whom he brought up his first double century (217 at Ahmedabad).

In 2003–04 the Australians again felt the wrath of Tendulkar's bat as he scored 383 runs at 76.60 in four Tests. Tendulkar recorded his highest Test score of 248 not out versus Bangladesh later in 2004.

He continued to be prolific and scored more than 100 against every Test-playing nation.

Tendulkar's final innings came in his 200th match in 2013 and it was a fine 74 against the West Indies at Wankhede.

Tendulkar holds the record by some margin for the most runs in Test cricket as well as the most centuries. He also holds the record for the most runs and centuries in international cricket (including Tests, ODIs and T20s)

He captained India 25 times for just four wins and nine losses.

In 1998 and 2010, Tendulkar was named leading cricketer of the year by *Wisden*. In 2014, India awarded him Bharat Ratna, India's highest civilian award. He is, of course, a member of the ICC Cricket Hall of Fame.

6. Brian Lara (WI)

Test Record

Bat	M	Inn	NO	Runs	HS	Avg	100	50	Ct
	131	232	6	11,953	400*	52.88	34	48	164

Bowl	M	Inn	Wkts	Avg	BBI	BBM	5i	10m	SR
	131	4	0	-	-	-	0	0	-

*not out

At his very best, it is arguable that Lara was the finest batter of his generation. Lara had a penchant for building massive scores rather quickly and with an elegance. He holds the record for the highest Test and First Class scores and, for a time, was the leading run scorer in Test cricket history before Tendulkar sailed past.

Lara was made captain of Trinidad and Tobago at just 20 in 1990 and he made his Test debut the same year, scoring 44 and six against Pakistan at Lahore.

He really announced his arrival in Test cricket in his fifth Test match in 1993 when he made 277 against Australia in Sydney. In the five Test series, he scored a total of 466 runs at an average of 58.25.

England toured the West Indies in 1994, and Lara struck 798 runs in the five Tests at 99.75 including the then-record high Test score of 375 at St John's. He also scored 167 at Georgetown.

When the West Indies visited England in 1995, Lara chalked up a series-leading 765 runs at 85 with three centuries in consecutive Tests.

Australia toured the West Indies in 1999 and Lara again led the way with 546 runs at 91 with a high score of 213.

In 2001–02, Lara crafted three centuries in three Tests against Sri Lanka and averaged 114.66 for the series including a double century.

Matthew Hayden had briefly taken the mantle for highest Test score from Lara, but he snatched it back by becoming the first and only Test player to score 400 as he scored exactly that, not out, again at St John's against England.

In 2005, Lara scored 393 runs in three Tests at 78.60 versus South Africa, and then 331 runs in two Tests against Pakistan with a best of 153.

Lara's final series was in Pakistan, and he went out on top as he led the runs aggregate for the West Indies with 448 runs in three Tests at 89.60 with a highest score of 216 in the second Test at Multan.

Lara captained the West Indies in three separate stints for a total of 47 matches with ten wins and 26 losses.

Post-cricket, Lara has done both coaching and commentary.

Lara was inducted into the ICC Cricket Hall of Fame in 2012.

7. Adam Gilchrist (AUS) wk

Test Record

Bat	Ma	Inn	NO	Runs	HS	Avg	100	50	Ct	St
	96	137	20	5570	204*	47.60	17	26	379	37

*not out

Adam Gilchrist hit the ball as hard as any player in the history of Test cricket. His Test strike rate is 81.95 which compares more than favourably with the greats of the game. His batting philosophy was simple: 'Just hit the ball.'

With the gloves, he was solid behind the stumps and briefly held the world record for most dismissals by a keeper in Test cricket.

Gilchrist was made to wait behind Ian Healy for his debut, but he grasped the opportunity with both hands. He eventually debuted in 1999, aged nearly 28, against Pakistan and scored 81 in his only bat, took five catches and made a stumping.

His second Test produced one of his three best in Test cricket, as he came to the wicket with Australia 5/126 chasing 369 for victory. He scored 149 not out off 163 balls and added 238 with Justin Langer to grab an unlikely win.

Gilchrist's second great innings came in 2002 in South Africa, where he scored an emotional 204 not out off 213 balls at Johannesburg. At the time, it was the fastest double century in terms of balls faced in the history of Test cricket. He followed it up with 138 not out in the next Test.

His third notable innings was against England in 2006 at Perth where he blasted a hundred off just 57 balls, missing Viv Richard's record by just one ball.

In between, Gilchrist scored hundreds against all the Test-playing nations, often at breakneck speed and often when Australia most needed him to produce. That doesn't include his countless influential knocks at the top of the order in ODIs.

Gilchrist's best two series with the gloves came with 24 catches and two stumpings both in the Ashes, firstly in England in 2001 and again at home in 2006–07.

He retired from Test cricket after the Indian series in the summer of 2007–08.

Gilchrist stood in as captain of Australia on six occasions for four wins, including the first Australian series win in India in 35 years in 2004.

An inductee in the ICC Cricket Hall of Fame, Gilchrist's voice can these days be heard from the commentary box.

8. Shaun Pollock (SA)

Test Record

Bat	M	Inn	NO	Runs	HS	Avg	100	50	Ct
	108	156	39	3781	111	32.31	2	16	72

Bowl	M	Inn	Wkts	Avg	BBI	BBM	5i	10m	SR
	108	202	421	23.11	7/87	10/147	16	1	57.8

A bowling all-rounder, Pollock relied on moving the ball both ways at a lively pace. Perhaps he underperformed with the bat over his Test career, but he holds his place in the 2000s XI for his bowling alone and any runs would be a bonus.

He also kept things tight and was difficult to score from, as his Test economy rate of 2.39 runs per over proves.

The Pollocks are a famed cricketing family in South Africa, with Shaun's dad Peter opening the bowling in the 1960s and his uncle Graeme being a member of the 1970s XI in this book.

Pollock was brought into the South African side for the 1995–96 series against England and although his Dad, Peter, was chairman of selectors there was no hint of favouritism. He showed he was up to Test standard by taking 16 wickets in the series including 5/32 in the Cape Town Test.

On the 1997–98 tour of Australia, Pollock picked up 16 wickets in five Tests and showed his fortitude with 7/87 in 41 overs on a perfect batting pitch at Adelaide.

In 1998, he collected a series-leading 29 wickets against the West Indies at home at 16.65 with three five-fors in the series.

Against Sri Lanka in 2001, Pollock scored his maiden Test hundred with 111 at Centurion.

Probably his best all-round series came in 2001 in the West Indies as he brought up his second Test century in scoring 302 runs at 75.50 and picking up 20 dismissals with a best of 5/28.

In England in 2003, Pollock collected 17 wickets in four Tests and also scored 205 runs at 68.33 to further underline his all-round potential.

England then toured in 2004–05 and Pollock dismissed 21 batters but couldn't stop England from winning the series and his best was 4/32. Pollock's last five for in Test cricket was October 2003.

Pollock's last Test was versus the West Indies in 2008 and he took 4/35 and 1/50.

Pollock captained South Africa 26 times in the wake of the Hansie Cronje affair, before handing the reigns to Graeme Smith, for 14 wins and five losses.

He has worked as a commentator and is an inductee in the ICC Cricket Hall of Fame.

9. Anil Kumble (IND)

Test Record

Bat	M	Inn	NO	Runs	HS	Avg	100	50	Ct
	132	173	32	2506	110*	17.77	1	5	60

Bowl	M	Inn	Wkts	Avg	BBI	BBM	5i	10m	SR
	132	236	619	29.65	10/74	14/149	35	8	65.9

*not out

With Jacques Kallis in the XI as the third seamer, there was a free spot for another spinner alongside Muralidaran. It came down to Anil Kumble or Harbhajan Singh (417 wickets at 32.46) but in the end Kumble was chosen as he has a slightly better record and his leg-spin complements Muralidaran's off-spinners.

Kumble was a quicker leg-spinner and his deliveries spat off the wicket rather than relying on flight to deceive the batters. He ended his career as the highest wicket-taker in Indian Test history and currently sits in fourth on the all-time list. Kumble also has the most five-wicket innings hauls for India and is tied with Ravi Ashwin for the most ten-wicket hauls in a match.

Debuting at Old Trafford in 1990, Kumble took 3/105 in the first innings and went wicketless in the second. It was two years before he got another opportunity, where he took three more wickets from Zimbabwe.

In 1993 he captured 21 English batters at home with a best of 6/64 and more or less cemented his place in the Indian side.

Australia toured India in 1998 and Kumble picked up 23 wickets in the three Tests with 6/98 his best bowling at Bengaluru in a losing effort.

In 1999, he took 21 wickets in two Tests versus Pakistan which included becoming just the second Test player (after Jim Laker) to take all ten wickets in an innings with 10/74 at Delhi and match figures of 14/149.

Kumble showed his grit and bowled with a bandaged broken jaw against the West Indies at St John's in 2002 for 1/29 off 14 overs.

He took a series-leading 24 wickets in Australia in 2003–04 with best bowling figures of 8/141 (match figures of 12/279) in the third and final Test in Sydney.

In the West Indies in 2006, Kumble captured another series-leading 23 wickets in the four Tests and bowled India to victory in the fourth Test with 6/78 at Kingston in a low-scoring affair.

At The Oval in 2007 Kumble managed his sole Test century, 110 not out, but went wicketless in the match.

Kumble took another 20 wickets in Australia in 2007–08, but by the end of the year had had enough and called time on his Test career.

Captaining India 14 times, Kumble had three wins and five losses. He also coached India for a period but stepped down after reports emerged which suggested he had an 'intimidating' style of man management.

Kumble was inducted into the ICC Cricket Hall of Fame in 2015.

10. Muthiah Muralidaran (SL)

Test Record

Bat	M	Inn	NO	Runs	HS	Avg	100	50	Ct
	133	164	56	1261	67	11.67	0	1	72

Bowl	M	Inn	Wkts	Avg	BBI	BBM	5i	10m	SR
	133	230	800	22.72	9/51	16/220	67	22	55.0

The leading wicket-taker in the history of Test cricket, 'Murali' goes down as one of the all-time great cricketers. However, as Dileep Premachandran wrote, 'Perhaps no cricketer since Douglas Jardine has polarised opinion quite like Muthiah Muralidaran. For the believers, he's among the greatest to ever spin a ball. For the doubters, he's a charlatan undeserving of the game's greatest records, responsible for changes in the laws that they think have legitimised throwing. What was undeniable was his ability to turn the ball sharply on just about any surface, and bowl the sort of marathon spells that would have seen a lesser man retire after five seasons rather than 18.'

Murali was much more effective at home with an average of 19.56 and strike rate of 50.8 versus 27.79 and 61.8 away. 612 of his 800 wickets came on the sub-continent.

He debuted against Australia in 1992 at Colombo and took three wickets. Murali picked up regular wickets thereafter, taking his first five-for against South Africa in 1993.

In the days when Sri Lanka were only accorded one Test series, in a single Test at The Oval in 1998 Murali took 7/155 and 9/65 to bowl Sri Lanka to victory over England.

Then, in 2000, Murali captured 26 wickets versus Pakistan in three Tests and repeated the dose with another 26 in three Tests against South Africa later that year with a best of 7/84 at Galle.

Zimbabwe toured in 2001–02 and Murali destroyed them with 30 wickets in three Tests at 9.80 runs per wicket and his best bowling in an innings of 9/51 at Kandy.

In 2004, Murali took 28 wickets in three Tests at home to the might of Australia including four five-fors and a best of 6/59 at Galle.

Murali added a further 26 in three Tests versus Bangladesh in 2007 at 10.84 with three five-fors, including 6/28 at Kandy.

His final Test came in 2010 versus India at Galle, and he collected 5/63 in the first innings to help Sri Lanka to a ten-wicket win.

All up, Murali took a world record 67 five wickets in an innings (30 better than second placed Shane Warne) and ten wickets in a match 22 times (12 better than again second place Shane Warne).

Murali has worked as a bowling coach in various capacities since his retirement from Test cricket.

Naturally, he is an inductee in the ICC Cricket Hall of Fame.

11. Glenn McGrath (AUS)

Test Record

Bat	M	Inn	NO	Runs	HS	Avg	100	50	Ct
	124	138	51	641	61	7.36	0	1	38
Bowl	M	Inn	Wkts	Avg	BBI	BBM	5i	10m	SR
	124	243	563	21.64	8/24	10/57	29	3	51.9

Glenn McGrath retired as the leading wicket-taker by a fast bowler in the history of Test cricket. He did not rely on outright pace but rather on a nagging line and length with seam movement both ways. His economy rate of 2.49 is miserly.

McGrath was also known for knocking over the big names in the opposition: he dismissed Michael Atherton 19 times, which is a record for the most times a batter has been dismissed by a single bowler. He also picked up Tendulkar 13 times and Lara 15 times.

He was catapulted into the Australian side against New Zealand in 1993 after an injury to Merv Hughes, and he picked up three wickets.

McGrath picked up his first five-for in the West Indies in 1995, taking 5/68 at Bridgetown and 6/47 at Port of Spain to help Australia to a historic series win.

In 1997, he collected 36 dismissals in the six Test Ashes series in England at 19.47, with his best bowling 8/38 at Lord's and 7/76 at The Oval.

Australia was back in the West Indies in 1999 and McGrath took a series-leading 30 wickets at 16.93 with four five-wicket hauls in an innings, including 5/50 and 5/28 at Port of Spain.

McGrath was again successful in England in 2001, adding a further 32 wickets to his tally at 16.93 with another four five-fors, including 5/54 at Lord's and 7/76 at Headingly.

In 2004–05, McGrath took 18 wickets in three Tests at 14.44 at home to Pakistan, including his best Test bowling of 8/24 at Perth.

He then dismissed another 18 batters at an average of 15.72 on the subsequent tour of New Zealand.

McGrath's Test career finished in the 5–0 drubbing of England at home in 2006–07, where he took 21 wickets with a best of 6/50 at the Gabba. He took a wicket with the last ball of his career.

He played on to the ODI World Cup in 2007 and was leading wicket-taker and player of the tournament as he helped Australia to a hat-trick of World Cups.

Since his playing career, McGrath has commentated but is best known for the McGrath Foundation, run in memory of his first wife Jane, which raises money to fight breast cancer.

McGrath is a member of the Australian and ICC Cricket Halls of Fame.

2000s Second XI

1. Graeme Smith (SA) c
2. Andrew Strauss (ENG)
3. Rahul Dravid (IND)
4. Mahela Jayawardene (SL) vc
5. Mohammad Yousuf (PAK)
6. Shivnarine Chanderpaul (WI)
7. Kumar Sangakkara (SL) wk
8. Chaminda Vaas (SL)
9. Brett Lee (AUS)
10. Harbhajan Singh (IND)
11. Makhaya Ntini (SA)

2010s and 2020s

The 2010s and 2020s to date has seen a close tussle for supremacy between Australia, India and South Africa. Australia has a win rate of 52%, India 51% and South Africa 49%.

Ireland played their first Test against Pakistan in Dublin in 2018 and lost by five wickets. Afghanistan played their first Test against India at Bengaluru, also in 2018, and were beaten by an innings but won their second Test versus Ireland by seven wickets.

The era also saw the introduction of the ICC World Test Championship, where points are available for every Test and the top-two sides meet in the final every two years. The first edition was played from 2019–2021 and India and New Zealand met in the final at Southampton. In a low-scoring affair, India made 217 and 170 while New Zealand made 249 in their first innings and then chased down the winning runs in their second to claim the title of world champions.

The second edition, played from 2021–23, saw Australia and India meet in the final at The Oval. Australia batted first and made

469 and then 8dec/270 and India responded with 296 and 234, leaving Australia winners by 209 runs.

There have also been four One Day International World Cups played during the era, with Australia winning two and India and England one each. England and the West Indies have each won two T20 World Cups while Australia and Sri Lanka have won one each.

England's Joe Root is the comfortable leader on the runs standings, nearly 2000 runs in front of Australia's Steve Smith who has the best batting average for the era. England are on top of the wickets tally as well, with Jimmy Anderson leading the way from countryman Stuart Broad.

The batting line-up for this era's XI virtually chose itself, with Alistair Cook and David Warner as the openers selected in front of a resurgent Usman Khawaja – although by the time his career is done Khawaja may have an undisputed claim to one of the opening slots. The middle order of Root, Smith, India's Virat Kohli and New Zealand's Kane Williamson is difficult to argue with, although AB de Villiers from South Africa and Australian Michael Clarke did average around 50 in Test cricket. But who would you leave out to leave space for them?

Anderson gets one of the fast bowling spots through sheer weight of wickets, while Australia's Pat Cummins and South Africa's Kagiso Rabada have such outstanding bowling averages and strike rates that they demand selection. This means fast bowlers of the calibre of Broad, Mitchell Starc and Trent Boult have missed out despite excelling during the era. The spinners position came down to a tussle between Ravi Ashwin and Nathan Lyon, with Lyon having a handful more wickets but Ashwin having a better bowling average (23.91 versus 30.35) and a better strike rate (51.3 versus 61.9). On this basis, Ashwin made the cut.

The wicketkeeper's spot was a decision between India's MS Dhoni, BJ Watling of New Zealand and Quinton de Kock of South

Africa. All three average around 38 with the bat (as does Jonny Bairstow) and Watling made the most dismissals by a keeper in the era. De Kock averages 2.367 dismissals per innings as against 2.086 for Watling and 1.912 for Dhoni. However, given Dhoni's influence on the team as the captain, the keeper's spot – and captaincy – has gone to Dhoni.

Most Runs in Period

Player	Mat	Inns	NO	Runs	HS	Ave	SR	100	50
JE Root (ENG)	137	251	20	11468	254	49.64	56.77	30	60
SPD Smith (AUS)	107	191	25	9634	239	58.03	53.59	32	41
V Kohli (IND)	113	191	11	8848	254*	49.15	55.56	29	30
AN Cook (ENG)	111	201	11	8818	294	46.41	46.93	23	37
DA Warner (AUS)	112	205	8	8786	335*	44.59	70.19	26	37
KS Williamson (NZ)	98	171	17	8498	251	55.18	51.44	31	33
CA Pujara (IND)	103	176	11	7195	206*	43.60	44.36	19	35
A Ali (PAK)	97	180	11	7142	302*	42.26	41.93	19	35
AD Mathews (SL)	100	178	25	7123	200*	46.55	48.04	16	38
FDM Karunaratne (SL)	89	170	7	6740	244	41.34	51.58	16	35

*not out

Most Wickets in Period

Player	Mat	Inns	Wkts	BBI	BBM	Ave	SR	5	10
JM Anderson (ENG)	140	263	547	7/42	11/71	24.04	55.6	25	3
SCJ Broad (ENG)	143	268	531	8/15	11/121	26.76	54.6	17	3
NM Lyon (AUS)	127	238	517	8/50	13/154	30.73	62.7	23	4
R Ashwin (IND)	97	183	499	7/59	13/140	23.92	51.5	34	8
HMRKB Herath (SL)	72	133	363	9/127	14/184	26.41	57.5	30	9
TG Southee (NZ)	92	175	361	7/64	10/108	28.46	57.9	14	1
MA Starc (AUS)	87	166	353	6/50	11/94	27.52	48.4	14	2
TA Boult (NZ)	78	149	317	6/30	10/80	27.49	54.9	10	1
K Rabada (SA)	62	112	291	7/112	13/144	22.05	39.2	14	4
RA Jadeja (IND)	69	130	280	7/42	10/110	24.42	59.5	12	2

Results

Team	Mat	Won	Lost	Tied	Draw	W/L
England	175	81	63	0	31	1.285
Australia	147	77	46	0	24	1.673
India	143	74	42	0	27	1.761
South Africa	118	58	38	0	21	1.526
New Zealand	112	47	40	0	24	1.175
Pakistan	112	44	49	0	19	0.897
Sri Lanka	122	41	52	0	29	0.788
West Indies	113	31	58	0	24	0.534
Bangladesh	79	16	51	0	12	0.313
Zimbabwe	34	5	26	0	3	0.192
Afghanistan	8	3	5	0	0	0.600
Ireland	7	0	7	0	0	0.000

2010s and 2020s XI

1. Alastair Cook (ENG)
2. David Warner (AUS)
3. Joe Root (ENG)
4. Steve Smith (AUS)
5. Virat Kohli (IND)
6. Kane Williamson (NZ) vc
7. MS Dhoni (IND) c wk
8. Ravi Ashwin (IND)
9. Pat Cummins (AUS)
10. Kagiso Rabada (SA)
11. James Anderson (ENG)

1. Alastair Cook (ENG)

Test Record

Bat	M	Inn	NO	Runs	HS	Avg	100	50	Ct
	161	291	16	12,472	294	45.35	33	57	175
Bowl	M	Inn	Wkts	Avg	BBI	BBM	5i	10m	SR
	124	2	1	7.00	1/6	1/6	0	0	18.0

Alastair Cook holds the record for most Test runs and most Test centuries for England, although Joe Root is closing in fast on both records. Cook also holds the record for most consecutive Test matches at 159.

Never an overly elegant batter, Cook had a steely determination to succeed at the highest level and won the respect of his teammates, opposition players and fans alike.

Cook made a century (104 not out) on debut in the second innings against India at Nagpur in 2006 to go with his 60 in the first innings. Later that year, he followed it up with two centuries versus Pakistan at home and averaged 57.57 for the four Test series.

In 2009 against the West Indies, Cook scored 209 runs in two Tests at an average of 104.50 and a top score of 160 at Chester-le-Street.

Cook anchored England's first victory in Australia in 24 years in 2010–11, scoring a series-leading 766 runs at 127.66 with a best of 235 not out made at Brisbane.

He followed this up with 390 runs in three Tests at home to Sri Lanka at an average of 97.50, including two centuries with 133 at Cardiff and 106 at Lord's.

Cook made his highest Test score versus India later in 2011 as he notched 294 at Birmingham, out chasing a wide delivery.

In 2012 in India, Cook's powers of concentration were on display as he scored centuries in three consecutive Tests to make 562 runs in three Tests at 80.28 with a highest score of 190.

England took on Pakistan in three Tests in the UAE in 2015, and Cook knocked up another series-leading effort of 450 runs at 90 including a top score of 263.

Cook's knack of logging big scores continued with 243 against the West Indies at Birmingham in 2017 and 244 not out versus Australia at the MCG in 2018.

His final Test was against India at The Oval in 2018 and he went out as he started with a century in his final innings, making 147 to go with his 71 in the first innings.

Cook captained England 59 times for 24 wins and 22 losses.

After cricket, Cook was a columnist and has worked for various charitable causes. He was knighted for his services to cricket.

2. David Warner (AUS)

Test Record

Bat	M	Inn	NO	Runs	HS	Avg	100	50	Ct
	112	205	8	8786	335*	44.59	26	37	91
Bowl	**M**	**Inn**	**Wkts**	**Avg**	**BBI**	**BBM**	**5i**	**10m**	**SR**
	112	19	4	67.25	2/45	2/45	0	0	85.5

*not out

David Warner was a pugnacious attacking opening batter who could be relied on to get the innings off to a quick start. He was a genuine star in all three formats of the game after starting his international career in T20 with a 43 ball 89.

However, Warner was denounced as the chief protagonist in the 2018 ball tampering scandal in South Africa and Cricket Australia suspended him for 12 months and stripped him of the vice-captaincy.

Chosen for his first Test in 2011 off the back of his T20 performances, despite having never played a First Class match, Warner scored his first Test hundred in his second Test with 123 not out (carrying his bat through the innings) at Hobart against New Zealand.

In 2014 in three Tests versus South Africa, Warner led the runs aggregate and averages with 543 runs at 90.50 with three centuries, including 135 and 145 at Cape Town.

Warner again led the way against the Kiwis in 2015 at home, where he scored 592 runs in three Tests at 98.66 with his then-highest Test score of 253 at Perth plus a century in each innings in Brisbane.

Pakistan toured Australia in 2016–17 and Warner contributed 356 runs at 71.20 in the three Tests. This included becoming just the fifth player to score a century before lunch on the first morning of a Test match as he brought up his ton in just 78 balls at the SCG.

Pakistan again wore the brunt of Warner's bat as he made 489 runs for once out in two Tests in 2019, including his highest Test score of 335 not out at Adelaide to go with 154 at Brisbane. His triple century came at a strike rate of 80.

Warner's output dipped slightly from this point but he still contributed, including a memorable 200 against South Africa at the MCG in 2022.

His final series came versus Pakistan in 2023–24 where he scored a credible 299 runs at 49.83 with a final century (164) in the first Test at Perth.

After his retirement from Test cricket, Warner has played on in T20 internationals and is planning full retirement later in 2024.

3. Joe Root (ENG)

Test Record

Bat	M	Inn	NO	Runs	HS	Avg	100	50	Ct
	137	251	20	11,468	254	49.64	30	60	188

Bowl	M	Inn	Wkts	Avg	BBI	BBM	5i	10m	SR
	137	140	65	43.87	5/8	5/33	1	0	81.2

In the early part of his career Root was considered as an opener for England but, with a more expansive game, it became evident he was destined for a spot at three or four. Root relies on precision and timing rather than brute strength to accumulate his runs.

Root is the leading run-maker of those still playing, and is closing in on Alastair Cook's record for most Test runs for England.

Debuting against India at Nagpur in 2012, Root made a measured 73 and showed he had the skill and determination to succeed at the highest level.

Root's maiden Test century came at home at Headingly versus New Zealand as he stroked 104 and averaged 60.75 for the series.

His first double hundred (an even 200 not out) was scored against Sri Lanka at Lord's in 2014.

He then led the way against India at home as he scored 518 runs at 103.6, including two centuries and a high score of 154 not out at Trent Bridge.

In 2016 versus Pakistan, he contributed a series-leading 512 runs in four Tests at 73.14 including his highest Test score of 254 at Old Trafford.

England toured Sri Lanka in 2021 and Root was again on top with 426 runs in just two Tests at 106.5 with scores of 228 and 186.

Later that year, India visited England and Root once again led the runs aggregate and averages scoring 737 runs at an average of 105.28 and a best of 180 not out at Lord's.

Root scored 396 runs against New Zealand at home in 2022 at 99 including two centuries, the best being 176 at Trent Bridge. When England visited New Zealand in 2023, Root added a further 319 runs at 106.33.

He had a solid Ashes series in 2023 with 412 runs in the five Tests at an average of 51.50 and one century (118 not out) at Birmingham.

Root was captain of England for a period after Alastair Cook before handing the reigns to Ben Stokes. He skippered his nation 67 times for 27 wins and 26 losses.

4. Steve Smith (AUS)

Test Record

Bat	M	Inn	NO	Runs	HS	Avg	100	50	Ct
	107	191	25	9634	239	58.03	32	41	180

Bowl	M	Inn	Wkts	Avg	BBI	BBM	5i	10m	SR
	107	62	19	53.05	3/18	4/83	0	0	77.3

When Steve Smith came into international cricket, his batting had many moving parts. He went away and tightened his technique to become the number one ranked batter in the world. Even today, Smith continues to tinker with his technique between series.

Another Australian to be lumbered with the 'best since Bradman' tag, Smith has scored heavily worldwide. He has all the shots, is sure footed against the spinners and particularly adept at the cut and pull against the faster bowlers.

He had his year out of the game as a result of turning a blind eye to the ball tampering in South Africa, and lost the captaincy he held dear. He was reinstated to the vice-captaincy position once he had served his two-year leadership ban.

Smith debuted as a leg-spinner who batted at eight in 2010 against Pakistan at Lord's as Australia searched in vain for the next Shane Warne.

It was two years later that Smith was chosen as an outright batter, and he made 92 versus India at Mohali. He brought up his first Test century (138 not out) soon after at The Oval.

In 2014–15, India toured Australia and Smith topped the runs tally and averages with 769 runs in three Tests at 128.15 with a hundred in each Test and a best of 190 at the MCG.

Smith scored his first double century against England at Lord's on the 2015 Ashes tour. He averaged 56.44 for the series.

In three Tests versus Pakistan in 2016–17, Smith racked up 441 runs at 110.25 with a best of 165 not out at the MCG to go with 130 at Brisbane.

Smith led the way in the 2017–18 Ashes with 687 runs at 137.40, including three hundreds with the best being his highest Test score to date of 239 made at Perth.

On his return from his suspension, Smith picked up where he left off against the English in England with another series-topping 774 runs in four Tests at an average of 110.57 with three more hundreds, including 211 at Old Trafford.

In Pakistan in 2022, Smith added another 226 runs at 56.50 but did not score a century. Later that year he added another undefeated double hundred against the West Indies again at Perth.

2023 was a quiet year by Smith's standards, with just three centuries highlighted by 110 against England at Lord's. He started 2024 brightly with 91 not out versus the West Indies.

Smith has captained Australia 38 times for 21 wins, a 55% win rate, and ten losses.

He now bowls only very occasionally, but is still a renowned slip-fielder.

5. Virat Kohli (IND)

Test Record

Bat	M	Inn	NO	Runs	HS	Avg	100	50	Ct
	113	191	11	8848	254*	49.15	29	30	111
Bowl	M	Inn	Wkts	Avg	BBI	BBM	5i	10m	SR
	113	11	0	-	-	-	0	0	-

*not out

No-one apart from Tendulkar has received the adulation from his home fans that Virat Kohli receives. Kohli burst onto the scene as a precocious talent and captain of India's world cup winning under-19 side. He has combined a technically correct batting approach with a zeal for fitness to dominate across all three forms of cricket. Kohli is now the leading century-maker in ODIs, passing Tendulkar at the 2023 World Cup.

Kohli has scored a century home and away against every Test nation he has played bar one in Bangladesh (he is yet to play Ireland or Afghanistan).

Debuting in 2011 in the West Indies, Kohli began slowly with a couple of fifties in his fourth Test. He was taken on the Australian tour that followed and in the third Test at Adelaide scored his maiden Test ton of 116.

A successful series at home to the Kiwis came next, with 212 runs in the two Tests, an average over 100 and another century.

Back in Australia in 2014–15, Kohli topped the runs tally for India as he knocked up 692 runs at 86.50 in four Tests with twin centuries at Adelaide and another two at the MCG and SCG.

Kohli led the overall runs aggregate and averages against England at home in 2016–17 with 655 runs at 109.16 and a top score of 235 at Wankhede. He followed it up with a double century versus Bangladesh at Hyderabad.

Sri Lanka toured India in 2017 and Kohli notched a century in each of the three Tests, with doubles at Nagpur and Delhi to score 610 runs at 152.50.

South Africa visited in 2019, and Kohli averaged 158.50 in the three Tests boosted by 254 not out – his highest Test score – at Pune in the second Test.

In 2019, Kohli scored 136 against Bangladesh at Eden Gardens but then had to wait over three years before his next century, 186 versus the Australians at Ahmedabad.

Kohli had a successful tour of the West Indies near the end of 2023, scoring 76 and 121 to average 98.50 and lead the averages for the series.

He has also captained India on 68 occasions, capturing 40 wins (a win rate of 58%) and suffering 17 losses.

6. Kane Williamson (NZ) vc

Test Record

Bat	M	Inn	NO	Runs	HS	Avg	100	50	Ct
	97	170	16	8490	251	55.12	31	33	88

Bowl	M	Inn	Wkts	Avg	BBI	BBM	5i	10m	SR
	97	67	30	40.23	4/44	4/44	0	0	71.7

Kane Williamson is New Zealand's most prolific batter, sitting at nearly 1000 runs in front of next-best Ross Taylor. Williamson's copybook approach to batting is unaffected by the T20 bug, yet he excels in all formats of the game. At the time of writing, Williamson is the number one ranked Test batter by the ICC.

His number of Tests played suffers from New Zealand playing only two or three Test series and not the four or five series that Australia, India and England play.

Williamson debuted in 2010 against India at Ahmedabad, and scored a hundred (131) in his first innings in a drawn match.

His next hundred (102 not out) came against South Africa at home in 2012 as he averaged 57.25 in the three Test series.

In 2013–14, Williamson scored 250 runs in two Tests at 83.33 versus Bangladesh, including 114 at Chattogram.

Sri Lanka toured New Zealand in 2014–15 and Williamson scored a series-topping 396 runs at 198 with his average boosted by 242 not out – his first double hundred – at Wellington.

Against Australia in 2015, Williamson knocked up a century in each of the first two Tests, with 140 at Brisbane and 166 at Perth, for a total of 428 runs at 85.60.

Versus Pakistan in the UAE in 2018, Williamson scored 386 runs at an average of 77.20 in three Tests, including 139 in the third Test at Abu Dhabi.

Williamson brought up his highest Test score of 251 against the West Indies in 2020 at Hamilton.

He followed this up with 200 not out against Pakistan at Karachi. Then, in 2023, he scored 215 versus Sri Lanka in Wellington.

In early 2024, Williamson scored 270 runs at 90 in two Tests against South Africa with a century in each innings in the Test at Mount Maunganui.

Williamson has skippered New Zealand 40 times for 22 wins and ten losses.

7. MS Dhoni (IND) c wk

Test Record

Bat	Ma	Inn	NO	Runs	HS	Avg	100	50	Ct	St
	90	144	16	4876	224	38.09	6	33	256	38

MS Dhoni probably ranks in the top-three most popular Indian cricketers of all time, along with Tendulkar and Kohli. Neither his batting nor keeping were textbook, but both were highly effective in Test cricket as well as in the shorter forms of the game.

Dhoni is also possibly India's most successful captain, with his side ranked number one in Tests for 18 months as well as winning the ODI and T20 World Cups. In all, he captained India in 60 Tests for 27 wins and 18 losses.

He debuted at Chennai in 2005 against Sri Lanka, where he made 30 and took a single catch. In his debut series, he averaged 37.25 and made six dismissals.

In his next series versus Pakistan, Dhoni scored his maiden Test hundred – 148 at Faisalabad – and averaged 59.66 with seven catches and a stumping.

When England toured in 2006, he held 13 catches and made three stumpings in just three Tests and had a top score of 64. Following this series, India toured the West Indies for four Tests and Dohni completed another 17 dismissals.

In 2009–10, Dhoni hit a purple patch with the bat, averaging 77.50 versus New Zealand, 107 against Sri Lanka, 89 versus Bangladesh and 81.50 against South Africa. He scored three centuries during this period, his best being 132 not out at Eden Gardens.

Australia toured India in 2013 and Dhoni made 224 at Chennai, his highest Test score and part of 326 runs at 81.50 for the series to go with nine catches and five stumpings.

In England in 2014, Dhoni had his most productive series with the gloves with 17 catches in five Tests as well as a batting average of 34.90 and a high score of 82 at The Oval.

Dhoni retired from Test cricket after the third Test on the 2014–15 tour of Australia where he took 13 catches and a stumping, playing in two Tests.

He played on in the shorter forms of the game until the 2019 ODI World Cup, but has continued in the IPL helping the Chennai Super Kings to success.

8. Ravi Ashwin (IND)

Test Record

Bat	M	Inn	NO	Runs	HS	Avg	100	50	Ct
	97	138	15	3271	124	26.59	5	14	32
Bowl	M	Inn	Wkts	Avg	BBI	BBM	5i	10m	SR
	97	183	499	23.92	7/59	13/140	34	8	51.5

The spinner's spot in this XI came down to a close call between Ravi Ashwin and Australia's Nathan Lyon. Both off-spinners, Lyon has a handful more wickets – but Ashwin's average is about four better than Lyon's and he strikes at 51.5 versus Lyon's 62.7. Ashwin's batting average is also more than double Lyon's (plus he has five Test centuries) so Ashwin has just got the nod.

Ashwin perfected his craft on the streets of Chennai, in particular the carrom ball where the ball is flicked out using a bent middle finger. In his first 16 Tests, Ashwin collected nine five-fors and he was the fastest bowler to 300 Test wickets and second fastest to take 400 wickets behind Muralidaran.

He had a debut to remember, claiming man of the match honours with 3/81 and 6/47 versus the West Indies at Delhi in 2011. Ashwin followed this up with another five for in the third Test to go with his maiden Test hundred of 103. All up he claimed 22 wickets in the three Tests.

In 2012, he picked up 18 wickets in two Tests against New Zealand with three five-wicket hauls and a best of 6/31. The following year Ashwin took 29 wickets in four Tests versus Australia with four five-fors and best bowling of 7/103 at Chennai.

Ashwin led the wickets tally in successive series in 2015, firstly with 21 wickets in three Tests against Sri Lanka, then 31 wickets in four Tests versus South Africa with a best of 7/66 at Nagpur.

In 2016 he again topped the wickets taken with 27 in three Tests in New Zealand, with his best Test bowling of 7/59, and then against England taking 28 wickets in five Tests with three five-fors.

When England toured in 2021, Ashwin was again on top with 32 wickets in the four Tests at an average of 14.71 and best bowling figures of 6/61 again at Chennai. Ashwin also scored a century at Chennai.

In 2023, Ashwin added a further 25 victims to his tally at home to Australia and then 15 in two Tests away against the West Indies, with his best being 7/71 at Roseau.

9. Pat Cummins (AUS)

Test Record

Bat	M	Inn	NO	Runs	HS	Avg	100	50	Ct
	60	85	12	1216	64*	16.65	0	3	31

Bowl	M	Inn	Wkts	Avg	BBI	BBM	5i	10m	SR
	60	111	263	22.40	6/23	10/62	12	2	46.6

*not out

Pat Cummins is a relentlessly effective fast bowler who has been ranked as the best bowler in the world and won the Allan Border medal for Australia's best male player in 2019.

Cummins debuted as an 18-year-old in South Africa in 2011. He took 6/79 in South Africa's second innings then made a cool 13 not out to help Australia to a series-equalling two-wicket win.

Injuries then intervened and Cummins did not play his next Test until six years later on the 2017 tour of India. He took eight wickets in two Tests but showing enough that he was going to be part of the Australian set up longer term.

Cummins led the Australian wickets tally with 23 in the 2017–18 Ashes and again on the 2018 tour of South Africa with 22 wickets in four Tests and a best of 5/83.

In the 2019 Ashes, Cummins led the wickets taken for either side with 29 at 19.62, although he did not take a five-for in the series.

India toured Australia in 2020–21 and Cummins was again the leading bowler for the four Test series with 21 dismissals at 20.04, but again picked up wickets consistently without a five-for.

Having been identified as a future captain, his rise to the position came earlier than expected when Tim Paine resigned shortly before the 2021–22 Ashes. The captaincy did not affect his form as he took the most wickets in the series for either side, with 21 in playing in four of the five Tests and a best of 5/38 at the Gabba in Brisbane.

He then picked up 12 wickets on the tour of Pakistan including 5/56 at Lahore to help Australia to a series win.

Cummins added another 18 wickets on the 2023 Ashes tour which included 6/91 at Headingly.

In the 2023–24 series versus Pakistan, Cummins claimed 19 poles in three Tests at an average of 12 with three five-fors and ten in the match at the MCG.

Cummins has captained Australia 26 times for 15 wins and six losses.

10. Kagiso Rabada (SA)

Test Record

Bat	M	Inn	NO	Runs	HS	Avg	100	50	Ct
	62	96	17	905	47	11.45	0	0	30

Bowl	M	Inn	Wkts	Avg	BBI	BBM	5i	10m	SR
	62	112	291	22.05	7/112	13/144	14	4	39.2

There were a number of players competing for this position. Australian Mitchell Starc, for example, would have given some variety with his left-arm fast bowling. Stuart Broad, who has over 600 Test wickets, was closely considered. However, Rabada's strike rate of a wicket every 39.2 deliveries at an average of 22.05 is impossible to ignore.

A strong and genuine quick, Rabada first came to the notice of South African cricket fans at the 2014 under-19 World Cup where he was the leading wicket-taker and helped South Africa to a win. In 2015 he claimed the best First Class bowling figures by a South African with 14/105.

Rabada made his Test debut later in 2015 against India at Mohali, where his first and only wicket was that of Indian captain Virat Kohli.

England then toured South Africa, and Rabada led the wickets tally for either side with 22 in the three Tests including 7/112 and 6/32 at Centurion.

Rabada again led total wickets when Sri Lanka toured in 2016–17, as he captured 19 dismissals at 17.15 including match figures of 10/92 at Cape Town.

In 2017, Rabada blasted out 15 Bangladeshi batters in two Tests with 5/33 and 5/30 at Bloemfontein in an innings victory.

Rabada was back on top of the wickets table when Australia toured in 2018, with 23 wickets in four Tests including 6/54 at Gqeberha, helping South Africa to a six-wicket win.

Another series-topping effort took place against India in 2021–22, where Rabada claimed 20 wickets at under 20 in the three Test series.

In 2022, Rabada added a further 14 wickets versus England in England, including 5/52, to get his name on the honour board at Lord's.

In two Tests against the West Indies in 2023, Rabada captured 12 batters at an average of 11 and a best of 6/50 at Centurion.

He followed this up in 2023–24 with 11 wickets against India at home at 14.72 with 5/59, again at Centurion.

11. James Anderson (ENG)

Test Record

Bat	M	Inn	NO	Runs	HS	Avg	100	50	Ct
	184	258	111	1351	81	9.19	0	1	105

Bowl	M	Inn	Wkts	Avg	BBI	BBM	5i	10m	SR
	184	343	695	26.34	7/42	11/71	32	3	56.7

James Anderson's longevity as a fast bowler is quite remarkable, as he bowled in Test matches into his 40s. He is the most prolific fast bowler of all time and sits third on the all-time list behind only Muralidaran and Warne.

Anderson's mastery of swing bowling is as good as any in the history of the game. His record is much better in the swing-friendly conditions of his home country, as his average is six runs better at home and his strike rate is 52.4 compared to 64.7 away.

Debuting at Lord's versus Zimbabwe in 2003, Anderson got off to a great start taking 5/73 in Zimbabwe's first innings. He took a further six in the next Test and was up and running.

However, it was not until 2008 when he had a dominant series at home and he took 19 wickets in three Tests against the Kiwis to lead the wickets tally for either side.

In 2010, he led the way for England with 23 wickets at 13.73 against Pakistan, including 5/54 and 6/17 at Trent Bridge for his best ever bowling in a match. Anderson followed this up with 24 wickets in Australia to lead the wicket-taking for either side and help England to a rare series win Down Under.

India toured in 2014 and Anderson was again on top with 25 wickets in the five Tests and a best of 5/53 at Southampton.

Anderson followed this up with 17 wickets in three Tests in the West Indies at 18, including 6/42 at Bridgetown in a losing effort.

In form against India at home in 2018, Anderson chimed in with 24 wickets, the best for either side, at an average of 18.12 and 5/20 at Lord's.

Anderson was again waiting for the Indians in 2021 and picked up 21 dismissals with another five-for at Lord's.

Since then, Anderson has picked up handy wickets when he has played for England but has not picked up another five-wicket innings haul, with his best being 4/18 in New Zealand.

2010s and 2020s Second XI

1. Usman Khawaja (AUS)
2. Marnus Labuschagne (AUS)
3. Hashim Amla (SA)
4. Michael Clarke (AUS) c
5. AB de Villiers (SA) vc
6. Ben Stokes (ENG)
7. Quinton de Kock (SA) wk
8. Stuart Broad (ENG)
9. Mitchell Starc (AUS)
10. Nathan Lyon (AUS)
11. Trent Boult (NZ)

Sundry Lists

Greatest All-Time XI

1. Jack Hobbs (ENG)
2. Sunil Gavaskar (IND)
3. Donald Bradman (AUS) c
4. Viv Richards (WI)
5. Sachin Tendulkar (IND)
6. Garry Sobers (WI)
7. Adam Gilchrist (AUS) wk
8. Imran Khan (PAK) vc
9. Malcolm Marshall (WI)
10. Shane Warne (AUS)
11. Sydney Barnes (ENG)

Greatest All-Time XI
One player from each era

1. Jack Hobbs (ENG) 1920s
2. Sunil Gavaskar (IND) 1970s
3. Don Bradman (AUS) 1930s c
4. Viv Richards (WI) 1980s vc
5. Steve Smith (AUS) 2010s and 2020s
6. Garry Sobers (WI) 1960s
7. Adam Gilchrist (AUS) 2000s wk
8. Keith Miller (AUS) 1940s and 1950s
9. Wasim Akram (PAK) 1990s
10. George Lohmann (ENG) 1800s
11. Sydney Barnes (ENG) 1900s

Greatest All-Time XI

One player from each Test-playing nation

1. Jack Hobbs (ENG)
2. Barry Richards (SA)
3. Donald Bradman (AUS) c
4. Sachin Tendulkar (IND)
5. Garry Sobers (WI)
6. Kumar Sangakkara (SL) wk
7. Andy Flower (ZIM)
8. Imran Khan (PAK) vc
9. Shakib Al Hasan (BAN)
10. Richard Hadlee (NZ)
11. Rashid Khan (AFG)
12. Kevin O'Brien (IRE)

Total of Batting Averages by Era

This list is made up by adding up the batting averages of all 11 players in an era. The Bradman-enhanced 1930s came out on top.

1. 1930s — 480
2. 2000s — 431
3. 1980s — 421
4. 2010s and '20s — 410
5. 1940s and '50s — 400
6. 1920s — 392
7. 1970s — 391
8. 1960s — 383
9. 1990s — 370
10. 1900s–WWI — 304
11. 1800s — 264

Best Test Win Rates by Era

Era	Best Nation	Win %
2000s	Australia	69
1940s and '50s	Australia	57
1930s	Australia	56
1800s	England	53
1980s	West Indies	52
1920s	Australia	50
2010s and '20s	Australia	52
1990s	Australia	50
Overall	Australia	48
1900–WWI	Australia	47
1960s	West Indies	37
1970s	Australia	36

The Author

Richard Smith grew up in regional Queensland where he developed his love of cricket as an enthusiastic but inconsistent opening batter at school. He grew a deep knowledge of the history of the game and its greats by choosing greatest-ever teams with his cricket-mad grandmother. Richard carved out a career in accounting and finance but has remained a cricket tragic and will happily debate the merits of his selections in World XIs with anyone. He lives in Brisbane, is married to Sarah, and they have two daughters; Alexandra and Georgia.

www.ingramcontent.com/pod-product-compliance
Lightning Source LLC
Chambersburg PA
CBHW031308150426
43191CB00005B/130